Sayer, James
Argumentation and debate:
principles and applications.

ARGUMENTATION AND DEBATE

Principles and Applications

ARGUMENTATION AND DEBATE

Principles and Applications

James Edward Sayer
Wright State University

15335 Morrison Street, Sherman Oaks, CA 91403

Printed and bound in the United States of America

Library of Congress Cataloging in Publication Data

Sayer, James Edward.
Argumentation and debate.

Includes index.
1. Debates and debating. 2. Persuasion (Rhetoric)
I. Title.
PN4181.S32 808.53 79-24519
ISBN 0-88284-102-5

Dedication

To Professor David A. Williams — a man who made debate fun and worthwhile.

Which is the way it's supposed to be.

CONTENTS

CONTENTS

Preface

Argumentation and Debate: is designed to acquaint you with the principles of argumentation and debate and to show their pertinence to all our argumentative encounters, formal (such as debates) and informal (such as daily conversations and decisions). To meet that twofold goal, this book is structured to take you through the unique experience that is argumentative communication.

Within this book, argumentation and debate are viewed as processes of communication, and the reader is reminded constantly that the tenets of effective public communication apply equally to all argumentative communication settings. This point is made most dramatically through the use of systems theory and through an examination of the nature of argumentation and debate in society.

The major elements of effective argumentative communication are delineated and exemplified through the use of historical and contemporary illustrations. In addition, each chapter concludes with a "Practicum" section, materials for study and activity for both in-class and out-of-class use to provide you with as many experiences as possible to improve your own argumentative and debate abilities.

Finally, the style and content of the book have been made as interesting as possible. Jargon has been held to the barest minimum, and the language employed is everyday, not "academese." I hope you like this book, because I have enjoyed my years of involvement in various argumentative communication activities, and I hope that some of my enjoyment will rub off on you.

Unit One

Argumentative Communication: The Philosophical Perspective

Chapter One

Argumentation and Debate: Definitions

* Definition of Argumentation
* Conviction-Persuasion Dichotomy
* Definition of Debate
* Debate as Advocacy and Inquiry
* Morality of Debating
* Values of Training in Argumentation and Debate
* Criticisms of Training in Argumentation and Debate
* Conclusions
* References
* Practicum

Both the study and the practice of argumentative communication have a history nearly as long as the recorded history of man itself. Centuries before the birth of Christ, residents of the many Greek city-states found that expertise in the formulation and delivery of argument was tied directly to their success and well-being in public life. Not only was oral skill necessary to carry on normal, daily conversation, but the ancient Greek court system depended exclusively upon verbal competence, as each member of society (male, that is) was expected to prosecute and defend his own legal case in court. There were no legal representatives; there were no attorneys. Each man had to speak on his own behalf. Argumentative communication was a central part of the existence within that society.[1]

Not surprisingly, the first great rhetorical theorists were men who trained others in the practice of oral advocacy — Corax and his pupil Tisias. These two men came to the fore out of necessity, because all men needed training for courtroom activity. Later, other teachers of rhetoric, known as Sophists, traveled the Greek countryside, instructing students in the art of oral discourse, and one of these, Protagoras, became the first to hold contests in argument for his pupils. Because of this practice, Protagoras has been called the Father of Debate, the man who originated argumentative contests nearly five hundred years prior to the birth of Jesus Christ.[2]

Today, the study of argumentative communication is much more complex and multifaceted than in the days of that ancient civilization. We live in the midst of a genuine communication explosion, and the need for the study and practice of argument is even more pronounced than it was several decades ago. We are bombarded daily with hundreds of arguments — from friends, relatives, teachers, salesmen, politicians, and dozens more. The study and practice of argumentative communication is of such significance today that the subject is discussed additionally in Chapters 2 and 3, but, for now, you should realize the study of argumentation and debate is not simply an academic concern. It is a study of importance that affects directly your life now and into the future; the study of argumentative communication is a study of life and mankind in our contemporary world.

Definition of Argumentation

Because the words *argumentation* and *debate* will be used a great deal throughout this book, it is necessary that a clear definition of each word be provided. For the purposes of our examination of argumentative communication, argumentation will be defined as: *the process of presenting persuasive information and conclusions to secure agreement with one's position*. This process means that an individual has a goal in mind (wanting you to agree with him) and that materials will be presented to you in the hope that such materials will cause the goal to be reached. Generally, argumentation entails the presentation of reasons (logicians often call these reasons *premises*) designed to have you agree eventually with a desired conclusion.[3]

Argumentation may be relatively brief ("Since she is the best cook, you ought to invite her to the potluck dinner") or may be very lengthy and documented. The following essay exemplifies such extended argumentation.

The Dangers of Nuclear Power

by Suzanne Lindsey

A young Mexican boy was walking down the street, when, looking down, he happened to spy a silver marble. Well, young boys like to collect marbles, so he picked up his new toy and put it in his pocket. When he got home he immediately fell ill, and his mother put him to bed. She took the silver marble and put it in a kitchen drawer. Both she and her young daughter also fell ill. When her mother heard that the whole family was sick, she came over to nurse them. Eventually, all four died. According to the book, *Poisoned Power* by Gofman and Tamplin, the silver marble was a Cobalt 60 source . . .from a nuclear power plant.

Following World War II, nuclear power was met with mixed reactions. Some people feared it as a danger to all mankind, but others championed it as a doorway to utopia. Eventually, the potential for greatness won out, and the American government promised us clean, cheap, and safe nuclear power. Well, they were wrong. And some of them were concerned enough to admit it. The first chairman of the Atomic Engery Commission, David Lilienthal, said, "Once a bright hope shared by all mankind—including myself—the rash proliferation of atomic plants has become one of the ugliest clouds overhanging America." So from the vantage point of over twenty years, let's examine the assurances given to the American people, and see if nuclear power really did turn out to be clean, cheap, and safe.

People might assume that nuclear fission is clean and non-polluting, because when you walk by a nuclear plant you don't smell smoke. But don't heave a sigh of relief for the environment yet. Nuclear fission does pollute—first of all with radiation. The government allows us a maximum does of up to 170 millirads each, but that standard was set decades before we realized the full dangers of radiation. Dr. Linus Pauling, in the book *Poisoned Power*, estimated that if the U.S. population was exposed to that acceptable level, the result would be 96,000 additional cancer deaths and up to 1,500,000 additional genetic deaths every year—at standards the commission considers safe. The commission replied that they would never allow anyone to be exposed to the allowable level anyway. But when concerned doctors and scientists asked for a show of sincerity, by lowering the acceptable level or by giving us a written guarantee that no one would be exposed to it, they refused absolutely.

Another pollutant from nuclear fission that no one can ignore is nuclear waste. A conventional pollutant takes millions of gallons to pollute a river. But according to *The People's Almanac*, just three tablespoons of plutonium contain enough radioactivity to induce cancer in half a billion people. And plutonium must be guarded with flawless vigilance for a quarter of a million years. No wonder plutonium is named after the lord of hell.

The August 5th, 1977 issue of *Science* warns that we can't guard those burial sites or even keep them marked that long. And in choosing a site, consider that 10,000 years ago the Sahara was fertile, the English channel was dry, volcanos were active in central France, and glaciers moved across the Earth. Now we are supposed to pick a site that for the next 250,000 years will have no water, no sharp or fragile rocks, no earthquakes, no landshifts, and no valuable minerals to attract future miners. This just can't be done. The National Academy of Scientists reviewed all of our sites, and warned that all of them would lead to eventual destruction of the environment.

Yet we still build more of these plants to produce more of this waste without knowing what we're going to do with it. Whenever we discuss this problem, the commission refers to the "legacy of guardianship" we are leaving to future generations. I would call it a curse. For we are cursing them with forced custodianship of our polluted wastes. And we are cursing them with something far worse, if anything happens to those tanks in the next few thousand years.

The early proponents of nuclear energy painted glowing pictures of the days when electricity would be so cheap, metering would hardly be worthwhile. In case you haven't noticed yet, that day still hasn't come. Despite massive subsidies, nuclear electricity is barely holding its own against fossil fuel electricity, which receives no federal assistance. Barry Commoner, in the book *The Poverty of Power*, points out that the capital costs of nuclear fission are increasing so fast that by 1985 it will be more expensive than coal. It will, therefore, have lost its only reason for existence.

Furthermore, nuclear fission is economically unreliable. The technology is so complex that the plants are shut down 40 percent of the time. Problems are usually common to several plants, so if one plant has to shut down, all the others have to shut down as well . . .for inspection.

The money funneled into nuclear fission to make it economically competitive with other energy sources reminds me of the man who woke up to find a dinasaur in his backyard. The dinosaur said, "Feed me." So the man fed the dinosaur, and he grew, and he grew, and one day he said, "Feed me. Otherwise, I will die and stink." The problem is, this dinosaur might try to take us with him. In *Perils of the Peaceful Atom*, Curtis and Hogan point out that no reactor can be both economical and safe. If we want safe reactors, we are going to have to build and operate them at a loss. If we want economically competitive reactors, we are going to have to compromise the safeguards.

So is nuclear energy safe? Insurance companies, who make money by assessing hazards, refuse to insure nuclear plants—at any price. Obviously, they are unable to believe the industry's promises of absolute safety. These promises are based upon the assumption of a low probability of an accident. But Dr. Edward Teller is known as the father of the hydrogen bomb, and he supports nuclear energy, but he still admits, "So far we've been extremely lucky. *But* with the spread of industrialization, and the growing number of simians monkeying around with something they do not completely understand, sooner or later a fool will prove greater than the proof—even in a foolproof system." Already we've had some narrow escapes. In 1966, they almost had to evacuate Detroit when the fuel at the Fermi plant started melting through it's casing. They had even started planning medical assistance in case the evacuation came too late. They *were* lucky.

The early proponents of nuclear energy may have believed it when they promised us clean, cheap, and safe nuclear power. But it's *not* what we received. Nuclear fission is contaminating, costly, and extremely dangerous.

As citizens, there's a lot we can do to help solve this problem. First of all, we have to act *now*, before we become economically dependent on nuclear fission. People who have organized moratoriums, petitions and demonstrations have kept nuclear plants out of cities before. Join these anti-nuclear groups—give them your time and money. And when the nuclear industry sets up these podium propaganda sessions, use your speech skills. Go to these meetings and ask questions. And make them answer.

Finally, don't try to sell a negative. We can't just cut down nuclear fission and offer no alternative in its place. Luckily, there are two energy sources that will work on a national level. Maybe I've given the word *nuclear* a bad name in this speech. But I've been talking about nuclear fission, which explodes the atom. Another alternative is nuclear fusion, which collapses it. Fusion is much safer and produces millions of times less radiation. And C. B. Reed in *Fuels, Minerals and Human Survival* points out that fusion wastes only 10 percent of its energy as a pollutant—whereas fission wastes 70 percent. And very importantly, fusion leaves no toxic nuclear waste. Fusion received 25 million dollars a year from the government. Fission—500 million.

But for those of you who simply do not want a nuclear plant anywhere on this planet, I have another solution. We have our own cosmic reactor 93 million miles away. At first we tried to use solar power to produce mechanical energy, and we failed. But in the last six years, we've switched our goal to electrical energy, and great strides have been made. A recent NASA-financed bulletin, "Solar Power as an Energy Resource," said that, given a fifteen-year research budget of 3.5 billion dollars, solar power could produce 300 percent of America's energy needs.

We have the reasons to fight, the means to fight with, and the alternative to fight for. We don't have to perpetuate a mistake. If we need a catastrophe to convince us we're in danger, then consider this—given the nature of radiation, our doom may be sealed twenty years before the first symptoms appear. By the time we can count corpses, it will be too late. Far from being the promised doorway to utopia, this magical energy source has turned into a costly trap. For our sake, and the sake of future generations, let's slam *this* door shut.[4]

Importantly, the reasons given in support of the argumentative goal may be logically sound or invalid, they may be heavily loaded with emotion, or they may depend upon the source credibility of the speaker or writer. Regardless, argumentation is *not* solely or exclusively based upon logic, syllogistic reasoning, or facts. The reasons in support of argumentative claims and conclusions may be of any nature, depending upon the communicator, the subject, the occasion, and the audience. Argumentation, like persuasion itself, is concerned chiefly with the process of securing audience acceptance of a communicator's message. To limit the study of argumentation to the principles of logic would overlook a vast array of communication activities and would force you to make superficial distinctions between the supposedly logical and the emotional.

Conviction-Persuasion Dichotomy

Reread the Lindsey essay concerning the dangers of nuclear power. Take your time in reading; examine its contents very carefully. Now, mentally list five of her *logical* arguments in support of her position. Compare your list with the lists of your classmates.

You should not be surprised to find that your lists differ; in some cases they may differ significantly. Why? Because people are different, they will see the same things from a different perspective. What is logical to you might seem to be totally illogical to me. Did you have an opinion about nuclear power before reading the Lindsey essay? If you did, your own opinion affected how you evaluated the logical nature of that essay. A member of the Stop Nuclear Development group would find the essay to be very logical and well-reasoned; however, an advocate of nuclear power would find the essay to be full of scare tactics and completely illogical in both structure and content. The essay is the same for all who read it; the words do not change on the page, but the interpretations and evaluations of the essay's content vary from person to person. That is why it is so difficult, if not meaningless, to describe or define argumentation in terms of its being logically based, as many people try to do. The definition of what is logical will shift from person to person.[5]

Some years ago, communication theorists attempted to distinguish between logical and nonlogical argument in what was called the conviction-persuasion dichotomy. In the simplest form of the distinction, conviction was considered to be a logical process, while persuasion was considered to be a nonlogical or emotional process. Shaw's *The Art of Debate* illustrates this claimed difference:

> Conviction is a process that appeals to reason in order to get understanding; and persuasion is a process that appeals to the emotions in order to get action. To be more specific: Conviction is a process by which the validity of all the proof in a case is made clear to the hearer; and persuasion is a process by which all the proof in a case is provided with interest and a motive for its acceptance.[6]

This dichotomy has found some acceptance with certain argumentation theorists, as attempts have been made to limit the study of argumentation to the principles and practices of logic. For example, Freeley has attempted to both define argumentation and to differentiate between argumentation and persuasion by revamping the central tenets of the old conviction-persuasion dichotomy:

> Argumentation gives priority to logical appeals while taking cognizance of ethical and emotional appeals; persuasion gives priority to ethical and emotional appeals while taking cognizance of logical appeals.[7]

You should note that both Shaw and Freeley have said essentially the same thing.

Perhaps the best way to demonstrate that trying to distinguish between logical and emotional appeals is a self-defeating activity is to consider the following case example.

Is It Logical or Is It Emotional?

> The famous American golfer Arnold Palmer is seen on your television screen in the company of a five-year-old boy in leg braces. The boy is trying to putt a golf ball, but his braces make it almost impossible for him to hit the ball squarely, even with Palmer's assistance.
>
> After 30 seconds of this scene, Palmer looks directly at the camera and says, "Joey sure tries hard, but he has a difficult time. But he never gives up. If you would like to help Joey and thousands others like him, pledge your fair share to the March of Dimes. With your support, you can help us eliminate the crippling ravages of birth defects."

Was that television spot logical or emotional in nature? Certainly, the sight of that young boy hobbling around with his braces would have a definite emotional effect upon most people. So, it was an emotional message, right? Yet, Palmer said that monetary contributions would aid in the battle against birth defects. More money means more research, increasing the chances that cures and preventative measures will be discovered one day. That was a logical message, right? Was that spot *both* emotional and logical?

The answer is yes to that final question. Both the elements of emotional and logical persuasion were present in that televised message; it is impossible to distinguish meaningfully between them in terms of their impact upon the viewing audience. As the receiver of that message, you would find yourself affected by both elements within the message as emotion and logic overlap into an effective public service presentation. Please note that both elements had the same goal: to get you to contribute money to the March of Dimes campaign. Both logic and emotion combined to pull you toward that desired conclusion; both elements functioned within the process of argumentation.

The conviction-persuasion dichotomy establishes a false delineation between factors that *in practice* cannot be easily separated. Although it is fairly easy to create a definition that carefully separates logic from emotion, in the realm of actual communication events that separation is practically impossible to distinguish clearly. This book is concerned with realistic argumentative communication as it occurs in our environment; this book does not adhere to the antiquated notion of the conviction-persuasion dichotomy. Though we might wish that all arguments were based on purely logical reasons, in reality argumentative encounters encompass both logical and illogical matters.

Definition of Debate

Having defined and exemplified argumentation, let us turn our attention to the second major element within argumentative communication: debate. Within this book, debate will be defined as: *the process of presenting persuasive information on behalf of or in opposition to a stated proposition or topic.* Since both argumentation and debate obviously overlap to some degree in the functioning of argumentative communication (both have the same goal of trying to secure audience acceptance of a message), there is one major structural difference between them: the process of debate guarantees response or refutation to an offered point of view. This difference was noted over fifty years ago in J. H. Gardiner's *Making of Arguments*:

> The essential difference between debate and written argument lies not so much in the natural difference

> between all spoken and written discourse as in the fact that in a debate of any kind there is the chance for an immediate answer to an opponent.[8]

In short, debate is an argumentative process with two opposing sides clashing over the same idea or topic. There is immediate response and feedback to the arguments offered by the participants in the debate; there is no such guaranteed immediate response in argumentation. Because of this difference, debate is generally an oral activity and argumentation is often thought of (as by Gardiner) as a written activity. However, this does not have to be the case. Immediate written responses between two opposing sides on the same topic would be classified as a debate, but this would be a most unusual and inconvenient argumentative encounter. Because the nature of debate requires immediate response to arguments, debate, especially academic debate, ought to be considered an exercise in oral communication.

In examining the nature of debate, it is necessary to distinguish between the two major types of debate structure: informal or everyday debate and formal or academic debate. The nature of each debate type is discussed below.

Informal Debate

Practically any argumentative encounter centering upon the same issue can be termed a debate. As such, many of your daily hassles could be considered informal debates. For example, a man and his wife have decided to replace the carpet in their living room, but they cannot agree upon the type of new carpet to buy. So, their discussion centers upon that issue — what kind of carpet should be purchased for the living room. The debate might proceed like this:

She: We ought to get a carpet with a low pile. That would be much better than our present carpet.

He: No, we really should buy a nice quality shag. It would make our house look classier and would give it a "rich" feeling.

She: But a shag carpet is almost impossible to keep clean. A low pile is much easier to maintain.

He: Yeah, but it looks like a putting green. It wouldn't add anything to the room. It would just look blah!

She: Okay, but I'll tell you now that our vacuum cleaner couldn't handle a shag carpet. We'd have to buy a new cleaner for that rug. Are you willing to spend $175 for a new vacuum cleaner?

He: $175?

She: That's right. That's what a good vacuum cleaner costs these days, the kind that will clean a shag carpet.

He: Hmmm, $175. You know, maybe a low pile carpet wouldn't be so bad after all.

She: Right, and not only would our old vacuum be okay, but a low pile carpet is much easier to keep clean.

He: And we'd save money too! Okay, we'll get a low pile rug. Where do you want to look first?

Both the husband and wife agreed upon the issue for debate — the purchase of a new living room rug — but they disagreed about the type of rug to be bought. She advocated the purchase of a low pile carpet, and he preferred a shag. She was concerned primarily with the ease of carpet upkeep; his concern centered on how the carpet would affect the appearance of the room. Notice that both had reasons in support of their positions, and agreement was reached finally when the wife introduced a reason (the money it would cost to buy a new vacuum cleaner) that overcame the reasons held by the husband. Their dialogue concerning the carpet certainly is an example of persuasive information on a mutually agreed-upon topic.

Formal Debate

Despite the fact that, as the preceding example illustrates, we spend a great deal of our lives engaged in debate, the word debate generally creates an image of formal debate structures, the kind found in legislative bodies like the U.S. Congress or in academic debates hosted by schools and universities throughout the country. Most likely, you are in a class now that is devoted to the study of formal academic debate; you may be expected to debate in the classroom against some of your classmates. Although the formal structure may be new to you, formal debating has a long history of practice in our Western civilization.

Formal debating was initiated in the fifth century B.C. by Protagoras, when he had his students take opposing sides on the same issue and give speeches on behalf of their respective positions. Medieval education was grounded firmly upon the use of formal debate (called forensic disputations and conducted in Latin) as a training device. In our own country, formal debating societies predated the American Revolution by more than fifty years, and the first so-called modern academic debates took place over one hundred years ago. Training in debate, then, has a long history, and your participation in an argumentation and debate class is part of a long tradition.

Formal debate differs from informal debate because it has established structural and time constraints. Formal debate forces its participants to select mutually exclusive positions on an issue; that is, one side must support the topic for debate, and the other side must oppose it. In a debate on the topic, "Resolved: that the United States should increase its defense spending," one side would argue in support of that statement, and the other side would speak in opposition to that statement. There is no middle ground, as often can be found within an informal or daily life debate.

In addition, formal debate closely restricts the amount of time one has to speak about the debate topic. Whether the particular time limit be four, five, eight, or ten minutes, that time limitation is enforced so every debate participant has an equal amount of speaking time. You may contrast that with the situation in most informal debates, wherein one person or one side often speaks more than the opposing person or side — a very inequitable situation. Formal debate does guarantee equity in time allotment, as exemplified in the Oxford style of contemporary intercollegiate debate practice.

First Affirmative Constructive Speech	ten minutes
First Negative Constructive Speech	ten minutes
Second Affirmative Constructive Speech	ten minutes
Second Negative Constructive Speech	ten minutes
First Negative Rebuttal Speech	five minutes
First Affirmative Rebuttal Speech	five minutes
Second Negative Rebuttal Speech	five minutes
Second Affirmative Rebuttal Speech	five minutes

You will note that each speaker has a total speaking time of fifteen minutes (one ten-minute constructive speech and one five-minute rebuttal speech); no one is provided more speaking time than any other person in the debate.

Whereas the process of argumentation is often a one-way communication activity as the message sender attempts to affect the beliefs or actions of the message receiver, the process of debate is a dynamic interaction of argument, counterargument, further argument, additional responses, and so on. Also, formal debate is staged with a third party present, to whom the arguments are addressed, to decide which person or side won the argumentative encounter.

Debate as Advocacy and Inquiry

By its very nature, debate, especially formal debate as practiced in academic settings, is an advocacy process in which one person or side advocates the acceptance of an idea and the opposition advocates the rejection of that same idea. There are some theorists, however, who prefer to look upon the process of debate as one of inquiry, not as a process of conflicting advocacy. Ehninger, for example, contended that debate was concerned with investigation of an issue, not with persuasive argument upon that issue, and that debate should be seen as a species of cooperation, not one of conflict.[9] The advocacy versus inquiry issue can be resolved by looking at formal debate in its entire context.

When debater A presents her point of view, the desired goal is to have a third party (judge or audience) accept that point of view and not the opposite viewpoint offered by debater B. Conversely, of course, debater B wants the third party to accept his position and not the position of debater A. In this sense, the process of debate is one of direct advocacy, as two opposing sides try to persuade the third party to accept their mutually exclusive positions.

However, from the third party's vantage point, debate may be seen as a process of inquiry, wherein the arguments of the competing debaters are assessed and evaluated so the best possible decision may be made. The judge, in effect, inquires as to whether he should agree with either debater A or debater B. Also, to develop the arguments and secure the necessary supporting materials in defense of their positions, the debaters have to engage in extensive research inquiries to secure the necessary information. So, debate does have its elements of investigation.

Therefore, formal debate can be viewed as a process of both advocacy and inquiry: advocacy of certain arguments and positions; inquiry into those arguments in search of the best possible decision. As the debaters engage in argumentative communication over whether or not the United States should increase its defense spending, for example, the dual process of advocacy and inquiry coexist. The process of inquiry predominates both before and after the debate and the process of advocacy predominates during the actual debate itself, but both are integral parts of the overall debate activity.

Morality of Debating

The formal debate structure forces its participants to examine and speak on behalf of both sides of any given issue. For example, in academic debate settings you would be expected to be able to speak for *and* against the debate topic. At one tme, you might be asked to support the notion that the United States should increase its defense budget, and at another time you might be expected to speak in opposition to such increased expenditures. Some individuals, however, have opposed this flip-flopping procedure.

Around the start of the twentieth century, such notable figures as Theodore Roosevelt and William Jennings Bryan took exception to the practice of having debaters both support and attack the same issue at different times. They claimed that such a practice was highly immoral, causing the student of debate to be literally two-faced in examining issues of public importance. Even some authors of argumentation texts contended that a two-sided approach to the study of argument raised ethical and moral questions, with several concluding that this approach should be avoided. In 1912, Gardiner offered this piece of advice:

> There is a moral or ethical side to practice in debating which one cannot ignore. It is dangerous to get into the habit of arguing lightly for things in which one does not believe; and students may be forced into doing this if great care is not taken in the choice of subjects and sides. The remedy lies in using, so far as they can be kept interesting, questions in which there is no moral element; but still better in assigning sides to correspond with the actual views and preferences of the debaters. Where a question of principle is involved no one should ever argue against his beliefs. . . . If you have clearly made up your mind on a question of public policy, you are in a false position if you argue, even for practice, against what you believe to be the right.[10]

The issue of the morality of debate is not limited to several generations in the past. During the 1954–1955 academic year, several American colleges and universities refused to allow their debaters to take part in debates on the national intercollegiate debate topic, "Resolved: that the United States should extend diplomatic recognition to the communist government of China." It was contended that no one could speak in support of that topic, because to argue that the government of Red China should receive official diplomatic recognition would be to uphold a totally immoral and unjustifiable position. The impact of the Korean War and the McCarthy era made it difficult for many schools to debate that particular topic.

Those who contend that debating both sides of an issue is immoral base their position upon two very large assumptions. First, there is the assumption that, on any given issue, only one side can be right or only one side is true. Many years ago, the followers of the great Greek philosopher Plato adhered to the position that there existed absolute truths, matters that were always correct regardless of time or circumstance. The Platonists had a difficult time isolating such absolute truths, and those concerned with the morality of debating would be hard pressed to demonstrate that one idea always is right, while the opposite idea always is wrong. All issues of daily life are flexible, changing from circumstance to circumstance. For example, we adhere to the notion that "to kill another is wrong," but this moral dictate changes under varying conditions. If someone tries to take your life, you have the right to defend yourself, including killing the aggressor if such action is found necessary. All court systems recognize the validity of self-defense and its related concept of justifiable homicide. Thus, to kill another is not always wrong under all conditions. Those concerned with the morality of debate assume that the issues of right and wrong never vary, but our own life experiences clearly indicate that such matters shift from one situation to another.

The second major assumption is that argument on behalf of a position with which you personally disagree somehow will warp or injure your attitudes and beliefs. Thus, to remain constant in your beliefs, you are asked to close your eyes to the arguments offered by those who disagree with you. Such a position is not only very limited in its consideration of what is right and true, but that position assumes that to change one's opinion is somehow immoral. On the contrary, to be able to see both sides of an argument provides the individual with the best perspective from which to make a final decision. By seeing all arguments, the individual can make a comprehensive and well-informed decision that is not shortsighted or limited in its view. In addition, seeing arguments from both sides strengthens the individual's ability to refute those arguments with which she disagrees. The more you know about your opponent's position, the easier it is to defeat that position.

The process of debate is not an immoral activity; it does not cause its participants to speak with forked tongues. Debate causes you to see the multiple ramifications of most issues, to see how intricate even the simplest decision really is. When you are engaged in debate, you do not make public statements that are etched in stone, nor do you take positions that you must defend for the remainder of your life. Instead, debate as a combined process of inquiry and advocacy opens your horizons of thought and imagination, allowing you to have a free and full view of the complex issues that face us today and will continue to face us tomorrow.

Values of Training in Argumentation and Debate

Volumes could be written about what you will gain from the study of the aspects of argumentative communication, but we shall limit our discussion here to seven of the major benefits.

1. See differing sides. The study of argumentation and debate causes you to see both sides of an issue, to see how complex most decisions are because of the multiple factors involved. Once you realize that no issues are simple, that no decisions are black or white, you will become a more cooperative individual in dealings with your fellow man. No one is always right or always wrong; the truth generally lies somewhere in between. By seeing both sides of issues, your viewpoints will be improved realistically and you will become more humane in life's activities — a definite personal benefit.

2. Increase awareness of issues. Because the study of argumentative communication involves the examination of many important issues and subissues, you will find that your awareness of these significant social concerns will be increased dramatically. The study of our country's defense expenditures, for example, will increase your knowledge not only of defense spending, but also of the related items of fiscal and monetary policy, other necessary federal expenditures, the efficiency and lack thereof in the functioning of the federal bureaucracy, and many others. You will become a virtual subject matter expert in those areas related to your debate topic. You will know more about that topic area than 99 percent of the general populace, and, importantly, your interest in that area will continue through the rest of your life.

3. **Increase research ability**. Since your arguments in support of or in opposition to a given issue must be substantiated by evidence, you will spend a great deal of time in the library researching the needed information for your debate encounters. Most individuals are ineffective researchers, spending a great deal of their library time in hopeless wandering through the myriad of bookcases. Your training in argumentative communication will, on the other hand, cause you to become most proficient at research, and you will discover that you can accomplish twice as much in less than half the time in doing research as your non-debate-trained friends. Of course, this skill will prove beneficial beyond your argumentation and debate class. Your increased research ability will pay dividends as you complete term papers and projects for other classes, and many former debaters have testified that their research training provided them with many advantages in their later studies in graduate schools and law schools.

4. **Improve analysis**. All major debate topics contain many issues that need to be addressed by those studying the topics. The examination of our country's defense expenditures entails a study of many related items that, at first glance, seem to have nothing to do with our defense policy. The study of argumentative communicaton allows you to see the many issues found within a broad topic and to see that most issues have multiple subissues within them. Thus, you will find that your ability to analyze (to be able to break down into component parts) ideas, arguments, and even the most complex theories will be greatly enhanced by the skills you develop in argumentation and debate. You will be able to isolate the important elements in materials presented to you; you will be better able to see how the various elements interact with one another. Whereas others grapple with vague generalities, you will be able to go the the heart of issues that confront you, saving time and improving your personal information-gathering and decision-making processes.

5. **Improve organization.** Because argumentative communication requires that you be able to deal with a variety of issues, subissues, and evidentiary materials, you will receive training in organizing your materials for maximum argumentative effectiveness. All the items generated by analysis must be grouped together in some type of reasonable organizational format so others might discover what you have found. Thus, argumentation and debate will improve your ability to organize, to put materials together so others will understand your point of view and agree with it. Your personal and academic life will be enhanced by this increase in your

overall organizational skill. It will pay dividends through the rest of your life.

6. Improve critical listening. All of us are bombarded daily with a variety of arguments — we are asked to buy this or that brand of toothpaste, support a certain political candidate, support or oppose a proposed policy or action, and so on. All of these daily requests are supported by arguments, reasons designed to convince us to go along with the desired course of action. If we do not discriminate carefully in agreeing with such pieces of argumentation, then we will find ourselves buying inferior products, supporting inferior candidates for public office, and agreeing to inferior personal life-styles. Therefore it is essential that we critically listen to and examine all such arguments, testing the validity of their claims. Training in argumentative communication improves your critical listening ability, making you a more thorough examiner of argument and a more objective consumer of public advertisement. Your life is affected directly by the arguments you accept and reject, and increased critical listening, aided by the study of argumentation and debate, will positively affect your decisions regarding such acceptance and rejection.[11]

7. Improve communication ability. Since the practice of argumentative communication is largely one of the oral give-and-take of arguments, you will find that your oral communication abilities will be heightened by your activities in an argumentation and debate course. Your verbal clarity, conciseness, and, in fact, all the items of functional communication will be improved by your training in argumentative communication. If you were to gain no other benefit beyond improved communication abilities from your argumentation and debate studies, the value of such a course would be immeasurable for the remainder of your life.

After completing this course, you will be able to list many other advantages you have gained from your studies, but these seven major advantages will be with you from this point forward. Argumentative communication is not a panacea, it will not solve all your personal and professional problems, but it will provide you with invaluable skills. Since argument is such a central feature in your life and in the lives of others, this course will be of significance to you now and in the future.

Criticisms of Training in Argumentation and Debate

Since argument plays such a large part in our lives, it is not surprising to find that there have been criticisms lodged against the study of argumentative communication as that study has been carried on in our nation's schools, colleges, and universities. Three such general criticisms may be isolated for our consideration at this time.

First, training in formal debate procedures has been condemned as immoral and unethical because of the practice of having debaters argue on behalf of both sides of a debate topic. However, as you have seen, this criticism assumes that there are absolute truths, that there are always clear-cut right and wrong ways of seeing and doing things. Common sense tells us exactly the opposite. Most issues are so complex that the best way to understand them is to study them critically from every possible perspective. Debate training is not immoral or unethical; in fact, training in debate is highly ethical in that it broadens your viewpoint, leaving no stone unturned in the search for truth as you may best find it.

Second, those who participate in formal debate tournaments have been criticized as being "trophy hungry," of being more concerned with winning debate contests than with anything else. Certainly, there have been and are those individuals who look upon debating as an ego trip and who want only to acquire trophies and plaques to show their friends how smart they are. But these individuals are a small minority of debate competitors; most seek benefits that go beyond the mere collection of trophies and other such memorabilia. Tournament debating requires many, many hours of research and practice, coupled with long trips on weekends that take up the majority of the debater's free time. To sacrifice so much requires that debating provide the competitor with more than a few engraved trophies.

Finally, training in argumentative communication has been accused of creating contentious, obnoxious individuals, the kind of people with whom most of us would not care to associate. These obnoxious types refuse to accept anything at face value, and they are on the constant lookout to do verbal battle with anyone over the most trivial of points. Unfortunately, being contentious and obnoxious are not character traits limited to those with argumentation and debate training; all sorts of people often are that way. Training in argumentation is designed to foster critical listening and judgmental skills, not mere contentiousness; training in debate is designed to develop healthy skepticism and functional advocacy, not boorish obnoxiousness. People who are contentious or obnoxious would be that way regardless of the effect of any training they might receive in argumentative communication. On the contrary, such training generally creates a respect for the views of others and a realization that no one individual has all the answers to a question — traits that are the exact converse of the offered indictment.

Although some people have abused those skills acquired via training in argumentative communication, the vast majority of practitioners have used these skills to improve their professional and personal lives, exemplifying the rationale for the development of this kind of study in the city-states of ancient Greece.

Conclusion

The study and practice of argumentative communication in which you are currently engaged has an interesting history from several centuries before the birth of Christ to the present day. By studying both argumentation and debate principles and procedures, you may expect to develop seven major skills that will aid you in your future personal and professional lives: (1) seeing both sides of an issue, (2) increasing your awareness of public issues, (3) increasing your researching abilities, (4) improving your analytical abilities, (5) improving your organizational techniques, (6) enhancing your critical listening powers, and (7) improving your overall oral communication abilities. Because the study and examination of argument is of central importance to everyday life, the skills gained from this course of study will prove to be invaluable to you.

References

1. For examples of arguments in Athenian law courts, see Kathleen Freeman, *The Murder of Herodes* (New York: W. W. Norton, 1963).

2. Bromley Smith, "The Father of Debate: Protagoras of Abdera," *The Quarterly Journal of Speech* 4 (March 1918) : 196–215.

3. Hence, the definition of argumentation offered herein is quite compatible with that favored by the National Developmental Conference on Forensics. See James H. McBath, *Forensics As Communication* (Skokie, Ill.: National Textbook, 1975), p. 11.

4. Suzanne Lindsey, "The Dangers of Nuclear Power," original essay presented with permission of the author.

5. See, for example, H. Sebald, "Limitations of Communication: Mechanisms of Image Maintenance in Forms of Selective Perception, Selective Memory and Selective Distortion," *Journal of Communication* 12 (1962), pp. 142–149. The difficulty in delineating between logical and emotional appeals caused Karlins and Abelson to conclude that there is a "lack of agreement among investigators on how emotional and rational appeals are to be defined and distinguished from each other." See Marvin Karlins and Herbert I. Abelson, *Persuasion*, 2nd ed. (New York: Springer, 1970), p. 37.

6. Warren C. Shaw, *The Art of Debate* (Boston: Allyn and Bacon, 1922), p. 247.

7. Austin J. Freeley, *Argumentation and Debate: Rational Decision Making* (Belmont, Calif.: Wadsworth, 1976), p. 8.

8. J. H. Gardiner, *The Making of Arguments* (Boston: Ginn, 1912), p. 213.

9. Douglas Ehninger, "Debating as Critical Deliberation," *Southern Speech Communication Journal* 24 (Fall 1958) : 22–30.

10. Gardiner, *Making of Arguments*, p. 230.

11. See Richard Huseman, Glenn Ware, and Charles Gruner, "Critical Thinking, Reflective Thinking, and the Ability to Organize Ideas: A Multi-Variate Approach," *Journal of the American Forensic Association* 9 (Summer 1972): 261–265.

PRACTICUM

To determine the significance of your argumentative communication, keep a three-day log of the conversations you have with others — friends, parents, teachers, and so on. Then answer these questions:

- How often did you attempt to affect another's beliefs or actions?
- How often did others attempt to affect your beliefs or actions?
- Did you present reasons to support those things you said; did other people present reasons to you?

You will find that you spent a great deal of time "presenting persuasive information and conclusions to secure agreement" with the positions you took — as did the people with whom you came into contact. Argumentative communication played a substantial role in your life in that three-day period.

2. Read the following speech by U.S. Senator Frank Church of Idaho (delivered on the floor of the Senate on October 4, 1977), another example of public argument. Compare and contrast this speech with the Lindsey speech presented within this chapter. Which speech is better documented? Which speech is more logically based? And which is more emotionally centered? Finally, which speech is better from your perspective, and why?

Natural Gas Deregulation: Gambling with Billions

Senator Frank Church

Mr. President [of the United States Senate], for two weeks the Senate has debated whether to continue controls on natural gas prices with a higher price allowed for newly discovered gas or to deregulate gas prices. I entered this debate supporting the pricing policy proposed by President Carter and I remain convinced that it is the best policy for our Nation and for my home State of Idaho.

To be successful, our national policy on natural gas pricing must establish a stable system of prices, provide incentives to stimulate new production and offer maximum protection from sudden inflationary surges in energy costs. The President's plan was carefully crafted to satisfy these requirements. In contrast, we are urged by proponents of deregulation to abandon regulation designed to reflect cost of production in favor of wide-open pricing, even for gas that is already in the market or under production. The cost differential between these two approaches is staggering. Supporters of deregulation urge that we transfer billions to the producers with no assurance that this would result in increased supplies.

Natural gas is of vital importance to many of Idaho's homes and industries. Natural gas and its products are widely used in agriculture — from fertilizer to food processing. Because of its clean burning nature, natural gas is often used in many processes where there is no readily available substitute. Thus, any boost in natural gas prices will not only increase the costs of heating Idaho homes, but will add to the already burdensome material costs faced by Idaho farmers. And the impact does not stop there, because we can anticipate higher costs for all food if natural gas prices are allowed to skyrocket.

There are several recent studies which point to the tremendous costs consumers will bear if we deregulate gas prices. A Congressional Budget Office study and a recent report of the Joint Economic Committee both found that deregulation will cost consumers about $10 billion per year above what the President's plan would cost. A typical January 1985 home heating bill is estimated to be $47 under the President's plan and $70 under deregulation.

Mr. President, most Idahoans would not object to paying more for gas if they thought this would yield greater supplies and insure deliveries when needed. Yet both of the cited studies show that the significantly higher prices of deregulation are not likely to produce substantial increases in production. This is so partly because the United States is already heavily explored and because we are unlikely to discover many more huge reservoirs of gas.

The argument for deregulation assumes that there is plenty of gas to be discovered if we will only give producers the money to find it. How then do we explain the fact that exploration activity has increased significantly under present prices and discoveries per well or per exploratory foot drilled have dropped dramatically? Federal Energy Administraton analysis of deregulation also reveals that it would cost consumers $72 billion more in the next eight years than the President's plan while increasing gas supplies only 2.5 percent over what the President's approach would yield. Is it worth $72 billion to increase supplies by 2.5 percent?

There is one effect of deregulation that is predictable. That is the fact that it would create huge windfall profits for producers. For example, we have already discovered large quantities of natural gas on Alaska's North Slope. That gas is now available and awaits congressional approval of a pipeline to transport it to Idaho and other markets. If prices are deregulated, this already discovered gas will cost Idaho and others billions of dollars more. It will represent a massive transfer from the pocketbooks of the consmer to the corporate bank accounts with no connection to increasing supplies. That is absolutely unnecessary. In contrast, the President's plan offers a substantial increase in price for new gas to stimulate exploration and development while controlling the price of already discovered gas. That is absolutely necessary.

Oil and gas companies are not being forced into bankruptcy. Gas exploration is occurring at a brisk pace. The President's plan is generous in its price for new gas. If a compromise is needed to resolve the impasse between the administration's proposal and unlimited costs under deregulation, then I will support it. But it should be clear that the President's plan is what we need.

We are not free to ignore these facts. Deregulation is an enormous gamble with poor odds. I cannot sanction such a risky unnecessary venture when the odds are so poor and the only guarantee is windfall profits for gas producers.

Chapter 2

Argumentation as Communication

*** The Communication Process**
*** The Reasoning Process**
*** Audience Primacy in Argumentative Communication**
*** Conclusion**
*** References**
*** Practicum**

To study argumentation and debate is to study the many elements of the human communication process. The significance of argumentative communication to the overall communication process was noted by Jerry Anderson at the 1973 National Conference on Argumentation:

> The study of argumentation is based on the premises that thoughtful deliberation, intensive research, rational analysis, and the testing of ideas through reasoned discourse provides a vital means of conflict resolution, attitude formation and change, decision making, and is also the process essential for thorough investigation and information processing. The student who firmly grasps principles of argumentation theory and exercises the ability to apply those principles as a consumer and source of communication will be best equipped to become a responsible citizen. The continuing strength of a democratic society depends on a public forum of competing arguments by informed, responsible and skilled practitioners of

argumentation in carrying out both logical and ethical duties in the communication process.[1]

The study of argumentation and debate, then, is an important study within your larger examination of the human communication process. The purpose of this chapter is to acquaint you with the basic elements of that communication process and to demonstrate the interrelationship of argumentative communication to that process.

The Communication Process

All basic models or structures of communication look essentially the same. Whether your studies emphasize oral communication, written communication, nonverbal communication, or even mechanistic communication such as that used by computers, there are *four basic elements* within the structure of the communication model:

Source refers to the initiator of the communication encounter, such as the *speaker* in an oral communication setting or the *writer* in a written communication situation.

Message refers to the *information* transmitted by the source through the use of the symbolic process we call language.

Channel refers to the *vehicle* by which the source transmits the message to another person or persons; the channel varies from one communication situation to another. For example, in a public speaking situation, the channel would be the air, because that is the vehicle that carries the message from the source to the receiver; the channel could be a newspaper, television, personal letter, radio, billboard, and so on.

Receiver refers to the *recipient* of the source's message, generally known as the audience in oral communication settings.

Those four elements are present in *any* communicative encounter.

In oral communication settings, the kinds of settings in which argumentative communication normally operates, a fifth factor additionally is present.

Feedback refers to the verbal and nonverbal *responses* of the receiver(s) to the message offered by the source.

This feedback may take the form of direct verbal response ("I don't think you know what the hell you're talking about") or less distinct nonverbal response (confused looks; yawning; uneasy fidgeting). Regardless of the particular type, feedback serves to indicate the receivers' reactions to the message, and it provides the source of the message with fairly clear information concerning the acceptability of the message to the audience.

The functionality of these communication components to the process of argumentative communication can be demonstrated by examining the following:

> **FRED** [initial *source* of message]: The United States should not have agreed to those treaties giving up the Panama Canal. After all, it is our canal; we built it and we maintain it. [*Fred's argument serves as the message.*]
>
> *Fred's message is transmitted by the air, the channel, to Martha.*
>
> **MARTHA** [*initial receiver of message*]: But, Fred, it really isn't our canal. After all, it is in the country of Panama. I don't think you'd like another country running some operation within the borders of the United States. [*Martha's response to Fred is feedback.*]

The biggest drawback to the study of the communication process is the tendency to look upon communication as a fairly simple undertaking. The five-part model of the oral communication process (source, message, channel, receiver, feedback) gives an inaccurate picture of the many factors involved in even the most seemingly simple communication encounter. The preceding illustration involving Fred and Martha does appear to be simple: Fred didn't like the Panama Canal treaties, but Martha did not accept his major reason for being opposed to those treaties. However, a lot more was going on than that simple illustration seems to indicate.

Perhaps the complex nature of communication may be inferred from the use of the word *process* (you should have noted that the phrase *communication process* has been used several times already in this book). A process is a compilation of factors that are constantly in motion, dynamic, and everchanging. A process is nonstatic and nonstationary; it constantly is in a state of change. The dynamic nature of a process stems from the interaction of its component factors, and the dynamic nature of the communication process may be seen by quickly examining the major factors that go into that process.[2]

The source of any message is not one-dimensional, but is, instead, most assuredly multidimensional, containing a variety of factors that influence both the makeup of the source as well as the construction of the message as put together by this individual. For example, Fred is affected by many *internal factors* that impact upon his communication encounters: his educational level and achievement; his vocabulary; his past communication experiences; the sum of his past life experiences; his cultural, hereditary, and environmental factors. The list of these internal factors is virtually endless, but the point to be made is this: the internal factors contribute to the shaping of Fred and all other people, causing him to act as he does, to believe what he does, and to say the things he does. All these factors interact within Fred simultaneously, therefore affecting everything that Fred was in the past, is now, and will be in the future. Thus, the source of any message is a most complex and difficult-to-understand item; the source is as complex and potentially confusing as the very nature of life and life's forces themselves. These internal factors often are examined by psychologists in the study of an individual's personality makeup.

Similarly, Fred is affected by a variety of *external factors* that enter the communication process whenever he interacts with another human being. These external factors include such items as Fred's image of the other person; Fred's own self-image as it is affected by how he believes others view him; Fred's past communication experiences with the other person; the nature of the situation that causes Fred and the other to interact communicatively; the role and status of both people; each person's attitude and predisposition concerning their communication topic; and so on. Again, such a list could be endless. These various external factors play a significant role in the communication encounter, controlling the overall encounter and affecting both what is said and what is not said within that encounter.

A third major factor in the functioning communication process is the presence of *message variables*, items relating to the nature of our language system. Since we use words to stand for or represent ideas, concepts, values, and objects, our language is of paramount importance in the communication process. However, all of us discover at an early age that the words we use may not carry the same meaning to others as we had intended. Language is very imprecise, and it is this lack of precision that causes many difficulties in communication encounters, or — to put it simply, just because I know what I meant when I said something does not guarantee that you'll get the same meaning from the language I used. If you wish to prove this point, go to several of your classmates and have them define what is meant by the word *liberal*. The many different and contradictory definitions that you will receive will indicate the importance of message variables to the communication process.

A fourth factor is that of *channel variables*. Although argumentative communication generally takes place in a direct speaker-to-speaker situation with the channel of transmission being the air to conduct the sound waves, you should be aware that the use of different channels has a significant impact upon both the nature and quality of the communication process. The mass media (television, for example) have a different impact than direct, one-to-one public speaking encounters. That is one reason why the various advisers to Gerald Ford and Jimmy Carter went to such great lengths preparing the setting and their employers for the presidential debates of the 1976 campaign. They recognized that the medium of television was not the same as direct contact with an audience, so appropriate changes had to be made to make certain that the candidates looked as good as possible on national television before tens of millions of people. In direct, one-to-one situations (like that between Fred and Martha), the people involved in the communicative encounter can interact with one another immediately, modifying and explaining their messages. However, such is not the case when the channel of transmission is indirect, exemplified by the broadcast media like radio and television. The speaker is not able to take advantage of receiver feedback — a most important difference.

Finally, the communication process is affected by *receiver variables*, the same items, both internal and external, that affect the source in any communication encounter. Like Fred, Martha is affected by her education, vocabulary, past communication experiences, past life experiences, and her cultural, hereditary, and environmental stimuli; she is affected by her image of Fred, her own self-image, her past communication encounters with Fred, the nature of the speaking situation, her and Fred's roles and status, and her various attitudes and predispositions.

By putting these many variables together, a realistic and complex model of *transactive communication* may be created, as illustrated in figure 2.1. Argumentative communication should be viewed as part of or as a subset of this overall transactive communication process. The same variables that function within general communication settings, such as daily conversational encounters, function within argumentative communication. There is a tendency on the part of some people to think that argumentative communication is fairly sterile, concerned only with purely logical arguments (whatever they are) that somehow restrict the use of emotion, biases and prejudices, images, and so on. That is simply not the case. Argumentative communication is as colorful and complex as any type of communication, and its goal is the same: to convey a message from one person to another with a particular purpose in mind.[3]

Figure 2.1

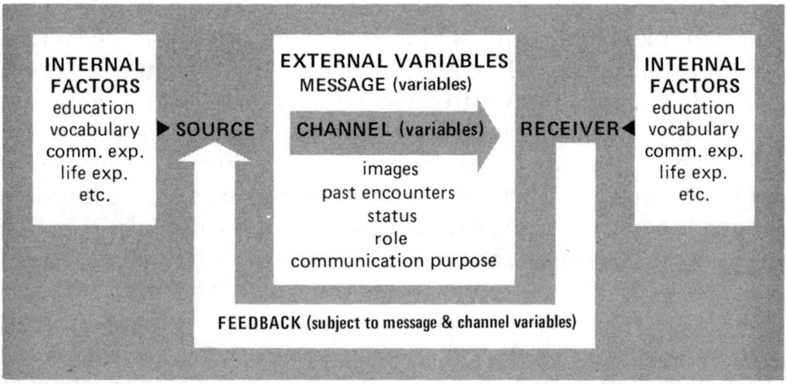

The Reasoning Process

The overriding reason why there has been a tendency to look upon argumentative communication as almost purely logical and, therefore, as more limited than transactional communication processes has been the notion that argumentation and debate are mainly limited to matters of a logical nature. The way one defines argumentation and debate will control the overall study of that type of communication, and the most prevalent notion has been that argumentative communication is a study of the principles of logic. For example, contemporary theorists Ziegelmueller and Dause drew this exact distinction when they defined argumentation as, "The study of the logical principles which underlie the examination and presentation of persuasive claims."[4] However, you should remember that argumentation has been defined quite differently within this book ("The process of presenting persuasive information and conclusions to secure agreement with one's position"); our operating definition does not restrict the study of argumentative communication in the main to the many principles of logic. The materials used in argumentation and debate do not have to be solely logical in nature.

Since the study of argumentative communication involves the giving of reasons to secure another person's agreement or action, it is necessary to examine briefly the human reasoning process. The purpose of this examination is not to delve into psychological theory, but to indicate the kinds of things that occur within the process of argumentative communication. To do so, a distinction must be drawn between logical reasoning and what we shall term *rhetorical reasoning.*

Logical (Formal) Reasoning

During the developmental period of rhetorical theory in ancient Greece, it was common to study oral communication hand-in-hand with dialectic or formal logic. Aristotle, for example, noted in *The Rhetoric* that rhetoric was the counterpart of dialectic and that "everybody to some extent makes use of both dialectic and rhetoric."[5] From that point on, it became the norm to study formal logic while simultaneously studying the principles of effective oral communication. The syllogistic disputations of early colonial America, the forerunners of competitive debate in this country, exemplified the proffered union of logic and public discourse, because those debates adhered strictly to the principles of formal logic and were conducted in Latin.

Although we no longer force debaters and practitioners of public argument to conform to the dull operating procedures of the syllogistic disputations, the reliance upon formal logic still remains constant in the general study of argumentative communication. The use of formal logic in the study of argument presupposes that man operates in the main logically; as Edward Corbett put it, we assume that "rationality is man's essential characteristic."[6] In implementing this assumption, the student of logical reasoning comes to revere the primary device of logical reasoning — the syllogism, the device developed primarily by Aristotle to analyze the reasoning process.

If you have taken a logic course or perhaps a course in philosophy, you have seen this classical example of the syllogism:

All men are mortal.

Socrates is a man.

Therefore, Socrates is mortal.

Every syllogism consists of three factors: a major premise (all men are mortal); a minor premise (Socrates is a man); and a conclusion (therefore, Socrates is mortal). In studying the structure of the syllogism in formal logic, you are primarily concerned with the validity of the syllogism; that is, does the structure of the syllogism allow you to reach the offered conclusion? Validity is determined by examining the structure of the components of the syllogism, and students generally are given a plethora of sample syllogisms for study to practice differentiating between valid and invalid types. Of course, rules exist for the determination of validity, rules that need to be applied to all syllogisms under scrutiny.

The study of the syllogism also entails the determination of the truth of the subject matter of the syllogism. Premises would be examined as to their truth—is it truthful to say, for example, that all men are mortal? If you could demonstrate that at least one man was not mortal, that one man would not die, then the truthfulness of the syllogism could be denied and the syllogism discarded. Importantly, a syllogism can be valid but not true; conversely, a syllogism can be true but invalid. This somewhat confusing paradox can be illustrated simply:

All A is B.
All B is C.
Therefore, all A is C.

That is a logically valid syllogism, but if, in reality, all A was not B, then it would be an untrue syllogism and of no logical value. Or, consider this:

All A is B.
All A is C.
Therefore, all B is C.

The materials contained within that syllogism might be true, but its structure lacks the proper "distribution of terms," thereby making that particular syllogism invalid and of no logical value — despite the fact that its contents might be true.

Syllogistic reasoning may be examined through the use of Venn diagrams, a pictorial approach to the study of argument. For example, the classical syllogism dealing with Socrates' mortality can be pictured as in figure 2.2. Notice that the circle encompassing all men is found completely within the larger circle of mortality, and, to demonstrate Socrates' relation to everything, Socrates is placed within the circle of being a man and within the circle of mortality. Similarly, the All A is B syllogism is described in a Venn diagram in figure 2.3.

Figure 2.2

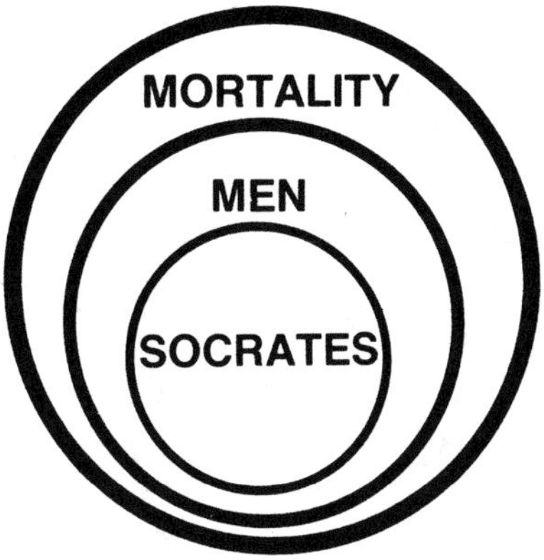

Figure 2.3

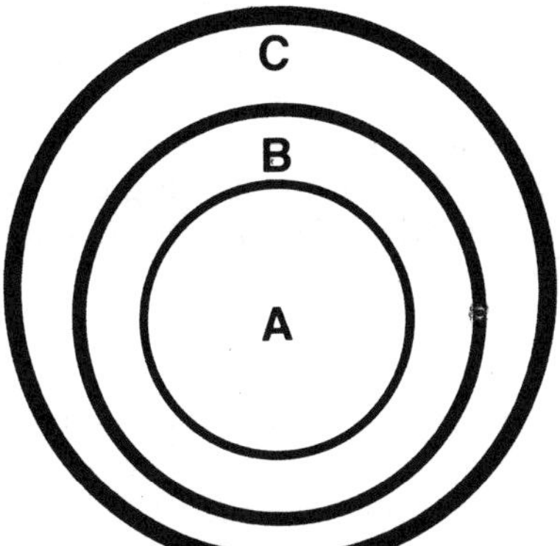

If, on the other hand, your premises were not universal statements but were limited particulars ("*Some* men are mortal"), then the Venn diagram would appear as shown in figure 2.4. Your task, as a student of logic, would be to find out where in those conjoining circles you would place Socrates. Is he a man who is mortal or is he one of those men who are not mortal?

The study of formal logic is fairly difficult and contains many important points and nuances that go beyond the intentions of this book. Although its study is beneficial to the serious student of

Figure 2.4

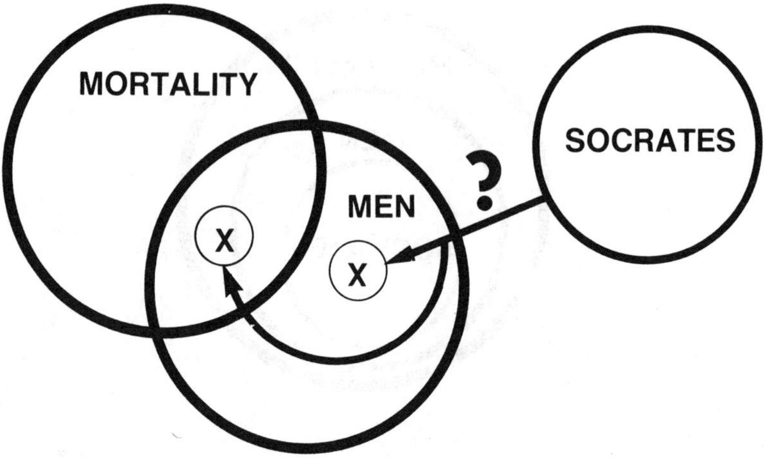

formal argument, formal logic tends to overemphasize rationality in the study of argument. This drawback was noted most clearly by contemporary argumentation theorist William Bennett:

> The rationality of man may be (or may not be) a good goal, but to train and educate students in a system (such as argumentation and logic) that presumes rationality is to weaken the effectiveness and relevance of the educational process.[7]

Although most classical scholars prefer to look upon man as a rational animal, even Edward Corbett was forced to admit that nonrational forces are important: "Ideally, reason should dominate all of man's thinking and actions, but actually, man is often influenced by passions and prejudices and customs."[8] Therefore, the study of realistic argumentative communication requires a knowledge about the human reasoning process that goes beyond the syllogistic models of formal logical processes. All elements of the reasoning process must be considered and placed within their functioning environment as they operate in various communicative settings. This more comprehensive approach will be termed rhetorical reasoning.

Rhetorical Reasoning

Although it is possible to agree with Hample in his analysis of Stephen Toulmin's model of argument that "arguments function syllogistically" in daily settings, it is insufficient to limit our analysis of the human reasoning process to the nature of formal logic.[9] What you or I choose to call logical will depend very heavily upon our particular biases and attitudes. When you read the Lindsey essay, "The Dangers of Nuclear Power," your decision concerning the strength or lack of her logical arguments was based heavily upon your predispositions about nuclear power. If you fear the development of nuclear power, you found her essay to be very logical; if you support the development of nuclear power, on the other hand, then you found her position to be quite illogical. This same logical-illogical dichotomy exists for Senator Church's speech on natural gas deregulation. Yes, real-world arguments function syllogistically, meaning that we tend to make decisions by proceeding from premises to conclusions, but those premises and conclusions often do not adhere to the syllogistic dictates of truth and validity. As Beardsley noted, "To argue is to invite a reader or listener to accept a conclusion because of the reason given."[10] In functional argumentative communication, the reason given may or may not conform to the structure of formal logic. The human reasoning process is multidimensional and much more complex than the limited view of formal syllogistic reasoning.

Reexamine the complex transactive communication model presented earlier within this chapter. Take careful notice of the many internal and external factors that affect one's communication with any other person. Every one of those factors, and many more not noted, come into play during each and every communication encounter. Since argumentative communication is but a subset of the overall communication process, the communication model itself indicates that there is more to the study of functional argumentation and debate than the study of formal logic. Those various internal and external factors color or affect how arguments are seen, interpreted, and evaluated. For example, if you have very little respect for me based upon our previous encounters, this lack of respect will affect your interpretation and evaluation of what I might say to you. I could recite the classical syllogism concerning Socrates' mortality — a valid and true syllogistic argument — but your lack of respect for me might cause you to reject my argument. If you say to yourself, "Man, this guy is such a big turkey, he'll never know anything that's right," then my formally logical argument will be ineffective. You will reject what I have to say, despite the fact that my argument conforms to the syllogistic structure.

Perhaps the best way to understand the functioning of the human reasoning process is to adopt Perelman's notion of quasi-logical argument.[11] Explained very simply, a quasi-logical argument is one that appears to be logical, despite the fact that the argument does not meet all requirements to be truly formally logical. Thus, the study of argument is not based upon the structures of formal logic, but is mainly based upon the operant human communication process. Another way of looking at the human reasoning process is to consider the Aristotelian enthymeme, Aristotle's system for studying real-world argument.[12] Unlike syllogistic reasoning wherein all the premises leading to the conclusion are clearly stated, enthymematic reasoning notes that a speaker's listeners will provide many of their own premises, which will either support or deny that which the speaker directs to them. People do not think or react in a vacuum; ideas, biases, and attitudes exist before the speaker initiates the communication encounter, and these preexistent materials will affect the acceptance or rejection of your argument. For example, the conclusionary argument that "people should love one another" is based upon the implied premise that each person has inherent value and worth. The acceptance or rejection of the premise will determine the eventual acceptance or rejection of the conclusion. Much of the current acrimony over the Equal Rights Amendment exemplifies this age-old notion of enthymematic reasoning. Although we might wish that decisions would be reached in accord with logical truth and validity, as Corbett noted, "Man is often influenced by passions and prejudices and customs."

Thus, the functional study of argumentative communication must be concerned with more than the limited study of formal logic. People accept as logical arguments that are structurally illogical; image often is given greater credence than substance; the imaginary often is preferred to the real—and argumentative communication is concerned with the totality of those dichotomies. Your study of argumentative communication will cover all aspects of the transactive communication process, examining a myriad of elements that cause others to agree or disagree with positions and decisions you advocate.

Audience Primacy in Argumentative Communication

The goal of argumentative communication is to secure the agreement of others with your point of view. Lindsey's essay on nuclear power was designed to get you to agree that nuclear power plants were dangerous and that development of such plants should be stopped. In Fred's argumentative encounter with Martha, his goal was to cause her to agree with him that the United States should not have approved those treaties giving the Panama Canal to the country of Panama. Senator Church opposed the deregulation of natural gas prices, and his speech was designed to increase support for his position. Argumentative communication, then, centers upon having an audience, be it one person or millions of people, agree with the position advanced by an argument. To be effective, argumentative communication must, out of necessity, be audience-oriented.

The totality of argumentative communication must be geared toward the audience. The wording of the argument, the language and materials employed to support the argument, the structure of the argument, in fact everything about the argument must be designed to fit that particular audience. The more you can learn about your audience, the better able you will be to frame arguments most appropriate to that audience. Arguments, in short, do not exist as separate entities unto themselves; they only have meaning and impact when they are presented to another person. Therefore, arguments must be tailored to coincide with that person's biases, attitudes, and beliefs; what may appear to be a perfectly good argument to you may seem to be sheer nonsense to the other person. Therefore, the successful practitioner of public argument will modify his positions to take advantage of that which he can learn about his audience. Later chapters within this book will provide various ideas designed to enhance the effectiveness of your argumentative encounters with others, but you must recognize that all argumentative communication is, by definition, audience-oriented. At all times, both before and during the presentation of argument, you must constantly ask yourself, "How is my audience going to react to this?" and, "How is my audience reacting to this argument?" By carefully scrutinizing audience feedback during the presentation of argument, you may make the proper modifications that will cause your argument to become acceptable to your audience. As with all communication, audience primacy must be considered the number one objective of effective argumentative communication.

Conclusion

Argumentative communication is but a subset of the overall transactive communication process, a process which is very complex and intricate. Since argument is affected by the totality of human communication factors, the study of argumentative communication must be more comprehensive than that limited to the study of formal logical principles. The full range of human communication factors must be considered in argumentative communication, but the practitioner of argument must put audience primacy at the top of the list of factors to be emphasized. Audience primacy must be of central concern to all practitioners of argument.

References

1. Jerry M. Anderson, "Argumentation and Education," in *Proceedings of the National Conference on Argumentation*, ed. James I. Luck (Fort Worth, Tex.: Texas Christian University, 1973), p. 5.

2. For an extended discussion of the factors of the communication process, see James Edward Sayer, *Functional Speech Communication* (Dubuque, Iowa: Kendall/Hunt, 1977), pp. 83–99.

3. See Richard E. Crable, *Argumentation as Communication: Reasoning with Receivers* (Columbus, Ohio: Charles E. Merrill, 1976).

4. George W. Ziegelmueller and Charles A. Dause, *Argumentation: Inquiry and Advocacy* (Englewood Cliffs, N. J.: Prentice-Hall, 1975), p. 4.

5. Aristotle, *The Rhetoric*, trans. Lane Cooper (New York: Appleton-Century-Crofts, 1932), p. 1.

6. Edward P. J. Corbett, *Classical Rhetoric for the Modern Student* (New York: Oxford University Press, 1965), p. 39.

7. William H. Bennett, "The Role of Debate in Speech Communication," *The Speech Teacher* 21 (November 1972): 282.

8. Corbett, *Classical Rhetoric for the Modern Student*, p. 39.

9. Dale Hample, "The Toulmin Model and the Syllogism," *Journal of the American Forensic Association* 14 (Summer 1977): 8.

10. Monroe C. Beardsley, *Modes of Argument* (Indianapolis: Bobbs-Merrill, 1967), p. 7.

11. See Chaim Perelman and L. Olbrechts-Tyteca, *The New Rhetoric: A Treatise on Argumentation* (London: University of Notre Dame Press, 1969).

12. See Aristotle, *Rhetoric*, pp. 154–181.

PRACTICUM

1. To develop your appreciation of the complex nature of the transactive communication process, recollect a recent conversation that you had with one of your friends. Now, answer these questions concerning that communicative encounter:

- What image did you have of the other person? (For example, did you consider her to be trustworthy and reliable — or the opposite?)
- How did you feel that the other person felt toward you? (For example, did she feel you to be trustworthy?)
- What factors caused you to communicate with the other person?
- Did you experience any confusion from language used either by you or the other person? Did you come away saying, "Why did I say that?"

By answering these questions, you will discover that that simple conversation was not that simple at all. You can imagine, then, how very complex an argumentative encounter can be, complete with its emotionally laden biases, prejudices, and attitudes.

2. One of the most unpopular military adventures undertaken by the United States was the Mexican War, a struggle that eventually brought the American Southwest under the control of the United States. Read the following extract from an antiwar speech presented to the United States Senate on 11 February 1847 by the famous Ohio senator Thomas Corwin. Since you are not emotionally involved with the issues presented within this speech, see if you can find the implied or unstated premises that underlie Corwin's arguments. How sound is Corwin's position? How many of his arguments would be viable today?

The Dismemberment of Mexico

Senator Thomas Corwin

What is the territory, Mr. President, which you propose to wrest from Mexico? It is consecrated to the heart of the Mexican by many a well-fought battle with his old Castilian master. His Bunker Hills and Saratogas and Yorktowns are there! The Mexican can say, "There I bled for liberty! and shall I surrender that consecrated home of my affections to the Anglo-Saxon invaders? What do they want with it? They have Texas already. They have possessed themselves of the territory between the Nueces and the Rio Grande. What else do they want? To what shall I point my children as memorials of that independence which I bequeath to them, when those battlefields shall have passed from my possession?"

Sir, had one come and demanded Bunker Hill of the people of Massachusetts, had England's lion ever showed himself there, is there a man over thirteen and under ninety who would not have been ready to meet him? Is there a river on this continent that would not have run red with blood? Is there a field but would have been piled high with unburied bones of slaughtered Americans before these consecrated battlefields of liberty should have been wrested from us? But this same American goes into a sister Republic, and says to poor, weak Mexico, "Give up your territory, you are unworthy to possess it; I have got one-half already, and all I ask of you is to give up the other!" England might as well, in the circumstances I have described, have come and demanded of us, "Give up the Atlantic slope — give up this trifling territory from the Allegheny Mountains to the sea; it is only from Maine to St. Mary's — only about one-third of your Republic, and the least interesting portion of it." What would be the response? They would say we must give this up to John Bull. Why? "He wants room." The Senator from Michigan says he must have this. Why, my worthy Christian brother; on what principle of justice? "I want room!"

Sir, look at this pretense of want of room. With twenty millions of people, you have about one thousand millions of acres of land, inviting settlement by every conceivable argument, bringing them down to a quarter of a dollar an acre, and allowing every man to squat where he pleases. But the Senator from Michigan says we will be two hundred millions in a few years, and we want room. If I were a Mexican I would tell you, "Have you not room enough in your own country to bury your dead? If you come into mine we will greet you with bloody hands, and welcome you to hospitable graves."

Why, says the Chairman of this Committee on Foreign Relation, it is the most reasonable thing in the world! We ought to have the Bay of San Francisco! Why? Because it is the best harbor in the Pacific! It has been my fortune, Mr. President, to have practiced a good deal in criminal courts in the course of my life, but I never yet heard a thief, arraigned for stealing a horse, plead that it was the best horse he could find in the country! We want California. What for? Why, says the Senator from Michigan, we will have it; and the Senator from South Carolina, with a very mistaken view, I think, of policy, says you can't keep our people from going there. I don't desire to prevent them. Let them go and seek their happiness in whatever country or clime it pleases them. All I ask of them is, not to require this government to protect them with that banner consecrated to war waged for principles — eternal, enduring truth. Sir, it is not meant that our old flag should throw its protecting folds over expeditions for lucre or for land. But you still say you want room for your people. This has been the plea of every robber chief from Nimrod to the present hour. I dare say, when Tamerlane descended from his throne, built of seventy thousand human skulls, and marched his ferocious battalions to further slaughter, — I dare say he said, "I want room." Bajazet was another gentleman of kindred tastes and wants with us Anglo-Saxons — he "wanted room." Alexander, too, the mighty "Macedonian madman," when he wandered with his Greeks to the plains of India, and fought a bloody battle on the very ground where recently England and the Sikhs engaged in strife for "room," was, no doubt, in quest of some California there. Many a Monterey had he to storm to get "room." Sir, he made as much of that sort of history as you ever will.

Mr. President, do you remember the last chapter in that history? It is soon read. Ah, I wish we could but understand its moral. Ammon's son (so was Alexander named) after all his victories, died drunk in Babylon! The vast empire he conquered to "get room," became the prey of the generals he had trained; it was dismembered, torn to pieces, and so ended. Sir, there is a very significant appendix; it is this: The descendants of the Greeks, Alexander's Greeks, are now governed by a descendant of Attila! Mr. President, while we are fighting for room, let us ponder deeply this appendix. I was somewhat amazed the other day to hear the Senator from Michigan declare that Europe had quite forgotten us, till these battles waked them up. I suppose the Senator feels grateful to the President for "waking up" Europe. Does the President, who is, I hope, read in civic as well as military lore, remember the saying of one who had pondered upon history long; long, too, upon man, his nature, and true destiny. Montesquieu did not think highly of this way of "waking up." "Happy," says he, "is that nation whose annals are tiresome."

Chapter 3

Argumentation and Debate in Society

* The Significance of Argumentative Communication
* Argument in Your Life
* The Nature of Argumentative Proof
* Conclusion
* References
* Practicum

In the preceding chapters, you have been given the definition and purpose of argumentative communication and shown its relationship to the overall transactional communication process. Within this chapter, the role of argumentative communication in society will be discussed, emphasizing the fact that the study of argument is no mere academic study but is one that has practical value and application to you in daily life. This chapter will present a theoretical justification for the existence of argumentation and debate in a free society, and then examples of societal argument will be presented and analyzed, the kinds of public argument that you use and, in turn, have used on you. President John F. Kennedy was once quoted as saying that the techniques of argumentative communication serve for us as "the tool of democracy." This chapter will support that viewpoint.

The Significance of Argumentative Communication

Perhaps the most outstanding characteristic of our society is the relative freedom to say anything and everything we want to say. As long as our words do not trample upon the rights and privileges of others, we are free to say whatever pleases us, to speak out on behalf of or against the policies and actions of others. Both law and custom have been controlled for more than two hundred years to guarantee the right to express, as Justice Holmes put it, even "the thought that we hate." The United States has stood as a stalwart beacon in support of the principle and policy of the freedom of speech. Free speech is perhaps the most essential element of the functioning American democracy.

Because of our commitment to free speech, our society concommitantly is committed to an open decision-making process, a system that encourages public participation in the process by which decisions are reached. The theory has been advanced that through the public examination of ideas and policy proposals, through the tools provided via argumentative communication, those final decisions reached will be the best of all possible decisions, a point indicated by Thomas Nilsen:

> We have come to value highly the processes of public debate wherein there is confrontation of case with case, where advocates challenge each other's information and conclusions. Such confrontation produces the kind of information and criticism of conclusions that makes possible more intelligent choices on the part of the listeners.[1]

It is not necessarily true that the more people involved in the making of a decision the more likely the results are to be constantly fantastic decisions (remember the old maxim that too many cooks spoil the broth); the odds favor better decision making in such an open system of inquiry and advocacy. Upon this basis, Ehninger and Brockriede approached the notion of "the value of critical choice and decision":

> A critical decision is more reliable than a decision that is arrived at uncritically, because it is based on a careful study of pertinent evidence and values. Not only does it have a better chance of proving true when put to the test or of working out successfully in practice, but it is able to withstand what John Dewey described as "the strain of further inquiry."[2]

The impact of an open system of decision making is clear: better final decisions generally result, because all proposed decisions are examined, critically evaluated, and stringently assessed as to their potential short-term and long-term effects. In putting all such potential decisions through these tests, the tools of argumentative communication serve society well. By examining the justification for policy decisions, by scrutinizing the materials that support those possible decisions, and by critically forecasting the results of all possible decisions, the processes of argumentation and debate allow you and the rest of the members of society to take an important role in developing beneficial approaches to the solutions of problems.

Not only does an open system of decision-making provide better results in the formulation and implementation of policy decisions, it also promotes the basic ethical responsibilities of a society founded upon the ideals of free speech and open public discussions. This inseparable link between practical value and ethical responsibility was seen by Dennis G. Day:

> Decision is meaningful only if there are alternatives from which to choose. . . . Thus, the prime requisite which must be met if debate is to provide sound decisions is that it be thorough and complete, that all arguments and information relevant to decision be known and understood. A commitment to debate as the method of democratic decision-making demands an overriding ethical responsibility to promote the full confrontation of opposing opinions, arguments, and information relevant to decision.[3]

Therefore, the critical tools of argumentative communication are significant in helping to develop sound decisions and in upholding the societal commitment to free speech and open decision making.

Unfortunately, there have been times in American history when information has been restricted, when there has been a minimum of public involvement in debate and discussion regarding proposed policy decisions. The Vietnam and Watergate eras of the 1960s and 1970s demonstrate the problems that can be generated when full, frank public discussion is prevented. Professor Jerome Wiesner, president of the Massachusetts Institute of Technology, surveyed our recent history and saw the link between poor decision making and the restriction of information flow:

> Many of the most decisively wrong policy errors of the last twenty years which exacerbated the cold war and led to many other bad decisions would probably not have been made if Congress and the people had been told even a small amount about the quality and character of the information these decisions were based on.[4]

A closed information system creates closed decision making, and such a system all too often leads to erroneous and harmful decisions.

Therefore, as you can see, your study of the essentials of argumentative communication is of significance to the functional operations of our free society. By researching all pertinent information and by critically considering all possible alternatives of actions, final decisions reached will be of a better and more thought-out quality. Certainly, the application of the principles of argumentative communication does not guarantee that errors will not be made; the processes of argumentation and debate are not panaceas for the solution of present and future problems. However, argumentative communication does provide the critical tools necessary for the most efficient and effective method of analyzing current situations and proposing viable actions for the future. Your study of argumentation and debate will prove to be very beneficial, for, as Russel Windes noted, "It is only good sense that in the process of educating young citizens to become a part of free society, we acquaint them with the methods of advocacy — the theory of argument and the practice of that theory in debate."[5]

As a final thought to the significance of argumentative communication to our society, the processes of argumentation and debate will tend to make you more tolerant of the views of others. It was noted in Chapter 1 that argumentative communication causes you to see both sides of an issue, to understand the perspectives of those who disagree with you. From a social standpoint, your being able to see the multifaceted nature of most controversial issues will improve your own humane tendencies, recognizing the inherent value and worth of the opinions of others. Obviously, such an attitude supports the social commitment to free speech; tolerance of opposing views aids in the maintenance of open discussion and improved information flow.

Argument in Your Life

The study of argumentative communication not only benefits the operation of our free society, it also serves your own interests very highly. As part of that society, argumentation and debate play an important role in your life, both as an initiator of argument and as a consumer of argument.

It would be an understatement to suggest that you engage in dozens of argumentative encounters every day. From the minute you get up in the morning until you go to bed at night, you come into contact with many people, and every such interpersonal contact provides a situation ripe for argumentative encounter. Consider this example from your life of only a few years ago:

Mother:	Come on, it's time to get up! Come on, it's almost eight o'clock!
You:	Okay, I'm up; I'm up.
Mother:	What do you want for breakfast this morning?
You:	Just some juice. I'm not hungry at all this morning.
Mother:	You've got to have more than juice. That's no way to start the day.
You:	No, really, I'll be fine. Juice is all I want.
Mother:	No child of mine is going off without a good breakfast. Now do you want bacon, some toast, an egg. . . .
You:	No, nothing. I just want a glass of juice. There's no sense fixing me something I don't want.
Mother:	Okay, but if you feel sick later on, don't blame me!

That does sound familiar, doesn't it? Well, that encounter truly was argumentative in nature. Both you and your mother had goals in mind; both of you supported your positions by giving a reason why your particular goal should be met. This argumentative encounter could be diagrammed as in figure 3.1. The argument ended when your mother relented, allowing you to have only juice for your breakfast, but it was no done happily ("If you feel sick later on, don't blame me!"). In a sense, you won this argumentative encounter, because you were able to achieve your goal, but your mother was not persuaded that your goal was a good one. In fact, she still felt that her goal was better for you in the long run.

Such a simple example demonstrates the truism that you engage in numerous argumentative encounters daily. Some of the issues are important (trying to convince your teacher that your final grade in this course should be higher) and some of the issues are

Figure 3.1

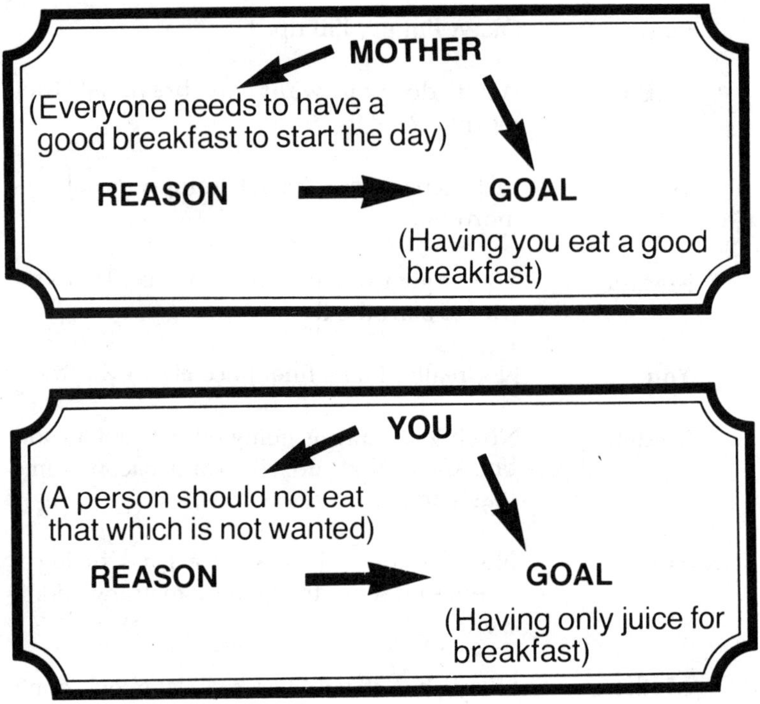

fairly trivial (orange juice is better than tomato juice for breakfast). Regardless of the particular issue involved, you engage in argument constantly, and, therefore, your study of the principles of argumentative communication will be valuable in your daily activities, providing benefits that you will discover every day of your life.

More importantly, argumentation and debate training will prove beneficial in your role as a consumer of argument in society. You are bombarded constantly with hundreds and thousands of arguments, arguments urging you to believe this or that, to buy this product, and to vote for that individual running for office. Statements from politicians, opinion leaders, persons in the mass media, and mass advertising actually serve as arguments designed to have you do something that will meet the goals of others. Therefore, knowledge of argumentative communication will improve your critical abilities to make better decisions concerning those arguments you are asked to accept. As a consumer of public argument, knowledge about such argument is invaluable.

You are bombarded with a plethora of political arguments, ideas that urge you to support a certain course of action or to support a particular candidate. The reasons given you to justify your support are argumentative in nature, and, as Howard Kahane wrote, "The person who understands how modern political campaigns are waged, and understands the devices and ploys used in campaign oratory, will be better prepared to cope with them."[6] For example, consider this piece of argument, presented in the form of a slogan, that was used to support President Woodrow Wilson's reelection campaign of 1916:

The Lesson is Plain:
If you want war, vote for Hughes!
If you want peace with Honor
VOTE FOR WILSON!

The argument contained within that slogan is very clear: if you want to avoid war, then you must support Wilson's reelection campaign. Conversely, if you vote for Hughes (Charles Evans Hughes of New York), then you will be voting to have the United States become involved in the Great War (World War I). Would you, as the consumer of that public argument, be willing to accept that argument? Assuming that you do not necessarily favor going to war, would you find yourself compelled by the power of that argument to cast your vote for Wilson? Hopefully, you would not be willing to accept that argument at face value; hopefully, you would recognize that that argument is much too simplistic to be sound. Since the issues surrounding possible American involvement in World War I are relative ancient history to you, you are able to look at that argumentative slogan objectively and dispassionately, discovering that the argument's simplicity makes it untenable. You would not find that argument to be sufficient in itself to cause you to support Woodrow Wilson.

That example is very dated; you have nothing at stake, because a 1916 argument means nothing of significance to you. However, contemporary political arguments are more meaningful, as you are part of the environment in which the arguments occur. For example, in early 1978, President Jimmy Carter said that we must combat the ever spiraling costs of energy, contending that this commitment must be "the moral equivalent of war." That is a contemporary argument, and it is one that you cannot view so objectively. You have lived through the period of skyrocketing energy costs; you have seen the prices for gasoline, home heating oil, natural gas, and electricity reach all-time highs. In a sense, you have been a victim of these energy costs, so you have an emotional response to Carter's argument. You might have found yourself saying, "You're damned right! It's about time somebody did something to stop the oil companies and utilities from giving us the short end of the stick!" Importantly, even though you are part of the argumentative environment, you still need to address the strength and worth of an argument as dispassionately as possible. Although you might instinctively agree with President Carter's positions, as a critical consumer of argument you need to assess carefully the justification and rationale for that position. In short, to be an effective consumer of public argument, you must stringently evaluate all arguments presented to you — all arguments, even those with which you might find yourself to be in agreement. Or consider these other political arguments of our recent past:

1. Supporters of Lyndon Johnson's 1964 campaign said that to vote for Senator Goldwater, the Republican party nominee for president, would commit the United States to thermonuclear war within days after the election.
2. Richard Nixon campaigned for the presidency in 1968 on the contention that he had a "secret plan" to end the Vietnam war that would provide us "peace with honor."
3. Certain national spokesmen said that the Watergate scandal was of little importance, noting that the president of the United States would never even consider lying to the American people.
4. Jimmy Carter campaigned for the presidency in 1976, contending that it was the federal bureaucracy in Washington that caused most of this country's problems.
5. Ronald Reagan opposed turning over the Panama Canal to the country of Panama on the grounds that the Cubans and the Soviets would keep us from using that shipping lane during wartime.

You may remember most of these arguments. Many of them seem either absurd or quite perceptive to us now, but that is an advantage that comes from hindsight. Unfortunately, in making decisions that affect us and others, we do not have this advantage of hindsight; we need to make the best possible, critically examined judgment concerning the future. To that end, critical assessment of political arguments is essential, and the study of the principles of argumentative communication will aid your critical assessment. As Kahane noted, you will be better equipped to cope with these important political issues.

Besides many political arguments, your life is full of arguments from advertisers, people who want you to spend your money for their particular products. Will a certain toothpaste enhance your sex appeal? Does that argument make sense to you? Do you believe that claim? Should you buy a brand of toilet tissue because it is squeezably soft? Should you eat a certain candy bar because it is named after an important baseball player? Should you use a particular brand of popcorn popper because it is advertised by a famous former football player? When you look at advertising, you really look at slick examples of public argument, and you should examine these claims as stringently as you would the claims offered by politicians. Billions of dollars are spent annually on mass advertising campaigns, chains of argument designed to influence both what you buy and how much you buy. And these arguments, too, need to be examined critically. The individual who unthinkingly buys a tube of toothpaste to increase his sex appeal dramatically also buys a very weak and unsupported argument.

You also face arguments from the mass media arena and from so-called opinion leaders, people whose thoughts and ideas have an impact upon the thinking of others. For example, during the late 1960s, one of the hottest national issues was the proposal to lower the voting age from twenty-one to eighteen, an issue that stirred a great deal of argument until its final adoption. Supporters of this proposed change said that anyone who might be called upon to serve in the armed forces (remember, the Vietnam war was going hot and heavy at that time) ought to be able to vote upon those policies that would so directly affect them. However, a large number of people opposed this change, fearing the impact that lowering the voting age would have on the United States. In April of 1969, syndicated columnist Don MacLean wrote a column entitled, "Why I'm Against Younger Voting Age," an excellent example of public argument, and one of such interest that it is reprinted here for your examination.

Why I'm Against Younger Voting Age

Don MacLean

There's a lot of talk about lowering the voting age — from 21 to 18. The young people are yelling for it and many politicians are going along with them because, well, because that's where the voters are, baby.

This doesn't mean any sensible politician really thinks an 18-year-old is old enough to vote. Not for a minute. It just means he hopes that when the kids do vote — be it at 18 or 21 — they'll remember he was for them.

Should the voting age be lowered, it'll amuse me to see that the kids, far from voting for kindly old Senator Whoosis, will instead vote for the current rock'n'roll star or protest singer. The kids almost deserve somebody like that as President, but the rest of us don't, and that's why I'm against lowering the voting age.

In fact, I think it should be raised — to about 25. While it is difficult to peg any particular age as that which most persons reach maturity, at least the age 25 suggests that the individual will have read something besides comic books and viewed something on television other than "Teen-age Dance Party."

Yet we have people like Senator Alan Bible (D., Nevada) who has introduced a bill to lower the voting age to 18 by amending the Constitution. He says things like, "If you're old enough to be a soldier, you're old enough to vote."

Well, bully for him, but I think the Senator (and anyone else who parrots that idiotic line) ignores certain facts. For one thing, while many kids are old enough to be soldiers, many of them are not old enough to take it in good grace. Otherwise, they would not be burning draft cards, having anti-draft rallies and running off to Canada.

Responsibility, i.e., responding to the draft when your number is called, is one test of maturity. So many of our youngsters have failed this test I'd be afraid to trust them with the vote. Besides, they'd just vote for any candidate who promised to keep their dear little necks out of the service.

I remember when I was 18 (it wasn't that long ago). On the day that I registered for the draft, I wasn't any more qualified to vote for President than I was to pilot a 707 over the North Pole. Old enough to fight, old enough to vote? Let's face it, an 11-year-old can fight: does that mean he should vote?

Remember, it was the youngsters who propelled Senator Eugene McCarthy into prominence. To me, this alone signifies that, as a group, 18-year-olds are not ready for self-government.[7]

You probably did not like the MacLean article; most of your classmates probably did not like it either. But can you develop sound reasons why MacLean's arguments should not be accepted? Or can you develop reasons why MacLean's arguments should be accepted? After all, that article was written to persuade you to agree that the voting age should not be lowered. Can you assess the argumentative weaknesses and strengths of that article?

You and I serve as consumers of public argument daily; therefore, it is essential that we be able to assess the viability of those arguments forced upon us. The study of the processes of argumentation and debate provides the skills needed to make such critical assessments, supporting Douglas Ehninger's view that "critical thought and deliberation are to be preferred not only in the life of the individual but in that of the group and of society, as well."[8] The study of argumentative communication will prove to be very useful every day of your life.

The Nature of Argumentative Proof

In examining the material support given public statements by various speakers, teachers of rhetoric in ancient Greece spoke of the use of proof — those bits of evidence and information that supported a speaker's position. Proof, in turn, was delineated into three categories: *logos*, the use of logical proof; *pathos*, the use of emotional proof; and *ethos*, the credibility or image of the speaker. While this separation of support materials is somewhat arbitrary, especially realizing that it is practically impossible to distinguish between the logical and the emotional in most situations, the importance of proof indicated that it was something deserving study in the preparation and presentation of effective oral discourse. Experimental research findings have supported the theories of the Greek rhetoricians. People actually demand that a speaker support or substantiate that which is said; they recognize the difference between a substantiated *argument* and an unsubstantiated *assertion*.[9] You can see this difference quite easily:

Heather: The United States ought to have a comprehensive medical care program to provide complete medical service for all its citizens.

Bill: Why? Why should we have such a program?

Heather: Because over forty million people right now cannot afford the medical care they need, and millions of children suffer yearly from the lack of medical attention. The United States Commission on Health in America developed those statistics after an exhaustive three-year study.

That was an example of a substantiated argument. This country needs to have a comprehensive medical care system (why?) to provide the necessary medical services for those who now are unable to afford such services.

Contrast that example with the following:

Mary: The United States ought to shut down the NASA space program.

Tom: Why?

Mary: Because it would be a good idea.

Tom: But why would it be a good idea?

Mary: Because it would be, that's all.

That was an example of unsubstantiated argument, a mere assertion that was not supported by any reason by Mary. You hear many such assertions every day, but they are of minimal argumentative value because (1) they are not supported and (2) many people refuse to accept them. Therefore, proof is an important factor in the construction of effective argumentative communication.

However, and this is a most important point, despite the fact that people demand that arguments be supported, many people cannot distinguish between sound and unsound support.[10] That is, many people cannot tell when proof actually supports an argument and when it does not. Many people cannot recognize discrepancies and contradictions between proof and argument. Unfortunately, for too many people the mere *appearance* of proof is enough; they accept arguments as sound because it appears that the arguments are appropriately supported.

The study of argumentation and debate causes you not to accept such faulty or nonexistent substantiation. You recognize that an argument's soundness is dependent directly upon both the quality and quantity of support that it has. There must be a direct link between an argument and its support, proof must uphold the argument or the argument itself must be considered unsound.

In the preceding chapter, we noted that the study of formal logical principles is of limited value to the practitioner of public argument. We do not reason or examine transactive human communication syllogistically. That does not mean, however, that there is no reasoning process in argumentation and debate. On the contrary, since people demand proof, the reasoning process is an important part of argumentative communication, but it is not the type of reasoning taught in classes on formal logic. Perhaps the nature of argumentative proof might best be described as *perceptual logic*, something that appears to be sound and tenable to those who hear an argument. Information that coincides with your beliefs, no matter how structurally invalid that information might be, often will be considered valid; arguments that are nightmares to formal logicians may appear to be very sound if you happen to agree with them. Studies in selective perception have demonstrated that people will accept, under certain conditions, what they want to believe and will reject what they do not want to hear or believe.[11] However, people tend not to accept or reject arguments or proof on the basis of syllogistic dictates.

The nature of argumentative proof, then, is that it must be audience-centered. To support your arguments, you must provide the kinds of material your audience wants to hear. Naturally, this raises many questions of ethics, an issue to be discussed in a subsequent chapter, but for now you must realize that arguments will not be accepted simply because you can support them with reams of information. Personal biases, prejudices, attitudes, and predispositions have a significant impact upon the acceptability of your arguments. Despite all evidence to the contrary, there still are people who believe that John Kennedy was not killed in Dallas in 1963; some continue to believe that he is alive, hiding out somewhere in South America. Those individuals have found or created their own proof to substantiate their opinion. In the everyday world of argumentative communication, you will have to deal with similar situations and arguments. That is why, in studying the overall scheme of argumentation and society, it is imperative that you heed William Bennett's words to "treat the audience as it is, not as someone wants it to be."[12] Although this book emphasizes the kinds of arguments and proof found generally in formal and academic argumentative encounters, there will be times in informal situations wherein these more formal principles will not be effective. Why? Because argumentative communication, like the transactive communication process itself, is made up of people dealing with people. And in the affairs of mankind, very little is certain.

Conclusion

The study of argumentative communication is important to you as an individual and as a member of a free society. Individually, the study of argument will prove to be valuable in your role as consumer of public argument, enabling you to assess better the claims offered by politicians, salesmen, and others who wish to affect what you think and do. As a member of society, argumentative communication supports this country's tradition of free speech and rational discourse, additionally upholding the virtues of free and open discussion in the decision-making process. A carefully thought-out and critically examined decision is superior to one reached hastily with little thought and examination. Similarly, arguments must be substantiated, underpinned by some form of proof. In all instances, arguments are superior to assertions.

References

1. Thomas R. Nilsen, *Ethics of Speech Communication*, 2nd ed. (Indianapolis, Ind.: Bobbs-Merrill, 1974), p. 74.

2. Douglas Ehninger and Wayne Brockriede, *Decision by Debate* (New York: Dodd, Mead, 1968), p. 3.

3. Dennis G. Day, "The Ethics of Democratic Debate," *Central States Speech Journal* 17 (February 1966): 6.

4. Jerome Wiesner, *None of Your Business*, ed. Norman Dorsen and Stephen Gillers (New York: Viking Press, 1974), p. 215.

5. Russel R. Windes, Jr., "Competitive Debating: The Speech Program, the Individual, and Society," *The Speech Teacher* 9 (March 1960): 99.

6. Howard Kahane, *Logic and Contemporary Rhetoric* (Belmont, Calif.: Wadsworth, 1971), p. viii.

7. Don MacLean, "Why I'm Against Younger Voting Age," *Tucson Daily Citizen*, April 28, 1969.

8. Douglas Ehninger, "Debating as Critical Deliberation," *Southern Speech Communication Journal* 24 (Fall 1958): p. 26.

9. See, for example, Robert S. Cathcart, "An Experimental Study of the Relative Effectiveness of Four Methods of Presenting Evidence," *Speech Monographs* 22 (August 1955): 227–233; James C. McCroskey, "A Sumary of Experimental Research on the Effects of Evidence in Persuasive Communication," *Quartely Journal of Speech* 255 (April 1969): 169–176; and Thomas B. Harte, "Audience Ability to Apply Tests of Evidence," *Journal of the American Forensic Association* 8 (Fall 1971): 109–115.

10. See the studies cited in Wayne N. Thompson, *Quantitative Research in Public Address and Communication* (New York: Random House, 1967), pp. 50–54. This was found also by Harte, "Audience Ability to Apply Tests."

11. See H. Sebald, "Limitations of Communication: Mechanisms of Image Maintenance in Form of Selective Perception, Selective Memory and Selective Distortion," *Journal of Communication* 12 (1962): 142–149; and David L. Paletz, et al., "Selective Exposure: The Potential Boomerang Effect," *Journal of Communication* 22 (March 1972): 48–53.

12. William H. Bennett, "The Role of Debate in Speech Communication," *The Speech Teacher* 21 (November 1972): 282. This suggestion fully supports the audience primacy concept so heavily emphasized in Aristotle's *Rhetoric*.

PRACTICUM

1. Take some time from your studies and spend one evening watching television — just the prime time hours (eight to eleven in the evening) will do nicely. Watch every commercial presented (both local and national in origin) very carefully, taking notes if you find that helpful. Once your viewing is completed, answer these questions:

- How many commercials did you see during that three-hour span?
- What types of products and services were you urged to buy?
- What kind of proof or substantiation was offered in support of those commercial arguments?

Now, after considering those questions, what commercial do you consider to be the best in terms of its argument? Does that commercial provide sufficient justification for your purchasing that product or service? Those are the kinds of questions you should ask of all commercial and political advertisements; seeking answers to them will make you a more critical and more effective consumer.

2. This chapter stressed the importance of free, unrestricted information flow to the functional decision-making process. Read the following argumentative essay, presented at the annual meeting of the Speech Communication Association in Houston, Texas, on Decembe 28, 1975, concerning the restriction of information through the use of executive privilege by the president of the United States. Discuss the many points considered within that essay, and then try to determine under what circumstances the doctrine of executive privilege should and should not be allowed.

Debate, Information Flow, and Executive Privilege: Some Pragmatic and Ethical Considerations

James Edward Sayer

As every observer of the recent Watergate hassle knows well, a main precipitatory factor in Richard Nixon's resignation from the office of the presidency was the decision by the United States Supreme Court in midsummer of 1974 against the president in the so-called Nixon tapes case. High-level conferences within the White

House had been audiotaped by the Nixon staff, ostensibly so that future Nixonian memoirs could be written with greater accuracy and drama than those of other presidents, but these very same tapes had been subpoenaed by the Watergate special prosecutor to serve as evidence in the ongoing Watergate conspiracy and break-in trials. However, President Nixon claimed that the confidentiality of White House decision-making sessions was threatened, and, in invoking the oft-used but ill-defined doctrine of executive privilege, refused to make the tapes available to the legal process, thereby leading to the confrontation between the special prosecutor and the president before the Court.

In ruling against the president in *U. S.* v. *Nixon*, the Court explained its position:

> We conclude that when the ground for asserting privilege as to subpoenaed materials sought for use in a criminal trial is based only on the generalized interest in confidentiality, it cannot prevail over the fundamental demands of due process of law in the fair administration of criminal justice. The generalized assertion of privilege must yield to the demonstrated, specific need for evidence in a pending criminal trial.

While civil libertarians took heart at the Court's decision and the subsequent demise of the Nixon presidency, one disturbing factor remained clear: the Court had, after years of evading the issue, acknowledged the legal and constitutional existence of the doctrine of executive privilege, a problem envisioned by *New York Times* columnist Tom Wicker:

> The problem is that in the doctrine of executive privilege now certified by the Supreme Court to have "Constitutional underpinnings," a President apparently could determine the scope of that area of secrecy for himself, and the privilege her asserted for it would be absolute, except in the unlikely event that it came into conflict with a higher, competing interest.[1]

Thus, executive privilege had not been eliminated by the Court's ruling; instead, its existence had been certified by the country's highest judicial tribunal, and the potential for future controversy had been increased by the decision. Instead of solving a problem, the Court's decision institutionalized it, and the need for further clarifying and delimiting of executive privilege is greater than before. The purpose of this paper is to examine both pragmatic and ethical reasons necessitating such future action, noting, as does "Supreme Court Review" editor Philip Kurland, that such action will have to be promulgated by the Congress.[2]

Pragmatic Considerations

First, it should be recognized that in the policy decision-making process, the pragmatic possibilities of viable policy options are increased by maximizing the informational input into these decisions. While it is not necessarily true that "two heads are better than one," it is still realistic to assert that, within limits, the viability of decisions increases concomitantly with the increase in the amount of informational input into the decision-making process itself. It was upon this basis that Ehninger and Brockriede approached "the value of critical choice and decision":

> A critical decision is more reliable than a decision that is arrived at uncritically, because it is based on a careful study of pertinent evidence and values. Not only does it have a better chance of proving true when put to the test or of working out successfully in practice, but it is better able to withstand what John Dewey described as "the strain of further inquiry."[3]

Therefore, if more individuals are involved in the making of the decision, the sheer involvement of many different viewpoints will enhance the quality of that decision.

However, decision-making at the federal level has become more and more centralized within the executive branch since the end of the Second World War,[4] and this centralization of power has been immeasurably aided by the president's use of secrecy and claim of executive privilege. The Congress and the American people have been systematically denied access to that information needed for the making of decisions; the executive controlled the information flow, or rather the lack of it, and, hence, controlled the decision-making process itself. The results have been negative of a twofold nature.

First, because of the restricted information flow and

subsequent limited nature of decision making, some unfortunate policies have resulted. While hindsight is always convenient in claiming that "such and such" would not have happened if more people had been involved in the making of decisions, the assertion of Ehninger and Brockriede in terms of improving the quality of decisions is still operable. Dr. Jerome Wiesner, president of the Massachusetts Institute of Technology, has overtly claimed that it was the lack of this information flow that directly led to policy decisions of a nonbeneficial nature:

> Many of the most decisively wrong policy errors of the last twenty years which exacerbated the cold war and led to many other bad decisions would probably not have been made if Congress and the people had been told even a small amount about the quality and character of the information these decisions were based on.[5]

Although one can dispute Dr. Wiesner's cause-effect analysis as "Monday morning quarterbacking," one can also look at the closed information system of the executive and ask how decisions could have been any worse with a free-flow system. A closed information system creates closed decision making, and, at least to Dr. Wiesner, such a system tends to promote erroneous decisions. Specifically, several individuals, including former Senator J. William Fulbright, have claimed that America's disastrous involvement in the Vietnam war could have been avoided within an open information system.[6]

Second, besides increasing the possibility of erroneous decisions, a closed information system encourages practices that are designed to falsify and justify those decisions, and this reaction has both pragmatic and ethical implications. Realizing that a closed information system has led to the pursuit of a nonbeneficial or erroneous policy, the decision makers then use this closed system to "cover up" both the results of the decisions as well as the process of decision making. By restricting the flow of information, it becomes relatively easy for the decision makers in power to subvert the perceived truth of the information and to promote distorted concepts of that information. In short, the current woes of "the politics of lying" became a direct offshoot of this closed information system, an effect noted within

American foreign policy by Arthur Schlesinger, Jr.:

> The secrecy system (for classifying and withholding information) instilled in the executive branch the idea that foreign policy was no one's business save its own, and uncontrolled secrecy made it easy for lying to become routine.[7]

Thus, a closed information system, aided and abetted by secrecy and the doctrine of executive privilege, tended to perpetuate its own evils. Limited access to the making of decisions led to nonbeneficial decisions, which, in turn, required the further extension of the closed system to prevent the discovery and subsequent political backlash of erroneous decisions, the doctrine of executive privilege has become a mainstay in the perpetuation of the closed information system as the executive branch tried to shield itself from outside scrutiny. An erroneous decision, therefore, could be endlessly perpetuated as the system itself prevented the correction of errors.

The cumulative result of policy errors and subsequent lying about those errors has been a marked decrease in the credibility of the government as seen by the citizenry. The closed information system created, as Senator Sam Ervin put it, "a virtual absence of accountability on the part of those who govern,"[8] and a decline in the desire to participate within the working of the system would be the final result. Reduced citizen participation within the operations of government further exacerbated the problem as the system became more and more closed unto itself. Government secrecy and the doctrine of executive privilege, then, have not been beneficial to the pragmatic operations of the American republic; in fact, they have created situations that run counter to the precepts upon which the republic is based.

Ethical Considerations

Besides raising pragmatic considerations, the restricted flow of information through the use of secrecy and executive privilege raises several ethical considerations as well. First, it should be noted that our society is, or ought to be, committed to responsible decision making through the testing process of debate — the public scrutiny of ideas and information upon which ultimate policy decisions rest. Through the process of debate, proposed courses of action are carefully investigated before-the-fact, thereby maximizing the probability that the policy selected will be the best of all alternatives, a probability clarified by Thomas Nilsen:

> We have come to value highly the processes of public debate wherein there is confrontation of case with case, where advocates challenge each other's information and conclusions. Such confrontation produces the kind of information and criticism of conclusions that makes possible more intelligent choices on the part of the listeners.[9]

Nilsen's statement is also important in that it highlights one of the critical necessities that must be satisfied if debate is to play a meaningful role in the overall decision-making process. Note that Nilsen requires the confrontation and evaluation of the policy makers' "information," the material upon which subsequent decisions or conclusions will be based. Only if we are able to test and evaluate this information will we be able to make those critical choices upon which our society depends. To operate effectively, an open system of information flow is essential.

Moreover, not only does the open system of information flow provide better practical results in the formulation of policy decisions, it also promotes the basic ethical responsibilities inherent to a society ground in the traditions of free speech and public discussion. This inseparable link between pragmatism and ethics has been noted by Dennis G. Day in 1966:

> Decision is meaningful only if there are alternatives from which to choose. . . . Thus, the prime requisite which must be met if debate is to provide sound decisions is that it be thorough and complete, that all arguments and information relevant to decision be known and understood. A commitment to debate as the method of democratic decision-making demands an overriding ethical responsibility to promote the full confrontation of opposing opinions, arguments, and information relevant to decision.[10]

Therefore, an open information system is necessary to uphold the ethical responsibilities found within our society.

"Freedom of speech" must be more than one's ability to speak his mind; freedom of speech also entails the availability of information upon which decisions are to be based. Those possessing "information relevant to decision" have the responsibility to make this information available to others to maximize the beneficial probabilities of the decision-making process.

However, the use of a closed information system, particularly through the now legitimatized doctrine of executive privilege, works counterproductively to the pragmatic and ethical requisites of American society. While most would give assent to the thesis that government should not lie to its people or to the separate branches within the government, without an open system of information flow there is no assurance that such will be the case. The case of the "Nixon tapes" clearly indicates an example of how executive privilege was used to prevent the disclosure of truth in the tangled Watergate affair. McBurney and Mills observed that an open information system provides the means "of separating the true from the false and the honest from the dishonest in such ways as to protect society."[11] Executive privilege serves to thwart that goal; the false and the dishonest are provided with a shield from which to operate.

Despite the fact that the doctrine of executive privilege actively works against effective decision making, President Nixon asserted in March 1973 that certain materials should be kept secret from Congress because their "disclosure might render damage . . . to the decision-making process,"[12] thereby completing a circular chain of folly. Throwing aside all considerations of ethical responsibility (a not uncommon posture for the Nixon administration), the president virtually claimed that freedom of discussion and debate was inimical to the interests of the United States, conjuring up the possibility that national security might be endangered by including the Congress and the American people in the policy decision-making process. Thus, pragmatic and ethical decision making was to be left to the president and to him alone.

This frightening statement should not be considered as an aberrative viewpoint of a man driven crazy by the lust for power, nor should the doctrine of executive privilege be considered only a manifestation of the Nixon administration. On the contrary, the use of this seamy doctrine has been on the constant increase:

> Modern Presidential government is symbolized by the frequency with which information is withheld from Congress at the sole discretion of the Executive. The Library of Congress reported in March 1973 that executive privilege had been asserted 49 times since 1952, includng 19 times by the Nixon administration alone. The Nixon administration has invoked the privilege at least twice more since March 1973.[13]

The use of executive privilege, then, has been relatively constant during the past twenty years; the Nixon administration merely used this device more often than had prior administrations.

What is even more frightening, however, are the implications of the Supreme Court decision in *U.S. v. Nixon*. Although overturning the president's claim of executive privilege vis-à-vis the Watergate tapes, the decision institutionalized and legalized the use of that doctrine. As Tom Wicker appropriately noted, the decision created a more enduring problem in that the determination of the scope of executive privilege was left to the president's discretion, thereby concretizing a system of restricted information flow within the government and from the government to the people. Unless the president were to transgress on higher interests (as Nixon had done with the "fair administration of criminal justice" in the Watergate tapes controversy), it appears that there does not exist any mechanism within the American system to preclude arbitrary and habitual use of executive privilege. The Court's decision can be utilized to work against the ethical requisites of open information flow and debate in society. An oft-asserted privilege has now been given constitutional substance, and the outlook for the future is bleak in evaluating governmental decision-making processes.

Therefore, what is needed is a clear definition and delineation of executive privilege as a viable tool of executive branch protection. While it is true that certain discussions and conversations must be kept secret to allow for full policy theorizing within the White House, it is also true that executive privilege must be limited to only those materials and conversations pertinent thereto. Without such delineation, the decision-making process will become more and more centered in the executive branch, aggravating a situation that has gotten out of hand during the past two decades. We must be concerned with this problem, concerned with the necessity of creating a system that minimizes the amount of information restriction within that system. The Congress must be prompted to action, because the alternative is too horrible: "Without free access to information and ideas, democracy suffocates and dies."[14]

Sayer Essay Footnotes

1. Tom Wicker, "Gratifying Mr. Nixon," *New York Times*, 26 July 1974, p. 33.

2. Philip Kurland, "Nixon and Executive Privilege," *U. S. News and World Report*, 24 December 1973, p. 23.

3. Douglas Ehninger and Wayne Brockriede, *Decision by Debate* (New York: Dodd, Mead & Co., 1963), p. 3.

4. Louis W. Koenig, "The Presidency Today," *Current History* 66 (June 1974): 250.

5. Jerome Wiesner, *None of Your Business*, ed. Norman Dorsen and Stephen Gillers (New York: Viking Press, 1974), p. 215.

6. J. William Fulbright, *Hearings on Executive Privilege, Secrecy in Government, and Freedom of Information*, April 1973, p. 79.

7. Arthur M. Schlesinger, Jr., *The Imperial Presidency* (Boston: Houghton-Mifflin, 1973), p. 356.

8. Sam Ervin, *Hearings on Executive Privilege*, p. 6.

9. Thomas R. Nilsen, *Ethics of Speech Communication*, 2nd ed. (Indianapolis, Inc.: Bobbs-Merrill, 1974), p. 74.

10. Dennis G. Day, "The Ethics of Democratic Debate," *Central States Speech Journal* 17 (February 1966): p. 6.

11. James H. McBurney and Glen E. Mills, *Argumentation and Debate*, 2nd ed. (New York: Macmillan, 1964), p. 12.

12. "Executive Privilege Issue Splits House Committee," *Congressional Quarterly*, 20 April 1974, p. 999.

13. Norman Dorsen, *None of Your Business*, ed. Norman Dorsen and Stephen Gillers (New York: Viking Press, 1974), p. 29.

14. Edward M. Kennedy, *Hearings on Executive Privilege* (Washington, D.C.: U.S. Government Printing Office, 1973), p. 15.

Chapter 4

Systems Theory and Argumentation

* The Nature of a System
* Systems Theory and Decision Making
* Systems Theory and Argumentative Communication
* Conclusion
* References
* Practicum

Whereas the preceding chapters in unit 1 have dealt with traditional argumentative communication elements, this chapter will focus upon a relatively new concept in the study of communication: systems theory. Since communication in general and argumentative communication in particular deal with a variety of factors and variables, you will find it helpful to examine the components of argumentative communication from a systems perspective. If nothing else, the application of systems theory to the study of argumentation and debate provides a most functional perspective from which to visualize and understand the interrelationship of the many factors involved in argumentative communication.

The Nature of a System

In discussing the nature of what is happening currently or the way things are now, we often make reference to the status quo or the *present system* in argumentative communication. Please notice the presence of the word *system*, because it indicates the important interrelationship of factors within that process. That is, components of the present system do not act independently, they are not complete entities unto themselves. On the contrary, systems thinking requires that you realize the integral interrelationship of the various factors that go into the makeup of that system, factors whose importance cannot be measured as single items, but as interacting items upon one another within the nature of the system. Perhaps the easiest way to understand the operation of a system is to consider the communication process that was discussed in chapter 2. As was delineated in the transactive communication model, figure 2.1 on page 32, the transactive communication process consists of:

internal factors affecting the source (education, vocabulary, and so on)

the source of the message

the message variables

the channel variables

external factors affecting both the source and the receiver (status, role, and so on)

the receiver of the message

internal factors affecting the receiver (education, vocabulary, and so on)

feedback

All those variables go into the makeup of the overall communication *system*; that is, they act *interdependently* to create the communication process. This is the best way to understand the functioning of a system: a system consists of the interdependent action of factors and variables to create a final product. A system is an amalgam of various functions that interact interdependently to create that system. The interdependence of components is of greatest importance in the functioning of a system. With that definition of a system in mind, we can examine the simplified model of a system in figure 4.1. As you can see by examining the systems model, there are six major functions that warrant consideration:

1. Input stage: there are a number of factors or variables that supply information to the system.

2. Differentiation: the factors within the input stage are different, separated from each other at this point within the system.

3. Throughput stage: the factors or variables obviously begin to blend, starting to come together and interact upon one another.

4. Integration: the factors now have come together, acting interdependently upon one another.

5. Output stage: the final product or end result, demonstrating the complete integration of the entire system.

6. Feedback: the system regenerates itself as new information is fed into the system and the process begins anew.

Figure 4.1

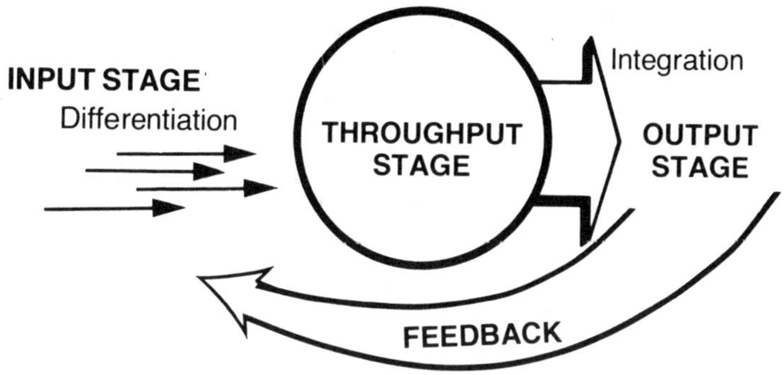

Let us now take the variables found to exist within the transactive communication process and place them within the systems model; the result is shown in figure 4.2. The various elements within the communication process enter the input stage differentiated, start coming together at the throughput stage, and then finally are fully integrated by the culmination of the systems operation at the output stage. The result is, of course, the transactive communication process itself. Thus, communication does not actually exist until those factors are *integrated* at the output stage. The systems model, then, clearly demonstrates the interrelationship of variables that exists within the functioning of most complex processes.[1]

Systems Theory and Decision Making

The relevance and application of systems theory to the making of decisions was noted by Professor Ralph Towne at the 1973 National Conference on Argumentation:

Figure 4.2

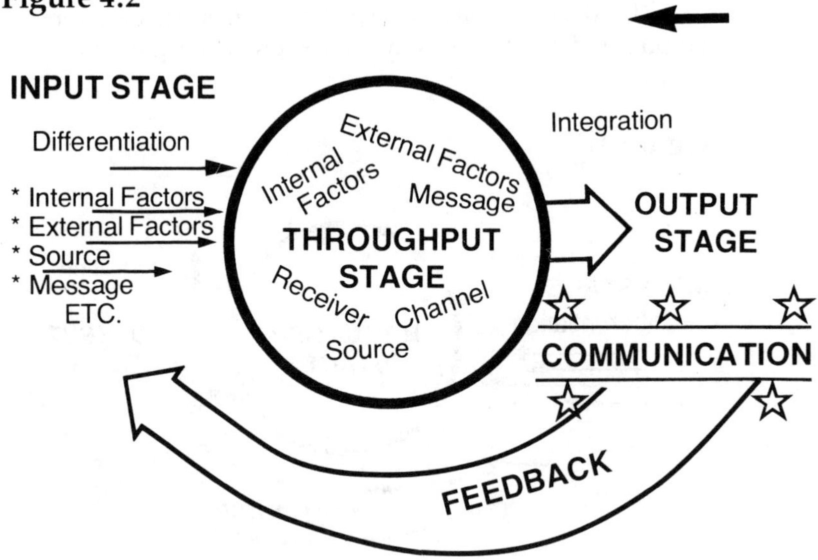

> The result of this complexity of situations that cry, and are being heard, for solutions is serious pressure on our methods of analyzing and solving problems. Previously, if you needed a bridge you built it as soon as you could convince someone to "foot the bill." Now, you must worry about all the traffic problems that the new bridge will cause in a particular neighborhood, whether there is space enough along with the bridge to have service facilities available, whether at rush hour the bridge can take care of the fifty or one hundred fold traffic increase over the remainder of the day. Etc. Etc. Etc. And, equally important, with a finite quantity of funds, material, and labor, is the bridge as important as the new hospital, the new library, or the new school for the community.[2]

Therefore, the decision to build or not to build that bridge is not a simple decision. Many factors are involved, factors that interrelate with one another, having influence upon the ultimate decision reached. Towne's example may be examined within the structure of our systems model, as shown in figure 4.3. The interrelationship of

Figure 4.3

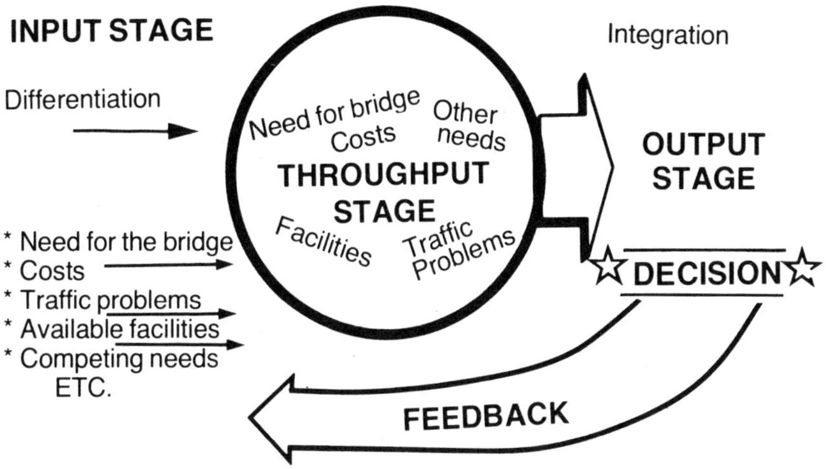

these factors allows us to study the entire complexity involved in building this particular bridge. After carefully considering this whole package, that is, integrating all the factors, we then can reach a decision as to whether or not we should build the bridge. Notice, however, that if new information is provided via feedback, then the system would be altered and the decision would be reconsidered.

Now let us examine a major system within the United States — the antipoverty program. The current antipoverty system contains many different programs and activities that are designed to combat the problem of poverty, programs such as food stamps, cash grants, in-kind benefits, job training, and so on. In sum, all these programs and activities constitute the status quo antipoverty system; figure 4.4 shows how it would look in the systems model. The integration of the various differentiated programs results in the creation of the overall status quo antipoverty system, and the overall system is the result of the interdependent interaction of the various functions within that system. The only meaningful way we can discuss our current antipoverty efforts is to recognize the functional interrelationship of the various component parts of the antipoverty system.

In making decisions concerning the antipoverty program, it

Figure 4.4

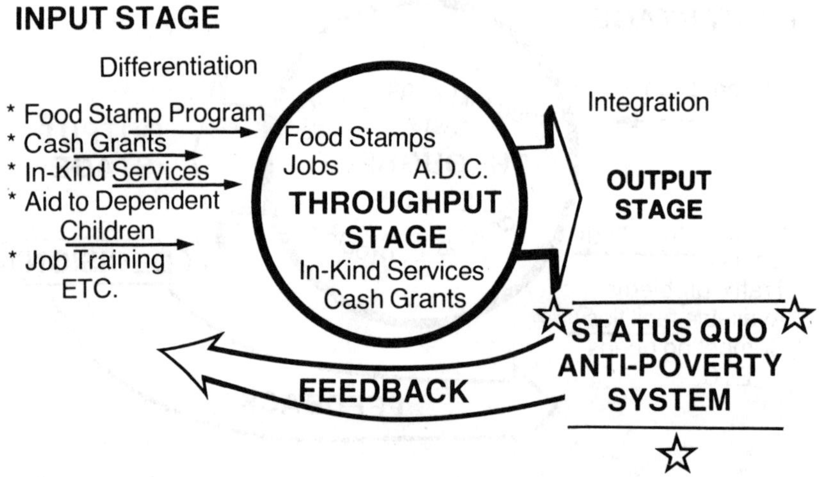

must be realized that any action taken concerning any part of the program will have an impact upon the other parts of the program. For example, if the amount of money provided through direct cash grants were to be reduced, there might be an increased demand for more food stamps and in-kind services. The elimination of job training for the poor might cause an increase in the need for food stamps, cash grants, and in-kind services. Expanding the food stamp program might decrease the amount of money needed within the cash grants portion of the overall program. Thus, any change made within the system will have an impact upon both the overall system and the component parts of the system.

If nothing else, the systems model should tell us two things about making decisions. First, there seldom is such an animal as a simple decision. As our example concerning the anti-poverty program indicates, there are a large number of factors that need to be considered in making decisions. While you might be quite upset about so-called welfare fraud and desire to reduce or eliminate the giving of money to poor people, you would have to realize that making such a decision would have a significant impact upon the other portions of the antipoverty program. Such a decision would increase the demand for food stamps and in-kind services, and you would have to be prepared to face such an increased demand in those areas. Decision-making, then, is a very complex and involved process.

Second, the systems model demonstrates the nature of multiple input, the fact that decisions are based upon a variety of factors and information. In chapter 3, we discussed the importance of argumentative communication and open decision making to our free society; the system model underscores this importance. By maximizing the amount of information we have before rendering a decision, we are prepared better to anticipate the impact of our potential decisions, and our ultimate decision will be the best possible decision because of our consideration of all these relevant functions. Systems theory shows us how important open information flow is to the making of solid, sound decisions.

Systems Theory and Argumentative Communication

The application of systems theory to communication activities occured within the past few years, [3] and the first full-blown application of the systems perspective to argumentative communication occurred even more recently.[4] However, practitioners of public argument, especially those engaged in competitive academic debate, have presented systems-type arguments for a number of years, although these arguments were not labeled as such.

Recognizing the interrelationship of functions within a system, it is merely common sense to recognize further that any proposed change within a system will have effects upon many, if not all, parts of that system. Similarly, supposed inadequacies found within any system can be caused by a variety of factors within that system and not necessarily by one factor. The interrelationship of factors is of great significance to formal argumentative encounters, and this significance can be exemplified by two major types of argument that occur within most debates.

First, when the affirmative advocates propose a change in the status quo, they contend that something is amiss with the present system. Often, they claim that some problem or harm exists that the status quo is unable to resolve; therefore, a new system is needed and justified to overcome this problem. However, in claiming that some problem exists, the affirmative advocates have the responsibility to prove *causality*—that something within the status quo is either (*a*) responsible for causing the problem or (*b*) responsible for allowing the problem to go unchecked. In either instance, the affirmative advocates must demonstrate a causal link between the status quo and the perceived problem, because without such a link there would be no justification to alter the status quo.

In analyzing such causal claims, adopt a systems perspective and remember that few results are caused by only one factor. Most situations have multiple causes; more than one factor is responsible for the presence of some undesired result. For example, one might contend that poverty is caused by the lack of money: "Give the poor six thousand dollars a year and the poverty problem will be solved." But will it? Is poverty more than merely the lack of money? A systems perspective would indicate that poverty is caused, certainly, by the lack of money, but it also is caused by inadequate education, lack of marketable job skills, poor spending habits, and many other factors. Poverty is not caused by one simple factor, but many affirmative advocates present justifications for changes in the status quo that are based upon such simplistic and unrealistic reasoning. Remember, multiple causality is an important argument drawn from the systems perspective that forces affirmative advocates to justify fully proposed changes in the present system. Conversely, of course, those attempting to defend the operations of the status quo need to be aware of the many programs and activities that go into present system decision making. Without such a systems awareness, any defense of the status quo would be unrealistic and ineffective. To defend the status quo antipoverty system, for example, the negative advocate would defend the totality of that system, not be limited to a defense of only one small part of that system.

The second major type of argument particularly relevant to the systems perspective is that of *impact*, often referred to as advantages, disadvantages, or program effects. Remember, any change within a system will have an impact upon both the overall system and the component functions of the system. Thus, changes made to solve a particular problem may create additional benefits (advantages) or they may create other problems (disadvantages). For example, giving all the poor people in this country six thousand dollars a year might overcome their lack of money, but it might also (*a*) cause rampant inflation that would (*b*) reduce everyone's, including the poor's, purchasing power, (*c*) further weaken the stability of the American economy, (*d*) increase the gold drain, and (*e*) destabilize the international economy of the Free World. That exemplifies resultant disadvantages that might come about when one so-called minor change is made within a system. However, additional advantages might result from giving the poor all that money: (*a*) consumer spending would increase, (*b*) resulting in increased production in the United States and (*c*) increased employment, (*d*) thereby strengthening the fiber of the American economy. Hence, it could be argued that both compelling disadvantages and advantages could be the result of the proposed change in the current antipoverty system. Any final decision would have to consider both types of potential impact.

Since academic debate is but a structured exercise in decision making, debaters ought to utilize the systems perspective in presenting, examining, and refuting arguments. Very few issues of public importance are simple; most are very complex and composed of many various factors and variables. Therefore, the debater should adopt a comprehensive viewpoint of the decision-making process, recognizing that the status quo and any proposed changes in the status quo are combinations of many differentiated and integrated factors. The more information that you possess about the construction of any system, the more reasonable, the more realistic, and—from an argumentative standpoint—the more effective will be your analysis of that system.

Conclusion

In considering policy systems and proposed alterations in those policy systems, the perspective provided by systems theory will be very useful to the practitioner of argumentative communication. Recognizing the unique interdependent interrelationship of functions that exists within systems allows the advocate to better understand the operations of the system, its problems, and the impact of any and all proposed changes within a system. Functional argumentative communication requires that a comprehensive view of the decision-making process be maintained, and systems theory is an important tool in the development of this comprehensive viewpoint.

REFERENCES

1. See Peter R. Monge, "Theory Construction in the Study of Communication: The System Paradigm," *Journal of Communication* 23 (March 1973): 5–16.

2. Ralph Towne, "An Expansion of General Systems Theory in Debate," in *Proceedings of the National Conference on Argumentation*, ed. James I. Luck (Fort Worth, Tex.: Texas Christian University, 1973), p. 14.

3. See, for example, Raymond K. Tucker, "General Systems Theory: A Logical and Ethical Model for Persuasion," *Journal of the American Forensic Association* 8 (Summer 1971): 29–35.

4. Bernard Brock, James Chesebro, John Cragan, and James Klumpp, *Public Policy Decision-Making: Systems Analysis and Comparative Advantages Debate* (New York: Harper and Row, 1973).

PRACTICUM

1. Since the adoption of Proposition 13 in California in late 1978, there has been great interest in reducing taxes at all levels of government — local, state, and federal. Some advocates have proposed reducing federal taxes by as much as 30 percent. To develop your understanding of systems analysis, assume that federal income taxes were reduced by 10 percent. Based upon current federal budgetary information concerning income and expenditures, what impact would such an income tax reduction have upon the many components of the federal budget? What areas would be beneficially affected by such a tax reduction? What areas would be negatively affected?

2. Another topical item pertinent to analysis by systems theory is the issue of capital punishment. Based upon information that you know or can obtain, answer these questions:

- Does capital punishment deter crime?
- Does the type of death penalty (hanging, gas chamber, for example) have a significant impact upon crime deterrence?
- What major factors appear to contribute to the crime problem in the United States?

Your answers to these questions should demonstrate the difficulty inherent in the decision-making process. There is no clear-cut relationship between capital punishment or its absence and the crime problem in this country. Based upon your answers, do you favor having a system of capital punishment? Can you justify your decision? Have you considered all the major functions of that system?

Unit Two

Concepts of Argumentation

Chapter 5
Probability: Basis of Argument

Chapter 6
Issues: The Crux of Argument

Chapter 7
The Burden of Proof, Inherency, and Presumption

Chapter 5

Probability: Basis of Argumentation

* Probability and You
* Rhetorical Reasoning and Probability
* Probability and Argumentative Communication
* Probability and the Construction of Argument
* Conclusion
* References
* Practicum

As we begin this second unit, you may look back upon the material covered in the preceding unit and find that the nature of argumentative communication has been defined and exemplified, that the relationship of that form of communicaton to the overall transactive communication process has been demonstrated, and that the significance of argumentative communication in your life and in the life of our society has been described. This initial chapter in the second unit deals with the element of probability, the primary reasoning factor that underpins all aspects of argumentative communication, both formal and informal, structured and unstructured.

Probability may be defined as: strong information or evidence to establish the likelihood that something happened, is happening, or will happen. Unlike the concept of certainty, wherein all materials are known that allow us to be completely sure of all observations and conclusions, probability deals only with particular known items or facts, causing us to reach incomplete or tentative conclusions. As will be demonstrated within this chapter, most of our decisions and actions are based upon probability; we seldom have the luxury of being certain about most things.

Probability and You

You are a student in a college or university—that is fairly certain. But what is not certain is the reason you decided to go to college. Why are you in school and not working at a full-time job? Why didn't you drop out of society and simply hitchhike around the country? Why didn't you join the armed forces? Again, why are you in school instead of being somewhere else?

We cannot speak about your motivation to go to college in particular, but it is possible to hypothesize why many of your classmates are in school and not working, bumming around, or enjoying a hitch in the armed forces. For many of them, the decision to go to college was based upon probability reasoning, specifically the probability that their lives would be better and happier if they furthered their education. They might have made their decision because of reasoning like this:

- I want to have enough money to lead a comfortable life.
- I want to have a nice home, a good car, and a job that is enjoyable and meaningful.
- If I go to college, I'll receive the training and skills I need

to find a good job, and that job will allow me to lead the kind of life I want.

- Therefore, my future happiness will be more secure if I go to college.

Note that there are no guarantees in those statements. Graduating from college will not ensure you or anyone else that you'll be able to find the type of job you want or are trained for. Even if you do get that type of job, there is no guarantee that you'll make enough money to lead that "comfortable life." Instead, that example of reasoning is based solely upon probability: it is *probable* that a college education will enable you to have the career you want with all its resultant benefits. You take particular courses in college based on probability, the probability that those courses will serve you well in acquiring the kind of educational knowledge and skill you desire. You read this book on the probability that you'll learn more about argumentative communication than you already know. In fact, the vast majority of important decisions you make during your life are based solely upon probability. You seldom make decisions based only upon some whim; very few of us make important decisions on the basis that if it feels good, we should do it. On the contrary, we tend to look at all the available information and then decide that probability supports our pursuing one course of action or another, exemplifying the contention of McBurney and Mills that "sensible people govern their lives by probabilities."[1]

You decide to marry a particular person on the probability that the two of you will be happy together. You decide to take job offer A instead of job offer B on the probability that the former will be better for you in one way or another. As a child, you decided that calling the neighborhood bully a nasty name would not be a smart thing to do. Why? Because, you reasoned, in all probability he would beat you up if you called him that name. Again, as with the decision to go to college, there are no guarantees, there are no certainties. Although Alvin and Sherry decided to marry because they felt they'd probably be happy forever after, there is no guarantee that the future will be pleasant for their relationship. You have no guarantee that job A will be better than job B; you were not certain that that bully would beat you up. Since you do not have a crystal ball, you cannot accurately forecast the future. All you can do is employ probability: examine the available information and evidence, and then make your decision upon that basis. You do exactly that all the time, often without being fully aware that you are doing it.

Even what you think you know about the past is based upon probability. Since you were not present at the Battle of Gettysburg, you cannot say that you know from firsthand experience exactly what happened there. All you can do is read various eyewitness reports, newspaper accounts, and the many writings of historians about that eventful battle. Then, based upon that information, you can only claim that you *probably* know what did occur, but you cannot say that you know *for certain* what took place. Former President Harry Truman was fond of saying that "the only thing new in history is that which you don't already know," and that was an observation of significance to the study of probability. If, for example, new information were to be uncovered, this new material might change your probability reasoning. Final decisions and judgments might be altered based upon that new information altering the probabilities involved. So-called revisionist historians do just that; their different or revised interpretations are designed to change the probabilities that we use in deciding what really happened in the past.

One of the most controversial issues of the past two decades has been the assassination of President Kennedy in Dallas on 22 November 1963. Based upon the information and testimony secured, the Warren Commission, a body of men appointed by President Lyndon Johnson to investigate the killing, reached the conclusion that, in all probability, Lee Harvey Oswald acted alone in shooting President Kennedy. Since the Warren Commission did not have all possible information concerning the shooting (Oswald was dead and there were no direct eyewitnesses who *saw* Oswald pull the trigger), its conclusion was one only of probability; it is not absolutely certain that Oswald was the lone assassin. If new information is uncovered that links other people or other weapons to that crime, then the probability statement might be altered. In fact, some researchers and writers currently claim that probability actually supports the notion that President Kennedy was killed by a band of conspirators, not by one individual acting independently. A present-day congressional committee has recently announced similar findings. Importantly, regardless of the conclusion reached, the question of who killed John Kennedy can only be answered by probability statements. We cannot know for certain.

The decisions you made yesterday, make today, and will make tomorrow generally are based upon probability. It is very rare for you to operate from a position of complete information or knowledge; you generally have to make decisions based upon incomplete information. Thus, you examine what you have and then decide to do something—and you hope that your decision based upon probability will turn out to be a sound decision.[2]

Rhetorical Reasoning and Probability

As you have seen, very few decisions are reached in accord with the dictates of formal logical reasoning. Since we do not reach decisions syllogistically, the application of formal logical reasoning is of limited value to the human communication process. Perhaps the most obvious reason why formal logic is of such limited value is that all of us make crucial value judgments concerning the acceptability of arguments or premises upon which decisions are made. For example, consider this syllogism:

All A is B.
All C is A.
Therefore, all C is B.

You might conclude that this syllogism has to be accepted without reservation. After all, the structure is valid; therefore, the conclusion ought to be acceptable. However, if you do not accept the notion that all A is B, then the entire structure of the syllogism falls apart. You will not accept the final conclusion that all C is B, because you have not accepted the major premise upon which the conclusion is based.

Now, consider this more substantive example:

All men are created equal.
Thomas is a man.
Therefore, Thomas is equal to other men.

Although the structure of this syllogism is sound, you may not accept its conclusion if you do not accept the notion that all men are created equal. If you believe that certain races or ethnic groups are superior or inferior to others, then you will not accept the idea of human equality, and, therefore, the conclusion will not be accepted. Or, taking "men" to refer to males rather than all humans, you might not agree that Thomas is a man. He might meet the biological requirements of manhood, but you might not think that Thomas is a *man* as you define that word. If Thomas is kind and sensitive, but you believe that a man must be gruff and steellike (the famous macho image), then you might say, "Thomas is not a *real* man." And, of course, you would not agree that Thomas was the equal of other men.

To further confound this situation, you might not have general agreement as to what "All men are created equal" means. Does it mean that they are equal under the law? Or does it mean that all men have equal physical attributes? If you apply the first definition, you might accept the syllogistic conclusion; if you apply the second definition, then you would not accept the conclusion, because, obviously, not all men have the same physical qualities of height, weight, strength, and so on.

The problem with formal logical reasoning, then, is that it does not account for differing perceptions, interpretations, and biases. Simply because the structure of an argument is sound does not guarantee that people will accept the conclusion drawn from that argument. On the contrary, people often render decisions that fly in the face of formal logic, but that is the beauty of the human communication process. In the affairs of mankind, very little is certain—except, perhaps, that the human reasoning and decision-making processes are not limited by the constraints of formal logic.

A second reason why formal logic is of limited value in human communication stems from the fact that we tend to make decisions about particulars, rather than about absolutes. Our basic reasoning process is limited to the information that we have or can acquire; it is very rare, indeed, when we can say that we have all the information regarding any future decision. We cannot say, in real-world reasoning activities, that all A is B, because we do not know everything about A or even about B. We may know a great deal about A, but we do not know everything—and this is a most important point: our limited information forces us to reach decisions based upon probability, not certainty. In rhetorical or communication-oriented reasoning, we tend to operate like this:

A probably is B.
C probably is A.
Therefore, C probably is B.

And that type of reasoning is significantly different from that taught by formal logicians.

When we make decisions based upon past events, as our prior illustration of the Battle of Gettysburg demonstrated, we operate only on that which is known. We cannot make judgments about that which is unknown. Thus, our decisions about what did happen is limited by what we are able to know, and we are compelled to say, "*It appears* that Jeb Stuart's tardiness led to the lack of Confederate success at the Battle of Gettysburg." We can only reach a conclusion based upon probability because we do not know all the factors that influenced the final outcome of that battle.

Similarly, decisions we reach concerning the future must, of necessity, be based upon probability. We cannot know all the present factors that do or should influence a decision; we most assuredly do not know about future factors that will be of significance to our decision. All we can do is use the information we have at our disposal to make the best probability-based decision for our future actions.

The study of communication is one and the same as the study of the actions and motivations of mankind. People are affected by a variety of influences—fear, hate, lust, greed, for example—a plethora of emotions, attitudes, biases, and prejudices. Each single person is so complex that there is no way to discover the reasons for all her actions and thoughts. Mankind is so complex that there is much more that is unknown than is known. Therefore, in dealing with the human reasoning process, we cannot deal with absolutes; we cannot say with any degree of assurance that all anything is anything. We can reach decisions based upon probability, but we cannot guarantee certainty. Since we generally deal with particular issues and particular bits of information, we cannot reach hard and fast absolute conclusions. Probability, then, is the foundation for the human reasoning process and the resultant reasoning that occurs in communication contexts.

Probability and Argumentative Communication

Since argumentative communication is significantly concerned with the decision-making process, it should not be surprising to you to find that probability is the foundation of argumentation and debate. Years before the birth of Christ, Aristotle noted that people do not argue over certainties, things that were of no question to them. Instead, people tend to argue or deliberate over issues of differing interpretation, items that are not clear-cut.[3] For example, people might not argue over the existence of poverty in this country. After all, a trip to the inner core of our large metropolitan areas or a trip to the Appalachian region will provide graphic proof that poverty does exist; there is no argument there. But there is argument over how poverty can be eliminated: give the poor money, guarantee adequate-paying government jobs, and so on—a plethora of differing proposals—and that is where the arguments take place.

Perhaps the best way to find the locus of argument is to imagine a straight line running from certainty at one end to possibility at the other. Somewhere in the middle of the line is the area of probability—and the locus of argument. To argue over issues that are certain is a complete waste of time. At the same time, we tend not to argue over mere possibility, because we learn at a very early age that practically anything is possible. Remember, not too many years ago certain experts loudly proclaimed that it was not possible for man to fly, it was not possible to split the atom, it was not possible for man to pole-vault over fifteen feet. Yet every one of those things has not only occurred but is now considered commonplace. Arguments over mere possibility assume far too many factors and unknowns, too much is left outside the decision-making process. Our arguments, formal and informal alike, generally center upon issues of probability.

Recall the essays and speeches reproduced in the first three chapters of unit 1; reread them to refresh your memory about their arguments. You should note now they present arguments of probability: given present knowledge and information, Lindsey concluded that, in all real probability, the continued development of nuclear power would be disastrous to this country and to our people. She marshaled information that supported her probability claim of future disaster. At the end of that essay, she wants you to agree with her that something must be done to stop this future probable disaster. The Lindsey essay is an excellent example of the interrelationship of argumentative communication and probability. The MacLean column concerning his opposition to the lowering of the voting age also exemplifies argument via probability as he envisions devastating results from the voting age's being lowered from twenty-one to eighteen.

Again, since our knowledge is limited by the fact that we do not have full and complete information regarding any one issue, our arguments and our conclusions and decisions drawn from those arguments must be based upon probability. We cannot argue certainty regarding the past; we cannot argue certainty for the future. Our argumentative attempts must be grounded upon probability—the use of available information and evidence to establish the likelihood that something happened, is happening, or will happen in the future.

To examine another piece of public argumentation for elements of probability, carefully read the following editorial from the *Arizona Republic*, a Phoenix newspaper, published 6 March 1972. At that time, students at the University of Arizona in Tucson were unhappy with plans to increase student fees to raise necessary monies to build a new parking garage on their campus. Student leaders demanded that students be allowed to vote on this issue and that fees should not be raised unless or until the students had approved of the proposed action. Many people were unhappy with those student demands, including the writer of the following editorial. Examine the arguments presented carefully; identify the probabilities within the editorial. Then, try to determine to your own satisfaction if the writer demonstrated sufficient probability to support the major arguments. Finally, and this is the hard part, try to discover what factors within you cause you to accept or reject the probabilities in the editorial.

Give the Students a Flat "No"

The Editors of the Arizona Republic

The state legislature had better show some backbone this week, and set University of Arizona student government leaders straight once and for all about who determines fees and policies at state universities.

It should give a flat and definite "no" to students who have appointed themselves as regents to govern the affairs of the university and set fees by vote of the students. Otherwise, legislators are going to find themselves in trouble with taxpayers, who are getting increasingly fed up with paying for youthful ingratitude and intolerance.

The U of A student government has demanded that legislators defer action on a proposed $11 million bond issue to finance construction of a 3,200-space, high-rise university parking garage until it can hold a campus election to get student approval of the fees to be charged.

Students have complained bitterly about parking problems at the Tucson campus for almost 10 years. Yet U of A student leaders reason that, since student fees would be increased $61 a year to underwrite the garage, students should be able to vote on the issue before it is taken up by the state legislature.

We sometimes wonder what kind of education produces such provincialism. The student position is naive and elitist. No election involving a fraction of the university's current enrollment could possibly address itself to the wishes and needs of thousands of students who will attend the university over the next several decades.

That is why the legislature established a Board of Regents to make university policy on a continuing basis. And it is irresponsible in the extreme for self-appointed student leaders, motivated by fleeting fancy, to propose the unprecedented usurpation of the Board of Regents' authority in these matters.

Student opponents of the fee increase have called its approval undemocratic without their direct consent. "We pay the bills," they declared. "And so we should make the final decision."

Nonsense, Has it never occurred to these self-centered and impudent students—many of them actually dilettantes, swelling the classrooms and forcing deterioration of academic standards—that they don't pay the bill at all?

Student tuition and fees are less than 32 percent of the $133 million annual operating budget of the state's three universities. Well over $100 million of that budget—like most of the original $350 million investment in land, plant, and equipment at the three campuses, and all academic capital improvements—is financed with tax money from the state general fund.

Arizona taxpayers have been more than generous about their commitment to higher education. And their return on that investment would likely suffer little if 10,000 or so of the state's almost 57,000 university students left the classroom and went to work for a change.

The taxpayers could very happily get along with about half of the approximately 8,000 nonresident university students, who are getting almost a free ride at Arizona's expense.

College students like to think they are adults. Most of them are 18, and voters. But we have coddled them for too long, providing them with frills and extras to sweeten up their college life that do not affect one whit the quality of education they are meant to be getting.

Even the U of A administration's garage proposal—prompted by student complaints about parking problems, and endorsed by students who have studied them—would not be necessary but for the inordinate number of students who drive, rather than walk or cycle the few blocks or miles each day to school.

Well, it's time for the piper to call the tune. And the small minority of vocal student critics—who, unlike the vast majority of sensible, hardworking university students, have been deluded by democratism to believe they are the rightful university decision-makers—must realize that the free ride is over.

Perhaps students will then stop expecting all their demands to be met, with no strings attached or obligation on their part, and for a change start acting like mature adults instead of whimpering adolescents.

The legislature should give a flat and definite "no" to the students' request that it postpone action on the U of A bond issue pending their own referendum on the matter. The students are asking legislators to give them authority delegated by law to the Board of Regents. And of all the unmitigated gall, that is surely unsurpassed.[4]

Hopefully, you noted at the very least that the editorial contained a great many value judgments, especially those dealing with the rights and privileges of university students. Your reaction to those value judgments directly affected your final reaction to the entire editorial and the writer's argument from probability. If nothing else, there is a very strong probability that few college students, today or tomorrow, would be happy with the tone taken by that editorial writer. Although you know nothing about the controversy that sparked the editorial except what you have read here, you have reached at least a tentative conclusion about that hassle. You have decided either in favor of or in opposition to the University of Arizona students, and your decision exemplifies what argumentative probability is all about: you reached a decision based upon the information available to you, deciding that *probably* the University of Arizona students were right or wrong in their demands.

Probability and the Construction of Argument

Because probability is the foundation of both formal and informal argumentative communication encounters, a brief word ought to be given the construction of effective argument. Most of our decisions function inductively in nature; that is, we tend to reach fairly broad decisions based upon particular bits of information and evidence. The Lindsey essay on nuclear power, for example, reaches a very broad conclusion (nuclear power development ought to be stopped) based upon several instances of disaster and several pieces of anti–nuclear power testimony from supposed experts. You obviously do not have the total story of nuclear power; the essay does not present the many positive factors about the continued development of nuclear energy. An effective, slanted case has been built that supports the idea that nuclear power is very dangerous and ought to be stopped.

Most of your argumentative encounters and important decisions function similarly. You deal mainly with specific items and then use those items to reach a conclusion or to justify a decision. Thus, to be an effective practitioner of public argument, you need to find and develop as many probability related factors as you can to support your intended conclusion. The use of examples, of the testimony of experts, and of the whole range of supporting materials discussed in unit 3 must be assembled together to develop an imposing, persuasive argument. People, by and large, demand that arguments be supported; they do recognize the difference between supported argument and unsubstantiated assertion. Therefore, by assembling as much supportive data as possible, you increase the probability that your audience will accept your arguments. The very reason for using evidence in effective argumentative communication is to increase the probability that your position will be accepted by your audience. No evidence or support means you have a low probability for argument acceptance—it's that simple.

The relationship of probability to the construction of argument is quite direct and may be pictured like this:

Evidence ⟶ Argument ⟶ Conclusion

The more evidence (good, sound evidence) and the more substantive arguments you present, the more probable it is that your conclusion will be accepted. Putting together an effective argument is a hard and time-consuming chore; therefore, to make the most of your efforts, you must construct your arguments so that their probability of acceptance is as high as possible. Formal argumentation and debate relies very heavily upon the great use of supporting evidence, evidence that enhances your argument from probability. It is the foundation for most of our daily decisions, and it is the foundation for all aspects of argumentative communication.

Conclusion

All of us reach decisions and take actions that are based upon probability: strong information or evidence to establish the likelihood that something happened, is happening, or will happen. Our careers, our interpersonal relationships, our entire lives are based upon a series of probabilities. Very little in our lives—past, present, or future—is certain. So many variables exist that to be certain of anything is a very rare situation. Thus, we reason, we argue, and we reach decisions based upon that which seems to us the most probable. The study of probability is the cornerstone of argumentative communication and of its component elements.

References

1. James H. McBurney and Glen E. Mills, *Argumentation and Debate*, 2nd ed. (New York: Macmillan, 1964), p. 17.

2. For an interesting discussion of the concept of probability, see Stephen Toulmin, *The Uses of Argument* (London: Cambridge University Press, 1969), pp. 44–93.

3. Aristotle, *The Rhetoric*, translated from the Greek by Lane Cooper (New York: Appleton-Century-Crofts, 1932), pp. 11–12.

4. "Give the Students a Flat 'No,' " an editorial in the *Arizona Republic*, 6 March, 1972, p. 6. Used by permission.

PRACTICUM

1. Interview five of your classmates, asking them the following questions:

- Why did they decide to attend college?
- Why did they decide to attend this particular school?
- What is their academic major?
- What is their career goal?
- What do they believe they will do after graduation?

You will find that the answers to these questions are based heavily upon probabilities. For example, your classmate may say he decided to attend this school because, "I ***probably*** couldn't afford to go four years at an Ivy League school because of the high tuitions," or because "I ***probably*** wouldn't have been accepted at one of the larger universities." After graduation: "I'll ***probably*** go to graduate school to get a master's degree"; "I'll ***probably*** look for a job"; "I'll ***probably*** get married." Now, ask yourself those same questions. How much of your life is based upon probability reasoning?

2. One of the most perplexing areas for decision makers is the American economy, that complex system of employment, unemployment, wages, prices, and a myriad of other factors. Certainly, everyone wants a healthy and sound economy, because all of us benefit, but that goal is most difficult to achieve. Because the American economic system is so complex and difficult to comprehend, it is not surprising to find completely differing attitudes and opinions on the same economic issue.

For example, let us pose a seemingly simple question: should the United States pursue a policy of full employment? Or, is a policy of full employment beneficial for the United States? Contradictory answers may be given. In his 1973 book, ***Economics*** (p. 407), Richard Gill, economics professor at Harvard University, found a full-employment policy to be beneficial.

> Insofar as . . .policies are successful in bringing the economy closer to its full-employment potential, they will have some favorable effect on growth. They will do this in the short run by speeding up the rate of growth as the economy moves from a below-full-employment to a near-full-employment level of output, and in the longer run by the presumably larger amount of investment that will occur at the higher levels of national output.

However, University of Notre Dame economics professors Charles Wilber and Kenneth Jameson reached the opposite conclusion in ***Alternative Directions in Economic Policy***, 1978 (p. 58):

> The attempt to maintain a steady full-employment expansion inevitably undermines itself. As full employment is maintained for any length of time, profits are eroded as bargaining power shifts in favor of workers and productivity declines as labor discipline weakens without the threat of unemployment.

Please note that no economist knows what will happen if we reach a state of full employment; economists can no more foretell the future than the rest of us. However, they, like us, do reason and reach conclusions from probability. Gill concluded that full employment probably would be beneficial to the economy; Wilber and Jameson reached a different probability-based conclusion.

Examine several recent issues of ***Business Week, Monthly Labor Review***, and ***Fortune***. Based upon what you read, do you now think that economic policies designed to foster full employment (the Humphrey-Hawkins proposal, for example) would be beneficial or harmful to the overall American economic system? Upon what probabilities did you reach your conclusions?

Chapter 6

Issues: The Crux of Argument

* **Definition of an Issue**
* **Discovering Issues**
* **Types of Issues**
* **Issues and Argumentative Communication**
* **Conclusion**
* **References**
* **Practicum**

We continue our discussion of the major elements of argumentative communication by examining issues, the foundation stones upon which argumentative communication takes place. The purposes of this chapter are to define what an issue is and determine how issues can be found in differing types of argumentative contexts, to discuss the varying types of issues, and then finally to apply the relevance of issues to argumentative communication. From this point on within the book, the ideas to be presented and considered will be of a less philosophical and theoretical nature than the materials covered previously. In addition, because the elements of actual argumentative communication are fairly sterile and meaningless when discussed in a vacuum, materials presented henceforth will be related increasingly to the activity of academic debate, the functioning laboratory for training and practice in effective argumentative communication.

Definition of an Issue

"What are the issues involved here, what are we dealing with?" "Come on, you're running too far afield. Stick to the issues!" "Ladies and gentlemen, the issue before us and this country tonight is plain. It is . . . ."

Do those quotations sound familiar? They should, because all of us have heard statements like them on many occasions, and each of us uses the word *issue* many times in daily conversation. Every election year you can expect every candidate to start her campaign for office by saying something like, "In my campaign, I shall not be concerned with individuals or personalities. I intend to stress the issues." Okay, that certainly sounds good, but what *are* issues? What are those things that candidates say they'll emphasize and that we are told to stick to?

In argumentative communication, an issue is *any question or disputed item upon which the final product or conclusion of the argumentative encounter is dependent.* That is, an issue is something central to the outcome of the argumentative encounter, and issues serve as the foundation of particular arguments. Viewed simplistically, you may look upon argumentative communication as a three-step process of issues (step 1) leading to arguments (step 2), which in turn lead to decisions or conclusions (step 3). Please remember that an issue must be a central part of the argumentative encounter; an issue must be something that directly affects the final outcome of that encounter. Thus, in any given argumentative situation, there are countless millions of possible ideas that could be discussed, but there are relatively few issues upon which the outcome of that argumentative encounter is dependent. Issues serve as the foundation for meaningful argument.

For example, in the current public debate concerning nuclear power plants, one primary issue is that of safety — are nuclear power plants safe or do they present a potent threat to those who live near them? At this time, that issue of safety is *the* paramount issue in the national debate over the viability of nuclear power, and resolution of that issue will largely determine whether or not the United States will continue its nuclear power program, modify it, or abandon it altogether. If the plants are finally judged to be safe, the development of nuclear power probably will continue (please note the probability statement; nothing is certain in the decision making of mankind); if, on the other hand, those plants are declared to be unsafe, then nuclear power probably will be dropped like a hot potato. Safety is the central issue of the ongoing nuclear power debate.

You settle arguments and make decisions based upon very similar issue analysis. Suppose you decide to buy a new car. Although many possible factors could enter into your decision to buy this or that particular car, only a few can truly be considered issues. Cost, for example, probably would be a major issue in your decision making. Although the car might have a color that appeals to you and a nice, soft upholstery, if you have to bankrupt yourself to handle the price, you'll probably decide not to buy that car. The car's gas mileage might be another important issue in your final decision. If the car can, as the old saying goes, "pass anything on the road but a gas station," you might decide that it would be too expensive to keep the car running, therefore deciding that that particular car is not the one for you.

Both formal and informal argumentative encounters and decision-making activities are based upon an analysis of issues — items of dispute or questions upon which the settlement of the dispute or the making of the decision is dependent. Issues are the foundation stones upon which argumentative communication takes place.[1]

Discovering Issues

Recognizing the central importance of issues to argumentative communication, the next point to be addressed is how issues are to be discovered. Before you begin to worry about the discovery of issues, one important point needs to be emphasized: you know more about your subject matter than you consciously realize.

One of the Roman Canons of Rhetoric many centuries ago, yardsticks by which effective oral discourse could be learned and examined, was the canon of *inventio*, translated as invention or the discovery of ideas. The ancient rhetoricians realized that every person was a virtual storehouse of information on any given topic and that this storehouse needed to be tapped for the speaker to find effectively and efficiently those ideas pertinent to that topic. To a large degree, the process of invention was one wherein the speaker examined his thoughts to discover known information concerning the topic to be covered.

Today, we generally refer to this internal examination of what we already know as *brainstorming*, and it is an excellent way to discover the issues to be found within a topic or problem area. In brainstorming, you allow your mind to run rampant, to consider any and all items that come to mind when you think of the topic area. Certainly a great many irrelevant ideas will come forth, but a large number of important ideas will be generated, too, and that is how issues can be discovered. To be truly effective, it is important that you follow several easy rules when trying to find issues through this creative and imaginative procedure:

1. Verbalize aloud whatever comes to mind. Simply saying it

can have a great impact upon later thoughts.

2. Write down whatever ideas you verbalize. This prevents your forgetting them later and provides you with a list for subsequent study and analysis.

3. Do not evaluate the worth of your thoughts and ideas as you brainstorm them. At this point you are interested in quantity of ideas, not quality.

If you follow these rules and allow your mind to associate one idea to another freely, you will be surprised not only by the large number of ideas on the topic you have developed but also by how much you know about the topic that you did not realize you knew. This procedure is very applicable to the operations of academic debate, especially in competitive interscholastic and intercollegiate debate with their broad and comprehensive topic areas. The generation of ideas via brainstorming is a most efficient method to begin your study of any topic or problem area.

After multiple ideas have been brought forth from your brainstorming exercise, an activity that you can do by yourself or, more suitably, in a group project with others to increase the number of ideas generated, the second step to be followed in the discovery of issues is to *analyze* that which you found during brainstorming. Now is the time to examine critically the materials you thought of, to probe what has been said. To analyze is to break something down into its component parts, to discover what factors go together to create something. For example, in examining the cost of running an automobile, you would find that there are several factors involved: the car payment, the insurance payment, gasoline expense, other maintenance expenses, and so on. All these combine to equal the cost of running your car, but each factor exists as a separate entity. Analysis, then, takes a general statement or thought and reduces it to its component factors, allowing you to have a more precise understanding of the potential issues involved in whatever you're examining. In essence, you are taking a system (cost) and delineating it into its components (insurance, gasoline, and so on) — an analytical systems approach.

Broad ideas are specified and particularized through analysis, by a careful study of each thought generated through brainstorming. What you discover through the process of analysis leads you to the final step of discovering issues — *research*, the search for external materials that crystallizes your discovery of issues. Up to this point, everything you have done has been internal, completed on your own and others' terms. You generated those ideas in brainstorming; you critically examined those ideas in analysis. Now you seek outside assistance in your study by finding materials pertinent to what you have already discovered. Through very basic library research, you will find information that supports, refutes, or modifies that which you discovered on your own. By initially reading general materials that relate to the topic or problem area and then reading information that is more particularized to meet those specifics discovered through analysis, you will have a comprehensive base of research knowledge that will allow you finally to discover the major issues at hand.

Thus, the process of discovering issues takes on the form of a funnel illustrated in figure 6.1. Your process from general thoughts to very specific ones is a primary example of reasoning by deduction. If you will follow this process, you will discover the major issues in any decision-making situation much faster and more efficiently than if you simply run to the library in the hope of finding pertinent information. Far too many beginning practitioners of argumentative communication make the mistake of going to the library too soon. If you do not have fairly specific ideas in mind when you begin researching, a great amount of time is lost wandering around stacks of books and magazines hoping that something will pop up and be of use. The discovery of issues must begin with your own thoughts and your own analysis. Researching should come only after you have thought through the problem very carefully.

Figure 6.1

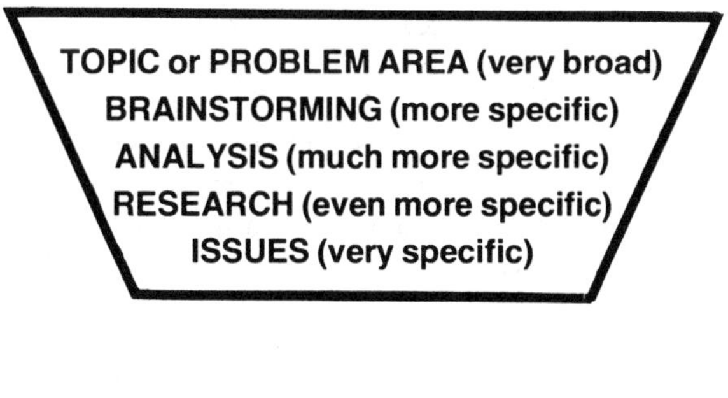

Types of Issues

Just as there are many types of ideas that can be generated on any given topic, there are differing types of issues for that same topic. Ideas are not the same, and not all issues are the same; in fact, some issues are much more important than others. For your study of the principles of argumentative communication, you should be aware of four types of issues that will be of significance to you.

First, *potential* issues are all issues that pertain to the topic or subject under scrutiny, including those that are found to be very important, marginally important, and completely unimportant — everything that relates to your topic in one way or another. Obviously, this is a broad category, probably the category of issue that is filled through brainstorming and, to a degree, by analysis. Subsequent research will indicate which issues are important or not, allowing you to proceed to the following two categories of issues.

Admitted issues are those that will not be disputed within an argumentative encounter, issues that are admitted by both sides. For example, in an academic debate dealing with the issuance of a guaranteed annual income to all Americans, an admitted issue would be that poverty exists within the United States. Even those who oppose a guaranteed income would not and could not dispute the existence of poverty; certainly, poverty does exist. Thus, the actual existence of poverty would not be a crucial issue in this encounter, because both sides would have to agree that to say "Poverty exists within the United States" would be to state a truism. An admitted issue is of little concern to the goings-on in argumentative communication, and an admitted issue is nothing but a time waster in the constraints of academic debate.

Main issues or *major* issues are those issues that spark dispute between the opposing sides in an argumentative encounter and are the central items upon which the outcome of the encounter will depend. Although the existence of poverty was found to be an admitted issue and hence of little importance in encounters over proposals to develop a guaranteed annual income scheme, the issue of *how* poverty was to be eliminated would be a very important or major issue. Should the poor be given money to raise them above the poverty level? Should the poor be given or forced to find jobs to raise themselves above the poverty level? Should the federal government be responsible for such antipoverty programs, or is this sort of action more appropriately the prerogative of the states and local communities? Answers to these questions deal with the important issue of how poverty should be eliminated and would be central to decisions regarding any guaranteed annual income proposal. Thus, the goal of your research is to discover these major issues, to distinguish major issues from the less important potential and admitted issues.

Finally, the last type of issue, a subset of major issues, is called *stock* issues, and these are those issues found most often within the operations of academic debate and traditional decision making. There are four such stock issues, which need to be considered in examining every topic and every problem area:

1. *Need.* Is there a need or rationale for such a change? Is there something wrong with the way things presently are that causes us to be compelled to make a change? Is there a warrant for change that justifies such a change? (Inherency — a major need subissue, is of such importance that it is discussed at length in the following chapter.)

2. *Plan or solution.* Is there a definite and concrete proposal that will solve the need? Can something specific be done to overcome the aforementioned rationale or warrant for change?

3. *Feasibility.* Can the plan be put into operation? Do we possess the capabilities to put the plan in operation? Do we possess the resources and technologies to implement the proposed solution?

4. *Advantage.* Will the implementation of the plan yield extra benefits? Besides solving the need, will the plan accrue other advantages?

Those four stock issues are of great importance in academic debate encounters—and in your day-to-day decision making.

Issues and Argumentative Communication

Functional and effective argumentative communication requires that issues be the foundation of argumentative encounters, thereby ensuring that decisions will be reached in accord with the merits of a case and not with irrelevant items or the personalities of the people involved in the encounter. Decisions that are based upon trivial matters or upon personality quirks tend to be erroneous decisions, the kinds of decisions in which we can place very little faith and trust. If, for example, you were examining the advantages and disadvantages of the proposed (at this writing) Equal Rights Amendment to the Constitution (ERA), arguments concerning the burning of women's undergarments and the abrasive personality of a Betty Friedan would be of no value to the question concerning the viability of the ERA. However, it must be admitted that in public discussion and debate, there exists often the temptation to deal with such irrelevant matters, to be concerned with items that are of minor importance to the central question at hand. The skillful practitioner of argumentative communication will try to avoid such irrelevant issues, keeping her attention focused on the major issues within public questions. Those issues should be the foundation of argument, as well as the foundation for the final decision reached.

In most of our daily decisions, as well as those positions taken within the confines of competitive academic debate, it is most useful to consider questions of policy placed before us in terms of the four stock issues delineated within the preceding section of this chapter. Need, plan, feasibility, and advantage are four benchmarks for both effective issue discovery and decision making. Questions that you face can be easily assessed in terms of those stock issues. Let us examine a case to exemplify their application, a normal daily decision-making question.

Question: Should I buy a new car to replace my 1972 Ford Maverick?

Application of stock issues

Need: Do I need a new car? Do I need to replace my Maverick?

Answer: My Maverick has had three major breakdowns in the past seven months. Repairs have cost me more than seven hundred dollars. The garage mechanic says its only a matter of time before the car falls apart. A new car, on the other hand, would be relatively maintenance-free. And I'd have sure, dependable transportation.

Plan: Can I replace my old car?

Answer: Yes. Several dealers are having car sales now before the new models arrive. I can trade my Maverick for a new Chevy Nova.

Feasibility: Would buying a new Chevy Nova be possible? Will I be able to afford to buy, operate, and maintain it?

Answer: Yes. My credit is good, and payments would be less than ninety dollars a month, less than I have been spending on the average just to keep my Maverick running. The total cost of operating the Nova is well within my budgetary limitations.

Advantage: Does buying a new Chevy Nova provide additional advantages over keeping my old car?

Answer: Yes. The new cars are all rustproofed by the Chevrolet dealer, meaning I wouldn't have to worry about the effects of snow and road salt in the winter. The Nova has a more pleasing color than my Maverick, and the Nova comes equipped with radial tires.

Decision: I shall replace my Maverick with a new Chevy Nova, because it provides better, more dependable transportation, is cheaper to operate, and it has the additional benefits of rust protection, a more pleasing color, and has much better tires. Therefore, I shall replace my Maverick with a new Chevy Nova.

By applying the four stock issues to a typical decision-making problem, you can render sound decisions, much sounder than those that are reached arbitrarily by whim or quick emotional judgment. In traditional, policy-centered academic debate, you may follow the same type of process as exemplified by the following:

Question: Should the United States implement a guaranteed annual income for all its citizens?

Application of Stock Issues:

Need:	Is there a need for a guaranteed annual income?
Answer:	Yes. There are more than thirty million people living at or below the poverty level, people who cannot afford the basics of food, clothing, and shelter.
Plan:	Can a plan be put together to implement a guaranteed income that will eliminate this problem of poverty?
Answer:	Yes. By giving cash grants to families whose annual incomes fall below the poverty level, every poor family will be lifted above that poverty level. This guaranteed income scheme can be handled efficiently through the computerized services of the Internal Revenue Service and controlled by the Department of Health and Welfare.
Feasibility:	Is a guaranteed annual income a feasible way to deal with the problem of poverty?
Answer:	No, because it does not guarantee that the poor will spend their cash grants for life's necessities. Besides, pumping that much money into the economy will increase inflation, thereby reducing the buying power of the dollar and, in effect, pushing the poor below the poverty level again.
Advantage:	Does a guaranteed annual income provide additional advantages over the current system's attempts at eliminating poverty?
Answer:	Yes. A guaranteed annual income is simpler and more easily administered than the present patchwork of cash grants, food stamps, in-kind services, and so on.

Decision: Because it appears that the impracticality of any guaranteed annual income scheme would (*a*) not really eliminate poverty in this country and would (*b*) heat up the inflationary cycle, it appears that the United States should not implement a guaranteed annual income.

In the formal advocacy setting of competitive interscholastic and intercollegiate debate, the opposing sides, of course, would present different interpretations and different supportive evidence for each of the stock issues. Those advocates on the *affirmative*, having the responsibility to support the debate question, would argue that, yes, there is a need for a guaranteed income that can be met with a feasible plan that also carries with it additional advantages. Those advocates on the *negative*, having the responsibility to oppose the debate question, would contend that there is no need for a guaranteed income, that any such proposal would be unworkable and infeasible, and that horrible disadvantages would result if a guaranteed income plan were to be implemented. Although some theorists are unhappy with this approach to the study of issues in argumentative encounters,[2] the application of those four stock issues to policy questions is a most efficient and effective method of discovering the major issues within the encounter and of guiding the decision-making process along rational and reasonable lines.

Conclusion

Meaningful argumentative communication requires that argument be grounded upon substantive items or issues, the very foundation of rational argumentative encounters. By carefully examining what you already know through brainstorming and analysis, and then by conducting specific research, you will discover the major issues within any important question confronting you. After these issues have been discovered, you want to limit your arguments to major issues, casting aside irrelevant potential issues and meaningless admitted issues. In policy-making decisions, decisions that confront all of us in daily matters and within the rigors of traditional academic debate, the four stock issues of need, plan, feasibility, and advantage should be used to reach and to accept or reject proposed decisions. When argumentative communication is grounded upon such issues, the arguments involved are solid and substantive, and the decisions reached tend to be better than those reached arbitrarily or through emotional whim.

References

1. For a fine discussion of the nature of issues, see Eugene R. Moulton, *The Dynamics of Debate* (New York: Harcourt, Brace and World, 1966), pp. 64–71.

2. See, for example, Robert P. Newman, "Analysis and Issues—A Study of Doctrine," *Central States Speech Journal* 13 (Autumn 1961): 43–54.

Practicum

1. Recall a decision that you have made recently — a decision to do something, to buy something, to go somewhere. As concretely as possible, recall those factors that prompted your decision. Those factors served essentially as the issues supporting or justifying your decision. Importantly, you should recognize that issues vary from person to person, that what is significant to you may not be significant to someone else. All of us identify issues daily in examining activities and actions that affect our lives.

2. One of the most important national matters of the past several years has been that of energy. Since the Arab oil embargo (OPEC nations) following the Yom Kippur war in 1973, perhaps the single most discussed national item has been America's ongoing energy crisis.

In assessing this country's energy problem, United States Senator Howard Metzenbaum (Democrat, Ohio) provided his view of the challenges facing United States energy policy in "America's Energy Challenge," a speech presented on 18 June 1977 to the Democratic Forum Energy Conference. Read Senator Metzenbaum's speech and then answer these questions:

- What issues (matters of central concern) did Metzenbaum find in assessing America's energy problem?

- What issues were most significant to the overall problem?

- What stock issues did Metzenbaum consider in his analysis?

- What issues did Metzenbaum fail to cover that you think are essential in examining the topic?

America's Energy Challenge
Senator Howard M. Metzenbaum

I, like 210 million Americans, agree with the president that our country is facing a tremendous energy challenge. There is no question that the continued well-being of our economy and our country demands that we reduce our dependence on foreign oil, as well as maximize the utilization of our domestic resources.

During the past several months, I have very carefully studied the president's proposals. I have attended extensive hearings — read detailed reports and studies — and met personally with many members of the administration's energy team.

Based on this study of the plan, I am convinced that the president has correctly stated the sense of urgency with which we must address the nation's energy problems. But while the president is correct in asking the Congress to expeditiously consider his energy program, I believe it is first essential that Congress carefully analyze all the alternatives available to us to increase production and conserve energy. It is the duty of Congress to closely scrutinize every aspect of the administration's plan — to offer constructive criticism — suggest alternative approaches — and to finally enact the best possible energy plan. For example, a careful examination of mandatory conservation programs may reveal that we can achieve the President's conservation goals without resorting to massive price increases and a complicated tax rebate program. Similarly, while it is necessary to provide oil and gas producers with adequate price incentives, it is impossible to intelligently determine a fair price without data pertaining to the actual cost of production and the amount of existing reserves. No such data exists today.

Last week, in his press conference, the president acknowledged that his plan was not infallible — that there are other proposals. He said: "We don't consider ourselves infallible. . .and I don't say that everything we propose has got to be passed just as though we put it forward." It is in this context that I will address my concerns with respect to the administration's plan and the need to consider alternatives.

To begin with, it seems that the administration's plans cannot achieve its stated goals. I am not alone in this conclusion. Many others, more expert than I, concur. Let me cite just a few:

1. A G.A.O. Study, issued less than two weeks ago, contained the following conclusion — *We believe that it is somewhat incongruous to ask Congress to establish a set of national energy goals, and then propose a national energy plan that is not expected to achieve them. . .we believe the plan should be redesigned to provide a reasonable opportunity of achieving the stated goals.*

2. A Congressional Budget Office Study reached a similar conclusion in a major report to Congress which stated: *[The] administration's estimates of the magnitude of input savings are over optimistic.*

3. In evaluating the administration's chances of limiting foreign oil imports to seven million barrels per day, Dr. Hans Landsberg, a senior economist at *Resources for the Future*, had a two-word comment — "*About nil.*" Continuing on this subject, Landsberg stated: "*Barring much more drastic conservation measures, this proposal will mean additional oil imports.*"

But this is not new to the administration. The plan itself projects that with full implementation, energy demand would still increase by a whopping 25 percent between 1976 and 1985 — *only 4 percent less than if no energy plan is enacted at all.*

The thrust of these studies is clear — almost without exception, every outside analysis of the administration's energy program has reached the same conclusion — the plan raises energy costs a total of $90 billion or more by 1985, but it cannot accomplish even its stated goals. Let's not forget that two presidents — President Ford and President Carter — both publicly stated that a $12 billion tax cut would provide a major stimulus to the economy. *Imagine the impact of an average consumer drain of almost that same amount each year for the next seven years.*

It is not enough, though, to criticize the administration's plan. I recognize this, and I will suggest several alternatives later in my remarks. A group of us in the Senate Energy Committee are presently exploring a number of different possibilities that we hope could attain the same objective expressed by the president without having so great an economic impact on the American consumer.

But first let me address what I believe is the fundamental problem in the administration's plan — its singular reliance on price as a means of stimulating production of domestic reserves and as a way of inducing conservation.

A careful study of the costs associated with the production of oil and natural gas clearly demonstrates that while greatly increased prices have provided producers with record profits, the increased profits have *not* been accompanied by noticeable increases in production.

In 1972, before the OPEC price increase, the average price for a barrel of U.S. crude oil was $3.39. Unbelievably, a recently completed in-House FEA study reported that even at this low price, Exxon's producing operation earned a 71 percent pretax rate of return on net investment. They were not alone. Mobil had a 49 percent rate of return; Amoco a 43.9 percent; and Gulf a 44.7 percent — all four figures based upon a $3.39 price per barrel.

These figures are particularly distressing when one considers that the average price of domestic crude is $8.50 — a price the administration now wants to raise to the OPEC cartel price of $13.50.

The national energy plan, on commenting on this price increase, masterfully understates the obvious: "This price should provide all the incentives needed for the development of new oil production in the U.S."

Indeed it should. It is bad enough that American consumers are forced to pay exorbitant prices — *but now these prices are to be set by the OPEC cartel — not the U.S. Government — not even the oil companies.* In short, the administration has asked American consumers to pay the OPEC monopoly price for domestic oil without any guarantee or reason to assume that increased production will follow.

As a matter of fact, there is every reason to believe that production will remain essentially the same despite increased prices. Dr. Walter Measday, chief economic advisor of the State Antitrust and Monopolies Subcommittee, recently testified that: "The [oil] companies have determined that it is not in their economic interests at this time to develop their leases."

The administration's proposal also provides a special bonus to producers of Alaskan oil without any justifiable reason. Only last month, Mr. O'Leary acknowledged that these revenues will amount to a windfall for the oil companies — more than $2 billion for British Petroleum, Arco, and Sohio.

Oil is not alone in its departure from any semblance of reasonable pricing. The price of new natural gas is tied to the BTU equivilent of crude oil delivered to the refinery — in common language, at $1.75 per MCF for new natural gas.

- This price is six and a half times the $.26 price agreed to by producers in a July 1971 FPC case "which would provide an incentive for substantial increases in exploratory and development activities."
- Three and a half times the last judicially approved "just and reasonable" price of $.52.
- Three times the $.60 range which an FPC staff report said should produce ample returns and incentives.
- And about 25 percent over the recently established $1.42 price which is presently being litigated in the courts — a case which the administration is now legislatively attempting to bypass.

There has been much made of congressional action with respect to the deregulation of natural gas. Many of us in Congress are strongly opposed to deregulation. But I must point out that the administration, by tying the price of natural gas to the BTU equivalent of oil, would effectively deregulate it in 1979 when mandatory oil price controls expire. Although the administration has announced its intention to extend oil price controls through 1985, no legislation has as yet been sent to Congress from the White House. If the administration is still of the same mind, then we should have that legislative proposal.

Last week, during a hearing before the Senate Energy Committee, I asked Mr. O'Leary how the administration determined the $1.75 price for natural gas. He responded that: "*The price was established through a 'give and take' by interested parties and was set to eliminate any uncertainty.*"

Having just listened to Mr. O'Leary's presentation, I'm still unclear why we can't have the same degree of certainty if we establish a $.52 price — or a $1 price — or even a $1.25 price.

But the facts are that the administration simply doesn't have the data to determine producer's costs, *despite their authority to get it.* When the chairman of the Energy Committee, Senator Jackson, recently asked Mr. O'Leary how soon the administration could get data with respect to the actual costs of discovery and production, his answer was: "*Three or four years.*"

I was a businessman for a long time and I know that no business would tolerate this kind of practice. This information is available. As a matter of fact, two weeks ago, I received a copy of a confidential accounting study of a major Gulf oil natural gas field. The study was conducted by the prestigious accounting firm of Price Waterhouse. *It showed that Gulf's average total exploration and production costs will be $.24 per MCF during the twenty-year contract. I want to note that the study was dated January 1976.* The $.24 per MFC price was broken down as follows:

- 10.09¢ for investment
- 8.6¢ for expenses
- 4.7¢ for royalty purchaser costs

These figures show beyond a doubt that high natural gas prices are not justified. While natural gas companies will respond to this by saying that these figures are the exception — I challenge them to prove their point. *Let them submit to Congress their detailed expense figures and profits on other contracts.*

When this $.24 price is compared with the administration's proposal to increase the rice of new natural gas to $1.75 per MCF, only one conclusion can be drawn — *skyrocketing profits for the natural gas companies.* According to the administration's own estimates, the nonrebated gas pricing provisions will increase producer revenues $15.3 billion by 1975 — an estimate based on the $1.42 figure currently challenged in court. While the administration makes this figure sound like a bargain for consumers when compared to the $86 billion cost of deregulation, it's like telling a person who has been robbed of $100 to be happy because someone on the next block was robbed of $600.

I want to emphasize that these profits do not go to struggling companies. *They go to Houston Natural Gas, whose earnings rose 35 percent in 1976 over 1975 — Texas Gas Corporation, whose earnings rose 35.7 percent in 1976 — and Columbia Transmission Company,* the pipeline subsidiary of the nation's largest integrated company, *whose earnings rose an amazing 85.5 percent in 1976.* They also go to the oil companies who own thirteen of the fourteen largest natural gas companies.

One of the major goals of the national energy plan is the acceleration of the development and utilization of coal. But the president's plan provides no safeguards against escalating coal prices — an omission which becomes all the more serious when we recognize that *since 1970, the average price per ton of coal has dramatically increased in some cases as much as 300 to 400 percent.*

This problem has been further exacerbated by the increasing move of the petroleum companies into the coal industry. A few facts illustrate this point: of the top fifteen coal companies, six are major petroleum companies. Twenty-four oil and gas companies control approximately 44 percent of the leased coal reserves — of these twenty-four companies, only eight actually are producing coal.

For example, Exxon controls the fifth largest amount of coal reserves held by an individual firm. But in 1975, Exxon produced less than three million tons, or only one thirty-third of 1 percent of its reputed reserves. A recent study I made indicated that in general, coal production has declined or failed to increase significantly when a previously independent coal company is acquired by an oil company. And that raises the entire question of whether or not the petroleum companies should be forced by law to get out of coal — uranium — solar — and other alternative energy resources.

- In 1976, the president said, "I support a legal prohibition against ownership of competing types of energy, oil and coal, for example."

- In 1977, Mr. Schlesinger, speaking for the president, said horizontal divestiture is not a priority.

I say to you today that while horizontal divestiture may not be a priority of the president's, *it is a priority of some of us in Congress.*

Earlier, I alluded to the total cost to consumers if the administration's plan was fully implemented — between 90 and 100 billion dollars by 1985. The price tag on the gas guzzler tax — $7.7 billion — the crude oil equalization tax — $15.3 billion — the standby gasoline tax — $39.7 billion — and oil and natural gas consumption taxes — $40.6 billion. If the rebates are not included in the plan, the cost could be as high as $222 billion. Whether or not these taxes and rebates will be legislated into law is the very issue before Congress.

The sums of money contemplated in the plan's tax proposal are, in a word, astronomical. But will they accomplish substantial energy savings? Alice Revlin, head of the Congressional Budget Office, in testimony before the State Energy Committee, stated that the wellhead tax, a provision which will cost consumers $15.3 billion in higher taxes and higher prices, *will only save 25,000 barrels per day out of a total of 17 million barrel per day — less than two one-hundreths of 1 percent.*

We could probably save this much if it rains during the July 4th weekend. The comptroller general, in a GAO report on the president's plan, concluded that the gap between what the plan can accomplish and its stated goals is even greater than the Congressional Budget Office study indicated.

But it is not enough for Congress to tell the American people that the president's energy plan will cost too much and accomplish too little. It is up to the Congress to provide its own alternatives which will bring about much-needed energy conservation. If we believe there is an energy crisis, and I do — and if we believe a wartime conservation effort is necessary, and I do — then *tough mandatory programs which fall equally on all Americans are necessary.* A gas-guzzler tax is not the answer. The Energy Policy and Conservation Act of 1975 provided minimum standards for fleets of cars. I believe we should apply these same standards to every new car, not just the fleet average.

Shouldn't we also be considering *a standby gas rationing program* which the president could put into effect if other conservation methods are ineffective? Or should we try to use mandatory means other than rationing? While I am not prepared to say which alternatives are best, I am prepared to say that there are other viable altermatives which would be more effective than higher prices alone.

Many of us in Congress are considering the elimination of natural gas pilot lights — a measure which could save as much as 3 percent of gas consumption alone — and a direction in which California has already moved. There are other possibilities — strict enforcement of the 55 mile per hour speed limit, a measure which the best energy authorities indicate could save as much as 4 percent of the total gasoline used in the country. The list goes on — mandatory insulation for all houses — mandatory industrial conversion from oil and gas to coal — all proposals that should be considered.

The message is clear — we can, and must, give serious consideration to tough mandatory conservation programs which can accomplish substantial energy savings *without massive and unjustified price increases.*

I salute the president and join with him in support of the enactment of a Consumer Protection Agency. But I urge him to show this same concern in the design of our energy plan — a plan which must be equally consumer-oriented. The American people are told that the excessive taxes they are being asked to pay will rebated to them. But now they are told that the administration isn't sure exactly how much, or in what way, this will happen. And the oil companies are now saying, "Give us fifty percent of the rebate to use for exploration." That would be tantamount to seven and one-half billion dollar extra bonanza for the oil companies.

We talk about equity — *but where is there equity when the president asks Americans to pay billions of dollars in higher prices and additional taxes, while the energy companies receive windfall profits. We talk about fairness — but what is fair about a program that doesn't place an equal share of the load on all Americans?* We talk about the need for a program that will quickly and significantly reduce energy consumption — *but what sense is there in enacting a plan that cannot accomplish its own goals?*

We need an energy plan that is fair to the consumer. We need a program that doesn't penalize one group at the expense of another. We need a program that will significantly reduce energy consumption without massive price increases. We need these programs now.

Congress cannot do it alone. Neither can the administration. Only by working together can we hope to enact a comprehensive plan that protects the consumer and accomplishes substantial energy savings. The time is now.

Chapter 7

The Burden of Proof, Inherency, and Presumption

*** The Burden of Proof: Its Definition**
*** The Importance of Inherency**
*** The Burden of Proof and Academic Debate**
*** Presumption: Its Definition**
*** Presumption and Argumentative Communication**
*** Conclusion**
*** References**
*** Practicum**

Recognizing that issues serve as the foundation of meaningful argumentative communication, we now may examine those factors prevalent in all argumentative communication encounters. This chapter details three such factors: the burden of proof, inherency, and presumption.

The burden of proof, one of the most basic elements in decision making and in academic debate contests, is an important foundation of the American judicial system. Anyone attempting to change the status quo or to alter the current state of affairs has the burden of proof — the responsibility to demonstrate that such change or alteration is justified. As in a court of law, the status quo is presumed "innocent" (no change is justified) unless and until proven otherwise.

Inherency, a subset of the stock issue of need, is a most complex and important element in justifying changes in present policies and actions. A warrant for change must be based upon proof that the status quo cannot overcome its problems or shortcomings; there must be an inherent reason within the status quo that causes the problem or prevents problem solution.

Presumption is the counterpart of the burden of proof. Since we tend to desire stability and tend to retain the way things are currently done, we presume that present goals, policies, methods, and attitudes are sufficient and that they should be retained until a compelling rationale is presented to force us to make a change. Presumption rests with the status quo; the burden of proof, then, falls upon those who wish to make some change within the status quo.

By studying the factors of the burden of proof, inherency, and presumption as presented within this chapter, you may determine who has what particular responsibilities in any argumentative situation.

The Burden of Proof: Its Definition

All of us tend to lead stable lives. We like to live in certain areas, we prefer some foods over others, we like to do certain things and not do others. And we tend to have our lives follow patterns: we like to get up at approximately the same time every morning, we like to dress in a certain way — in short, we like to know what to expect **tomorrow, the day after, and indefinitely into the future. We do like** to have stability.[1]

However, you know from your own experience that nothing remains stable forever. The ongoing life process constantly changes, and our desired stability often is seen to be threatened. When you are asked to make decisions such as whether to move to another house or whether to change jobs, your stable life pattern directly is faced with the possibility of change. Similarly, major policy decisions that affect our governmental units, our society as a whole, and our fellow citizens are decisions that affect stability. For example, when we consider the viability of adopting some sort of guaranteed income scheme, we come face-to-face with change, changing from our current system of welfare payments and so on to a new system of a guaranteed annual income. In all such proposals for change, whether personal (things that affect only you or your family) or much larger (things that may affect everyone in society), the burden of proof in such decision making is present. In the study of argumentative communication, the burden of proof is defined as **the responsibility of the advocate proposing change to justify completely the proposed change.**[2]

Our personal actions and our social systems are structured so change is not seen to be necessarily good. We seek stability in our own lives, and the overall social, political, and economic structure also seeks a similar degree of stability. Thus, whenever any person or any group proposes that we make changes in the way we believe or act, that person or group has the burden of proof and the responsibility of completely justifying making the proposed change(s). The way things are now—everything that goes on in the present—is called the present system or the status quo. Proponents of change, therefore, wish to make alterations in the status quo by changing something within the status quo, and all such proposed changes must be justified and their proponents must shoulder the burden of proof. Perhaps the following example will clarify the nature of the burden of proof.

Status Quo:	poverty exists within the United States; local, state and federal governmental bodies have programs designed to combat poverty (cash payments, food stamps, and so on).
Proposed Change:	to replace the current system of antipoverty programs and projects with a national guaranteed annual income to eliminate poverty finally within this country.
Burden of Proof:	rests with those advocating the implementation of the guaranteed annual income. They must justify replacing the status quo with their proposed policy.
Justification:	to uphold the burden of proof, those advocating change must demonstrate a need or rationale for making the change, a method whereby change can be practically implemented, and the method must not be so disadvantageous as to overwhelm the supposed benefits of the new system.
Decision:	will be based upon how successfully the proponents of change uphold the burden of proof by justifying the proposed change.

That example should demonstrate not only the importance of the burden of proof to the decision-making process but also the continued importance of the four stock issues discussed in chapter 6. Notice that the justification necessary to uphold the burden of proof rests very largely upon the stock issues of need, plan, feasibility, and advantage. Unless those issues are met adequately, then there is no justification for change, the burden of proof has not been supported, and change, therefore is not warranted. All major decisions should be subjected to that type of scrutiny.

Our system of justice depends upon the notion of the burden of proof to a large extent. Anyone accused of a crime, for example, is presumed to be innocent until he is proved to be guilty. The prosecuting attorney, the individual accusing you of the crime, has the responsibility to uphold the burden of proof. She must demonstrate that you did commit that crime, that you no longer may be considered an innocent party. You see, until that time, the status quo is that you are innocent, you have not been convicted. To change the status quo, to show you to be a criminal and not innocent, the prosecutor must uphold the burden of proof. She must prove that you are guilty, but you do not have to prove you are innocent; you need only blunt the prosecutor's case sufficiently to prevent your being proven guilty.

Similarly, the status quo in personal decisions and in major national decision-making situations is presumed to be good, just, innocent, and correct, until those advocating change prove that making such a change is completely justified. When an insurance salesman tries to persuade you to change life insurance policies, the salesman has the burden of proof to justify that change. When you try to persuade your teacher to change your final grade in a course, you have the burden of proof to justify the teacher's changing your grade. When the Carter administration proposed to return the Panama Canal to the nation of Panama, the Carter administration had to uphold the burden of proof by justifying that change in American foreign policy. In all situations, those desiring change in the ways things are currently done must uphold the burden of proof; they must be held accountable for justifying any proposed changes.

The Importance of Inherency

In formal decision-making processes, especially academic debate, there is one issue that goes along, quite literally like a horse and cart, with the responsibility of the burden of proof — inherency, perhaps the most vital issue in all formal argumentative encounters.

Basically, to meet the issue of inherency, those who advocate change must go one step beyond showing that change is justified, they must also demonstrate that the rationale for change is *inherent*: that the staus quo cannot overcome the shortcoming, problem, or harm found to be within it. That is, the advocate of change must prove that the present system cannot solve its own problems, which would, of course, totally eliminate the need or warrant for change.

In the preceding section, the nature of the burden of proof was exemplified by examining the justification for a proposed guaranteed annual income system. You might remember that such a system was justified on the grounds that *(a)* poverty ought to be eliminated in the United States but that *(b)* the present system's many antipoverty programs had not eliminated the poverty problem. Thus, since the present system's efforts against poverty were not effective, the implementation of a guaranteed income would be justified to solve a problem that the present system apparently was incapable of solving. That example illustrates the proper upholding of the burden of proof to justify a proposed change.

However, before rushing off to implement some type of guaranteed income scheme, the rational decision maker would ask whether or not the present system's inabilities to eliminate poverty were inherent, demanding proof that the status quo somehow was prevented from ever overcoming the problem of poverty. Simply because poverty exists does not prove that the various existent antipoverty programs will not eventually overcome the poverty problem. Truly to justify the change to a guaranteed income system, the proponent of change must demonstrate that the present system cannot, in all probability, solve the problem in the future; that is, the proponent of change must demonstrate that the problem within the status quo is inherent and can only be overcome by changing the system altogether.

This demand that the proponent of change demonstrate that the rationale for change is inherent is good common sense. Since we tend not to change our way of doing things unless or until we are compelled to make a change, it is imperative that the rationale for change be so compelling that there is no other alternative in solving the problem with which we are faced. For example, if it could be proven that the many current antipoverty programs could be altered or modified somewhat to eliminate our poverty problem, it would be absurd to throw over that system in favor of a new and completely untested guaranteed annual income scheme. We know how the present system works, but we do not know how a guaranteed income system would work because it has not been utilized in this country. Therefore, if the programs within the present system could be made to function effectively in the elimination of poverty, common sense would dictate that the known present system be kept and that the unknown guaranteed income not be implemented in its place. You make the same type of decision in daily situations:

Problem:	Your car is getting miserable gas mileage; your gasoline bills have more than doubled in the last three months.
Proposed solution:	Get rid of your old car and buy a new car that has EPA-tested better gas mileage.
Inherency:	Can your old car be fixed to overcome the gas mileage problem? Can your old car be fixed to eliminate the current problem?
Answer:	By having a minor tune-up, your gas mileage will be improved, returning your gasoline expenses to their prior acceptable level.
Decision:	You keep your old car, deciding to have a tune-up to restore your lost gasoline economy.
Rationale for decision:	You know how your old car works. It has given you dependable transportation. You enjoy driving it, and your friends enjoy riding in it. However, you have no such knowledge about any new car you might buy. Therefore, by having the tune-up restore the desired gas mileage, it makes better sense to retain your old car and not to buy a new car.

Both personal decisions and major national decisions, therefore, contain the important issue of inherency, an issue that must be met by proponents of change to justify adequately making any proposed change.

In formal argumentative settings as exemplified by academic debate, there are three major types or kinds of inherency that proponents of change use to justify changes in policies and systems. Inherency can mean more than just one idea. The three types of inherency are structural, gap, and attitudinal, and each is explained briefly.

Structural inherency is the type most often used to justify change within a contest debate encounter. This type of inherency claims that there exists a structural flaw within the status quo that prevents the system from overcoming the problem under discussion. For example, in dealing with the problem of poverty, the advocate of change might contend that certain laws or regulations preclude the present system's ability to eliminate poverty. Various welfare requirements, residency requirements, and the like might be seen as actual impediments to the goal of elimination of poverty in the United States.

A second type of inherency claimed by advocates of change is called gap inherency or priority inherency. Unlike structural inherency wherein the claim is made that part of the actual structure of the status quo prevents the problem from being solved, gap or priority inherency claims that there is a lack of coverage of the problem within status quo programs to deal with the particular problem under consideration. For example, because of the relative newness of the home energy crisis, some have claimed that there are not enough governmental regulations over the selling and installation of various home insulation materials. These critics claim that many homeowners are being ripped off through inferior materials and workmanship because there are insufficient governmental controls over the home insulation industry. This complaint illustrates gap inherency; that is, there is a gap within status quo laws, powers, programs and so on that allows the problem to remain unsolved.

The third type of inherency is the most difficult type of inherency with which to deal — attitudinal inherency. This type of inherency claims that it is not the structure of the status quo that creates the difficulty but the existing attitude of the status quo (ideas, philosophies, goals) that prevents the system from alleviating the particular problem under discussion. The proponent for change contends that the status quo is virtually incapacitated by this negative attitude, thereby justifying the implementation of a new proposal not handicapped by this poor attitude. One might contend, for example, that the various antipoverty programs are ineffective now and will continue to be ineffective in the future because major decision makers have negative, "who cares?" attitudes about the poor people in the United States. Thus, a new system is needed to overcome this disabling attitude.

Regardless of the type of inherency argued, the general issue of inherency itself is the most critical issue within any formal argumentative encounter. In academic debate, those advocating change could win every issue within the debate, but, if they were to lose the issue of inherency, they would also lose the ultimate debate decision. Inherency is of central importance in formal argumentative communication settings.

The Burden of Proof and Academic Debate

The structure of academic debate creates two opposing sides who contest a central question, generally a question of policy (should we or should we not do something). As explained fully in chapter II, the debate question is generally phrased as a direct declarative statement, for example, Resolved: that the power of the presidency should be significantly curtailed. Within this structure, those advocates occupying the position of the *affirmative* have the responsibility to uphold the burden of proof; they must completely justify doing that which is called for in the statement of the debate topic. The speakers on the affirmative, then, must present solid reasons why a change from the status quo is warranted, and, in so doing, they must deal with the all-important issue of inherency, demonstrating why the status quo cannot eliminate the rationale for change by its own devices.

To give you a clear idea how both the burden of proof and the issue of inherency are covered by affirmative speakers, the following example of an affirmative speech is presented for you to read and to study. While reading through the arguments and evidence presented to substantiate those arguments, ask yourself these questions:

1. Does the affirmative presentation provide a sufficient amount of proof to cause you to agree that there is something wrong with the present system?

2. Is the problem presented by the affirmative of such a magnitude that you believe a change is warranted?

3. Does the affirmative presentation adequately demonstrate that there are sufficient structural problems within the status quo that preclude that system's being able to eliminate the problem isolated by the affirmative?

4. Does the affirmative present a proposed policy change that, in all probability, would eliminate the problem identified earlier by the affirmative?

5. Finally, after reading the entire affrimative presentation, do you believe that the affirmative speakers have adequately upheld both the burden of proof and the issue of inherency? What weaknesses did you see in the nature and structure of the affirmative's argument?

The following speech was prepared for a debate on the topic, Resolved: that the power of the presidency should be significantly curtailed. The affirmative speakers had the responsibility to justify why presidential powers ought to be curtailed and how, specifically, those powers ought to be curtailed. As their problem area, they chose to isolate the presidential practice of impounding funds, that is, failing to spend money for various programs that had been approved and appropriated by Congress.

Against Presidential Impoundment

As George Danielson observed in June of 1973, "...There is only one effective way to solve the impoundment problem, and that is to take away the executive's power to impound by making it literally impossible for him to do so." Because Tom and I share Mr. Danielson's concern with the unauthorized presidential impoundment of appropriated funds, we stand firmly resolved: that the power of the presidency should be significantly curtailed.

Curtailment of the unauthorized presidential impoundment of funds is justified by consideration of three major areas of analysis.

Consideration I:
The unauthorized impoundment of appropriated funds is nonbeneficial

Our first major consideration analyzes the resultant effects of unauthorized presidential impoundment of appropriated funds and is based upon a two-part supportive substructure.

A. *Impoundment is significant*

Statistical analysis of the monies impounded by the various presidents indicates the scope of the problem. During the mid-1960s, for example, President Johnson impounded some $10.6 billion in congressionally appropriated funds, a figure supplied by Nebraska Congressman Dave Martin during the 1973 Impoundment Reporting and Review Hearings.

Arthur Schlesinger has noted in *The Imperial Presidency* that, by 1973, President Nixon had impounded $15 billion and that this action "had affected more than a hundred federal programs [and had been equivalent] to about 17 to 20 percent of controllable funds."

In just the past ten years, presidential impoundment of funds has totalled over $70 billion. And when one considers the fact that nearly every president has used this power, that its use has been on the steady increase during the past thirty years, and that President Ford has recently threatened to impound billions more, then one is able to see the magnitude of the problem.

B. *Impoundment is harmful*

The unauthorized presidential impoundment of appropriated funds is given further nonbeneficial impact by the resultant harms from such action that can be noted in qualitative and quantitative terms. The extent of this impact is illustrated in the following two independent areas:

1. *Education*

The role of the federal government in higher education was explained by Robert C. Calkins of the Brookings Institute: "The active interest of the federal government in higher education has been aroused in recent years as never before, primarily because of the critical importance of higher education to national security, technological progress, and economic growth. These pressing problems, like others, require highly trained personnel. American leadership in the coming years, and perhaps even American survival, depend in large measure on the provision of top quality education beyond the high school level. . . ."

However, despite the importance of federally aided higher education, and despite congressional appropriations to fill this need, President Nixon impounded millions of dollars earmarked for higher education. And the harmful result was crystallized by Congressman Madden of Indiana: several million students throughout the country would have to curtail their education.

2. *Conservation and environmental protection*

Recognizing the importance of preserving and

improving our environment, Congress has, in recent years, appropriated large sums of money to achieve this goal, but, here too, unauthorized presidential impoundment has left its mark. Florida Representative Claude Pepper noted in 1973 that Congress had voted to fund the Environmental Protection Act with some $11 billion over a period of two years. However, President Nixon impounded $6 billion of these funds, over 50 percent of the program's entire support.

An example of the concomitant impact of this action was provided by Senator Dick Clark of Iowa who noted that some 90 percent of Iowa's water pollution is caused by soil erosion and chemical runoff; and the program designed to solve this problem was eliminated by the unauthorized presidential impoundment of funds. In addition, Senator Clark has noted that "water and sewage grants for dozens of Iowa communities presently polluting our streams have ended by presidential decision."

Please remember that these two areas — education and conservation and environmental protection — are but two examples of the nonbeneficial results of unauthorized presidential impoundment. Congressman Madden noted that impoundment has affected programs dealing with housing, health, transportation, hospital construction, and many more. Remember: over $70 billion impounded in just the past ten years with the promise of more to come.

Consideration II:
The unauthorized impoundment of appropriated funds is nonjustifiable

Despite accruing the above-noted resultant nonbenefits by impounding Congressionally appropriated funds, presidents and their staffs have attempted to justify such unauthorized actions on various grounds. Our second major case consideration provides an analysis of these rationales and demonstrates their nonviability.

A. *Unauthorized impoundment of funds is not justified in combatting inflation*

The most oft-used presidential rationale for unauthorized impoundment is that such action was necessary to combat inflation. However, careful examination of the statutes upon which this claim is based reveals the executive rationale to be insufficient.

1. *Employment Act of 1946*

Often the president attempts to justify impoundment in terms of his responsibilities under the Employment Act of 1946. However, expert analysis denies this rationale. The *Yale Law Journal* of July 1973 noted that ". . . if Congress meant in the Employment Act to direct the president to achieve that goal (controlling inflation) by impounding whatever funds he felt were unessential, it seems likely that it would have made the empowerment explicit . . . this section can hardly be read to declare that the fight against inflation is to take precedence over any other aim of national policy, much less over other specific legislation."

Thus, the Employment Act does not justify impoundment. In fact, as Louis Fisher noted in the *Buffalo Law Review*, impoundment goes contrary to the purpose of the act: "The Employment Act of 1946 was enacted as an instrument for countering a possible postwar depression. Maximizing purchasing power, a primary goal, was to be attained by promoting employment and production. Impoundment has precisely the opposite effect."

2. *Anti-Deficiency Act*

A second statute upon which the president tries to justify impoundment in combatting inflation is his authority under the Anti-Deficiency Act. Again, however, the *Yale Law Journal* makes clear the fact that no such rationale is viable: ". . . A reading of the Act makes clear that it gives no support to the impoundments currently in controversy. The Anti-Deficiency Act provides . . . that the executive branch shall so appropriate as to assure that they last for the full period of time for which they were intended by Congress." The preclusion of program deficiencies is not the same as combatting inflation; this rationale is inadequate.

B. *Unauthorized impoundment of funds is not justified in maintaining the debt ceiling*

Presidents have also attempted to justify the unauthorized impoundment of funds by claiming that such action was necessary to maintain the existent debt ceiling. The *Yale Law Journal* denies this justification: "The mere existence of a ceiling clearly provokes no unavoidable statutory conflict.... The impoundments currently in controversy took place while the debt level was at least $16 billion below the ceiling, and thus derive no support from the ceiling law . . . .(The debt ceiling cannot be read as a grant of power to impound whatever monies the president chooses.)"

Conclude the analysis of our second consideration by turning to Congressman Anderson: "Of all rationales used for impoundments, the two that deal with inflation control and remaining within the debt ceiling have been the ones that have been used to eliminate programs that were found to be unneeded by the administration.

"But it turns out from my study of this particular report that only $40 million of all the impounded funds have been impounded for those two purposes alone."

Thus, the affirmative analysis claims that not only do presidential rationales fail to provide support for unauthorized impoundment of funds, but also that the track record of their usage — $40 million out of $70 billion — fails to support their justifiable validity.

Consideration III:

The unauthorized impoundment of appropriated funds is inherent

Having seen that the unauthorized presidential impoundment of appropriated funds is both nonbeneficial and unjustified, we turn to our third consideration that indicates the present system's inability to solve the total problem. This inability is noted by considering two lines of analysis.

A. *The 1974 Impoundment Control Act is ineffective in its structure*

1. *It institutionalizes impoundment*

Under the procedures of the 1974 Impoundment Control Act, the president is given authority to impound funds. In short, the status quo legitimizes the use of this power and institutionalizes the harms noted above.

2. *It provides only after-the-fact control*

Under the new law, congressional action on presidential impoundment occurs only after the impoundment power has been utilized. Congress can act only after the fact, after the monies have been impounded.

The inherent problem with this after-the-fact check is that it does not eliminate the nonbenefits of impoundment. As Congressman Matsunaga noted in 1973: ". . . Even if the

Congress should disapprove of a presidential impoundment within sixty days [as the law provides] there would have been as much as fifty-nine days of impoundment, which in some cases could even kill the program."

Thus, the Impoundment Control Act cannot guarantee the elimination of the harms; it provides only after-the-fact control.

3. *It provides no guarantee of congressional action*

The Impoundment Control Act does not guarantee that the Congress will offset presidential impoundment by disapproving the impoundment. Although the mechanism for an after-the-fact check exists, there is no guarantee that it will be used. In either case, the harms or nonbenefits continue to be realized: either the harms will occur before Congress can act, or Congress will not act and the harms will continue.

4. *It provides for compound impoundment*

Finally, the Impoundment Control Act is structurally deficient in that it allows for compounded impoundment decrees. As noted in the *Congressional Quarterly Almanac*, "The President might withhold funds indefinitely by repeating the notification process if approval for an impoundment action was not granted after the first sixty days."

Thus, the law itself provides a perfect self-circumvention measure. The president is therefore able to continue to impound funds even under the new law that was theoretically designed to preclude such action.

B. *Judicial checks are structurally ineffective in controlling impoundment*

Having seen that existent legislation is structurally incapable of guaranteeing the elimination of unauthorized impoundment, we turn finally to a consideration of the structural ineffectiveness of judicial control in this area. Note in an overview that there is no controlling Supreme Court decision concerning the viability of impoundment; the Supreme Court has not acted within this area. But note further that:

1. *Supreme Court decisions are not necessarily binding upon the president*

This observation is supported by Robert Hirshfield who noted in 1967 that "the Court's infrequent ex post facto pronouncements regarding the limits of presidential authority have little direct effect in any case, and since no judicial decision is self-enforcing they are always essentially lectures rather than injunctions." Further, Robert Scigliano noted in 1971 that "the Court's interpretations of the Constitution are not necessarily binding upon the President, nor upon anyone else. It is the Constitution that the President swears to support, and not what the Court says about the Constitution."

Thus, even when and if the Supreme Court rules upon the viability of unauthorized impoundment, there is no guarantee that the Court's decision will halt such impoundment.

2. *Lower-court rulings have been nondefinitive*

Compounding the ineffectiveness of judicial control over impoundment is the fact that there is no guarantee that lower-court rulings will move to eliminate the harms accrued from unauthorized impoundment. *American Libraries* noted in February of this year that "seventeen suits have been filed against seventy-three federal education fund impoundments and the government lost in the five suits decided at the lower federal court level."

Therefore, this piece of evidence is important in two respects. First, it indicates that not all unauthorized impoundments are taken to judicial review for decision and, second and more importantly, that in several instances the harms resulting from impoundment have been allowed to stand. Thus, judicial control cannot guarantee the elimination of the problem.

Therefore, in light of these three considerations, we present the following three-plank affirmative proposal to be enacted by appropriate federal legislation and/or Constitutional amendment:

1) The president will be prohibited from impounding any appropriated funds for which he does not have specific, statutory authorization.

2) A congressional committee will:

a) determine if any past impounded funds are still held by the U.S. Treasury, and, if so

b) shall use these remaining funds for the affected programs. Allocation will be based upon a costs/benefits criterion.

3) This proposal will be enforced by all necessary means, including impeachment.[3]

After reading that sample affirmative presentation, you should have concluded that, at that point, the burden of proof had been shouldered adequately and that the inherency indictment, at that time, was sufficient to justify change. However, your conclusions would be altered somewhat once refutation to those affirmative arguments was presented. But, at that point, by the conclusion of the affirmative presentation, there was sufficient justification to consider changing the status quo.

Before concluding our discussion of the burden of proof and its corollary issue of inherency, one final dichotomy needs to be revealed. Whereas those advocating change (for example, the affirmative in an academic debate) must uphold *the* burden of proof, *everyone* within an argumentative encounter must uphold *a* burden of proof. That is, all parties to an argument have the responsibility to support and substantiate all arguments put forth. All have the responsibility to do research to document their positions. In short, the old debate maxim of "he who asserts must prove" is quite true.

Presumption: Its Definition

The application of the theory of presumption to decision making and argumentative communication was noted most clearly over a century ago by a famous cleric and rhetorical theorist, Richard Whately, in his book entitled *Elements of Rhetoric*. His delineation between the burden of proof and presumption vis-à-vis argumentative communication is of such importance that this specific definition ought to be studied by contempory practitioners of argument:

> According to the most correct use of the term a "Presumption" in favour of any supposition, means not (as has been sometimes erroneously imagined) a preponderance of probability in its favour, but, such a preoccupation of the ground, as implies that it must stand good till some sufficient reason is adduced against it; in short, the Burden of Proof lies on the side of him who would dispute it.
>
> There is a Presumption in favour of every existing institution. Many of these (we will suppose, the majority) may be susceptible of alteration for the better; but still the "Burden of Proof" lies with him who proposes an alteration; simply, on the ground that since a change is not a good in itself, he who demands a change should show cause for it.

> No one is called on (though he may find it advisable) to defend an existing institution, till some argument is adduced against it.[4]

Thus, presumption may be defined as the preoccupation of ground by existing attitudes, policies, and procedures. It is this presumption, then, that those who advocate some type of change must overturn in upholding the burden of proof.

Perhaps the nature of "the preoccupation of ground" may be best explained by the application to the poverty problem. Presume that at this particular point in time there are various local, state, federal, and private programs designed to combat poverty in the United States. These programs literally do *occupy the ground* of our current battle against the ravages of poverty. Both the problem itself and the current measures utilized to combat the problem make up what we call the status quo. However, you might feel that these various measures are inadequate or ineffective; you might desire a change in our policies so that a guaranteed income might be used to overcome this problem. If so, you would have the responsibility of overcoming presumption by substantiating a rationale for change through the upholding of the burden of proof; for example, you might propose a guaranteed income to replace current antipoverty programs, prove that it would eliminate the poverty problem, and justify changing the status quo. Thus, the burden of proof must overturn presumption to affect the status quo so that the desired change may be justified. If, on the other hand, the burden of proof is not upheld adequately, then presumption will remain, meaning that the status quo will not be changed or altered.

Importantly, "presumption" does not imply that the status quo is perfect, that everything is functioning smoothly; it means only that that is the way things are and the way they'll remain unless or until a change is justified. Presumption, then, is the way it is, while the burden of proof deals with the way things ought to be. All existing policies, goals, attitudes, and so on are presumed to be good: we presume your innocence when you are brought to trial *until* you are found guilty of a crime; we presume that current antipoverty programs are working adequately until they are proven to be otherwise.

Presumption and Argumentative Communication

In the formal argumentative setting of academic debate, the burden of proof is the responsibility of the *affirmative*, those advocating a change in the present system. Presumption, however, rests with those on the *negative*, those who support the status quo and who oppose the change offered by the affirmative speakers. Thus, academic debate balances the burden of proof against presumption, exactly the way those two factors are counter-balanced in real-life situations and decision-making processes.

To uphold the burden of proof, the affirmative must present a substantiated rationale for change, generally adhering to the four stock issues of need, plan, feasibility, and advantage; the issue of inherency also must be carried by the affirmative to prove that the status quo cannot rectify its own problem. To support the factor of presumption, the negative speakers must (*a*) defend the operations of the status quo and (*b*) refute the charges lodged by the affirmative. The negative may utilize those four stock issues to demonstrate that there is no justification for change, and the negative may argue that the problem is not inherent, that the status quo can take care of problems indicated by the affirmative.

To exemplify the counterbalancing nature of presumption and the burden of proof, part of a championship debate is presented for your study. While this is not the complete debate, it does provide you with a fairly clear example of how the affirmative attacks the status quo, thereby upholding the burden of proof, and of how the negative supports the status quo, thereby upholding the burden of proof, and of how the negative supports the status quo and attacks the arguments of the affirmative, thereby supporting presumption. The following is the transcript of the first affirmative presentation and the first negative presentation of a debate on the topic, Resolved: that executive control of United States foreign policy should be significantly curtailed. You should notice that both affirmative and negative speakers utilize a large amount of evidence to support their arguments and that the organization of their arguments is quite intricate.

Presumption vs. burden of proof: A sample debate

First Affirmative Constructive

Richard Lewis, Harvard

Frankly, I want my mother. [*Laughter.*] "All the people who lined the streets began to cry, 'Just look at the Emperor's new clothes. How beautiful they are!' Then suddenly a little child piped up, 'But the Emperor has no clothes on. He has no clothes on at all!' " In 1947 the United States created the Central Intelligence Agency and donned the cloak of secrecy to pursue communism. Experience has proven the cloak we donned was nothing more than the Emperor's new clothes, hiding far less than we have long pretended and exposing America to peril.

Because Joel and I believe it is time we all recognized the American emperor's mistake, we stand resolved that executive control of United States foreign policy should be significantly curtailed. We believe the executive should be prohibited from carrying out covert operations, that is, attempts to tamper with the structure of any country or institution in the conduct of foreign policy while concealing our involvement.

Our first contention: Discovery of covert operations undermines American objectives; discovery of covert operations undermines American objectives. There are three dimensions to the harm. First, discovery strengthens communism; it strengthens communism. when America is discovered attempting to dictate a nation's political future, that nation resists our influence by enlisting communist support.

Consider these two examples: One, Laos. In 1958 the CIA spent $310 million in a covert attempt to defeat the Communist Pathet Lao and elect a pro-Western cabinet. Noted journalist Fred Cook wrote in 1961: The inevitable consequence, once the plot was exposed, was a crushing election victory by the Communists who then used American foreign aid to support Communist battalions. Discovery of our operation thus promoted communism. But the CIA was not content. Unable to purchase a pro-Western government, it installed one with a military coup in 1961. Enraged at the United States and now backed by communist power, the ousted leaders began to carve up the country. In three years America had sacrificed Laos to communism, a serious setback in itself. But this defeat also made a long-term contribution to communist strength elsewhere — in Vietnam. The *New York Times*, April 25, 1966: Following the CIA fiasco, "Pro-Communist Laotians . . .were never again driven from the border of North Vietnam, and it is through that region that the Vietcong . . . have been supplied and replenished . . . ."

Our second example is Burma. Since 1949, the CIA had directed thousands of Nationalist Chinese troops who had siezed a Burmese province and were preparing to invade mainland China. When American responsibility was exposed in 1952, Burma abandoned her pro-Western stance, renounced American aid, and moved closer to Peking. The *New York Times* concluded that nothing, nothing so helped the Communists in Burma as discovery that the CIA had directed the colony of Nationalist Chinese troops. Discovery strenghtens communism, and that's our first subpoint.

Our second subpoint: Discovery injures the innocent; it injures the innocent. When a CIA agent suffers as a result of underhanded tactics, it can be said that he knew what he was getting into. But when innocent people are harmed — people who are unaware that they are part of an international intrigue — then clearly a basic moral standard has been violated, and that we cannot tolerate. Two examples: One, private organizations. Using the National Student Association as a propaganda weapon, the CIA secretly funded that organization. Unaware of the source, the NSA gladly accepted the money. Disaster came with discovery. As newsmen dug deeper, hundreds of other private institutions — unions, charities, and churches — were identified as unknowing recipients of CIA funds. Professor Richard Hunt of Harvard described the result: The exposure of CIA connections undermined the independence of countless innocent organizations; the work of many private institutions abroad was jeopardized, reputations were injured, careers were shattered, and charitable foundations were shaken. thus, scores of innocent individuals were gravely injured simply because the CIA chose to use them.

But more sinister cases have come to light. Our second example: Berlin, 1954. Taking young and easily influenced students, the CIA plunged them into the explosive postwar German underground, directing them in secret maneuvers in preparation for an invasion of East Germany. When the operation was discovered, it was the students who suffered. Louis Hagen, writing in *The Secret War for Europe*, notes that the world "...had to watch the sad aftermath of this [CIA] affair. Scores of these misled youths were arrested in East Germany as alleged...provocateurs and were sentenced to terms of up to nine years' hard labour." No more than pawns in the Cold War, innocent people suffer as the CIA escapes to plot further operations. Our second subpoint: Discovery injures the innocent.

But we pay yet another price when covert operations are discovered. Our third subpoint: Discovery threatens the peace; it threatens the peace. There is a danger of retaliation whenever the communists discover the origin of plots against them. A perilous incident occurred in Formosa, 1954. The CIA masterminded guerilla attacks on the Chinese mainland from Taiwan, and the Red Chinese reacted with violence. Fred Cook comments: Having isolated the origin of the operation, Red China blasted Quemoy and Matsu with heavy artillery. The United States and China had been pushed to the point of open conflict. Mr. Cook concludes: The world stood dangerously close to total war. Professor Paul Blackstock of Chicago stated our conclusion: Our covert operations have created major threats to peace. Our first contention: Discovery of covert operations undermines American objectives.

Our second contention: the only way to prevent discovery is to end all operations; the only way to prevent discovery is to end all operations. Our first subpoint: Discovery of some operations is inevitable; discovery of some is inevitable. Officials in the field, allied operatives, and the American press have all leaked news of covert operations. And, of course, given the nature of our society with its freedom of speech and press, these sources cannot be silenced. That was the conclusion of President Kennedy quoted by Theodore Sorensen: Discovery of covert operations, he said, is inevitable in an open society.

But communist counterintelligence also guarantees discovery. General Bedell Smith, the late director of the CIA, frankly admitted that any agency engaging in covert operations can safely assume that some of its activities will be penetrated and compromised by the enemy. Some operations, therefore, will inevitably be discovered.

Of course, the fact that some will be discovered argues only for stricter control to abolish them. Our second subpoint explains why such control is impossible: There is no way to tell in advance which operations will be discovered; there is no way to tell in advance. History proves the point. Obviously no one would mount an operation knowing full well that it is going to be discovered. Yet time and again operations come to light with no consistent pattern of disclosure. They are discovered, large and small, at home and abroad, in success and failure. There is no singular characteristic triggering discovery which we can isolate and eliminate. So we cannot control operations to eliminate just the ones that are going to be discovered.

If we want to eliminate discovery, we must end all covert operations — good and bad. And the reason we should do so is our third contention: The harm of discovery outweigh the value of continuing all operations: the harms of discovery outweigh the value of continuing all operations. Now Joel and I realize the CIA has often done what it set out to do. It has overthrown governments and it has fixed elections. But the critical question is, do these activities make any significant contribution to American foreign policy? Two experts, both of whom were associated with the CIA in official capacities, answer no. Turn to Professor Edwin Reischauer, President Kennedy's foreign policy adviser. In 1967 he wrote, "The sort of covert... activity. . .associated with the CIA is of value only in relatively weak. . .countries — and even then only for short range purposes." Or turn to Roger Hilsman, former director of the Bureau of Intelligence. He wrote, ". . .covert action was really nothing more than a gimmick. In very special circumstances, it was a useful supplement, but nothing more."

So continuing all operations would make an insignificant contribution to our foreign policy objectives. And yet our first contention indicates that discovery of covert operations significantly undermines those objectives. The conclusion is obvious. Professor Reischauer makes the final judgment: On balance, covert political activities carried out by the CIA are clearly a net loss, a net loss, to the United States. For this reason he concludes, ". . .the CIA should not be engaged in political activities but should be limited to its original function of intelligence gathering."

To that end, Joel and I propose the following plan: One, covert operations will covert operations will be abolished; be abolished. Two, a court will be established to enforce this law; a court of enforcement. Three, participation in or direction of a covert operation will constitute an act of treason and will be punishable as such; participation or direction punishable as an act of treason.

"Still in all the people started to whisper to one another that what the child said was so. 'The emperor doesn't have any clothes on. A little child is saying it and it is true.' The Emperor began to squirm, and all at once he knew that what the people said was right." [*Applause.*]

First Negative Constructive

Mike Miller, Houston

Frankly, I wish I was debating Rich's mother. [*Laughter.*] However, I would like to direct your attention to the gentlemen's rationale for change. Before I do so, David has one question. He would like to know who is going to appoint this particular court or commission.

With this in mind, consider what the gentlemen from Harvard tell you. They tell you, first of all, that discovery of covert operations is detrimental. Now first, I would make the observation that the gentlemen haven't really defined *discovery* for us. What the gentlemen have shown is suspicion, and I would suggest that discovery in the radical term — that is, proving something about the CIA — is nearly impossible. Discovery is nearly impossible. We can turn to the CIA itself, a publication in 1961. It notes that "...the Central Intelligence Agency does not confirm or deny published reports, whether good or bad; never alibis; never explains its organization; never identifies its personnel. . .and will not discuss its budget. . . ." I would suggest, first, that the gentlemen have little more than suspicion throughout the entirety of their examples. They claim that the communists say that the CIA was involved in certain plots to overthrow them. That's quite probable. They do not point out that the CIA admits that these people were operatives, and I think that is a major consideration.

With this in mind, consider what the gentleman tells you. He tells you, first, that we strengthen communism, and he gives you two examples of where we strengthen communism. I would suggest two basic things. First, look at both the gentlemen's examples, Laos and Burma. I would suggest in neither state do we have a communist form of government. First, look at the case of Laos. The gentlemen admit that we have a tripartite government that is neutralist.

Secondly, look at Burma. I would suggest, number one, Burma is officially neutral. I would suggest, number two, that Burmese neutralism is favorable to the interests of the United States. Let's turn first to Mr. A. Doak Barnett on the Council on Foreign Relations in 1960. He notes, "Since late 1958," — which I want you to remember is the same year as the supposed CIA operation — "a subtle change has been taking place in Burma's neutralism. While continuing to adhere to a policy of nonalignment, Burma's new military leaders. . .have steadily strengthened their ties with the West." I would indicate as did Harold Hovey, former director of the Military Assistance Program, 1965, that ". . .United States military equipment," for example, "has been provided to Burma under sales arrangements begun in 1958 and renewed in 1961," despite all the supposed strengthening of communism that took place in that particular state.

But the gentlemen then go back to Laos and indicate to you that there was a harm in Vietnam. Note the assumption that Harvard makes here. They assume because Laos now has a three-party government, the North Vietnamese are capable of infiltrating through Laos. Now I want the gentlemen to indicate to me in any shape, form, or fashion, that even a pro-United States government could police the entirety of the Laotian jungle and prevent that infiltration. The gentleman simply doesn't have a point here; it doesn't necessarily strengthen communism.

Number two, the gentlemen tell you that the National Student Association, for example, is an instance of where CIA operations involve unknowing persons. Note, number one, there is no way of knowing whether they should be involved or not, whether there was actually an operation or not. It is quite possible under this particular proposal for the Soviets or Chinese or anyone else to claim that anyone in a particular country is involved with the CIA, and there is no way of denying it, either under the affirmative proposal or under the present system.

Consider, however, the National Student Association and student movements around the world. I would suggest that we do gain an advantage by subsidizing those particular movements and should maintain that option. Amaury de Reincourt, consultant to the Foreign Policy Research Institute, noted on page 111 of his 1968 book, *The American Empire*, "Often enough, the CIA assists the enemies of the United States' allies, and by doing it secretly, avoids antagonizing those allies while keeping all its options open for the future and undercutting Communist influence." He notes the involvement of students in anticolonial type rebel movements. I would suggest that is a definite advantage, and I would suggest the advantages outweigh the losses in that particular point. I think I'm as qualified as Mr. Reischauer to make that particular judgment.

Number three, the gentlemen tell you that discovery of particular operations threatens the peace. Now note the example that the gentlemen give you. They give you the example of Formosa. Now note, the Chinese on the mainland and the Chinese on Formosa have been carrying on these particular operations — fighting against each other — since 1946. I don't think the CIA created the enmity between Chiang and Mao. I indicate, number two, that we would requre some utilization of intelligence research over Red China. And I indicate to you, number three, that it is quite probable that spies would be treated the same way as guerrillas. Note that the gentleman talks about the shellings. He in no way proves that Chiang Kai-Shek couldn't send guerrilla operations over there anyway, and the world still wouldn't be pushed to war. I don't think Harvard has a warrant in this particular contention.

But here the gentlemen present their most important contention. They tell you that, in order to prevent discovery, we must end all covert operations. And here the gentlemen tell you that operatives can be detected. And note what the gentlemen say here. They say that operatives in this particular operation can be detected by similar operatives. Now the question arises in my mind, as I am sure it does in yours, exactly why we alienate everyone, exactly why we harm the innocent, exactly why we alienate these countries, when the Soviet Union does the same thing in the particular field. I think we need to maintain the option for that particular reason. Mr. Reincourt, previously cited, 1968: "Since it is difficult to fight an opponent without using his own best weapons, the Americans were quickly driven to duplicate, to a certain extent, the Soviet apparatus" for conducting covert operations. I would suggest we need to counterbalance it. I would also suggest once again — and this is most important — that anyone can be called by anyone else an operative, and there is no way to disprove that even under Harvard's proposal because it is not going to do much good to show a Soviet police agent a copy of the new law.

All right, now consider the third basic point. Here the gentlemen tell you — and I want you to note this, this is a subjective value judgment that the gentlemen make — they tell you that the harms of covert operations and the discovery of covert operations outweigh the gains. Let's consider some of the gains. First of all, let's consider a general trend. Now I think this is particularly important. Mr. Amaury de Reincourt, previously cited, in 1968: ". . .It is certain that an increasing number of covert operations are carried out with considerable success; past successes testify eloquently, although they are less publicized than the failures. . . ." We are suggesting, therefore, that there is an increasing trend for covert operations of the United States to be more effective. The gentlemen simply make that particular judgment on the basis of past failures. At no time does their authority or do the gentlemen from Harvard actually draw the correlation between the two. They say, here is the political value, here is the political loss. Harvard cannot make that particular moral judgment.

But just to show you that we are not short on moral judgments ourselves, I would suggest to you that we have an authority that's just as good as Mr. Reichauer who suggests to you that there is a reason, and that the actual costs-benefits ratio is in favor of the present system. Here we turn to Mr. Charles Jacobs, professor of political science at Vassar, in 1966. He notes, "That the CIA has at times been mis- or uninformed is obvious, but this is a hazard common to all government agencies; to suggest that [the covert operations of] the CIA be abolished, or even closely scrutinized by the normal governmental agencies, is to deprive ourselves of an unpleasant necessity in the era of the cold war." I suggest that Harvard makes this particular value judgment.

Now let me document some of the successes. We turn once again to Mr. Riencourt in 1968. He notes, in the case of Indonesia, that there is a distinct possibility that during the coup of 1965 the CIA had a distinct connection between the opponents of President Sukarno, forcing him to do what it wanted. Consider Reincourt's conclusion: It is plausible to assume that the CIA might have had a finger in the Indonesian pie when President Sukarno was overthrown in the 1965 military takeover; it is naive to assume that the CIA, after attempts to overthrow Sukarno in 1968 and at other times, had nothing to do with the coup. I would suggest Indonesia is very important. The gentlemen tell you it's only small areas. Remember that Indonesia is one of the major areas in the Southeast Asia island chain, has all resources, etcetera, and was in danger of communist takeover.

Now look at our own hemisphere. I would suggest we have been successful here too. Turn to Mr. Amaury de Reincourt, previously cited: ". . . In 1962 and 1963, the American Federation of State, County, and Municipal Employees had turned its International Affairs Department over to the CIA to be used as a base for strikes and subversive activities aimed at the overthrow of Premier Cheddi Jagan's proto-Communist regime in British Guiana — which was duly accomplished . . .in . . .1964, thus avoiding . . .a new Cuba" in the Western Hemisphere.

The gentlemen give you examples; we give you examples. The gentlemen give you a conclusionary piece of evidence; we give you a conclusionary piece of evidence. The basic difference is that Harvard cannot guarantee that their particular harms will necessarily be met by the adoption of their proposal. We can guarantee some successes in the future. We can guarantee a probability that those successes will be good. We have to take the criticism either way. We suggest, therefore, the basis for United States policy should be to gain the most advantage from covert operations, which are necessary, and that we can do with the present system. [*Applause.*][5]

Before that particular debate began, it was presumed that everything was okay with the status quo, that the executive branch's control of American foreign policy was a functioning, beneficial system. However, after the first affirmative speaker indicated a variety of problems in and suggested modifications of that system, that prior presumption was in doubt. The affirmative adequately upheld its burden of proof. Concomitantly, the negative, then, had the responsibility to resupport presumption by both defending the status quo and attacking the arguments presented by the affirmative. Those two debate speeches clearly illustrate the counterbalancing nature of presumption and the burden of proof. Both examine the four stock issues, but both reach different conclusions. Presumption argues that there is no need to change, there is no practical plan to effectuate change, and that any change would be disadvantageous; the burden of proof contends that there is a need for a change, that there is a practical plan to effectuate change, and that such a change would be advantageous. You'll read more about these counterbalancing burdens in chapters 12 and 13.

Conclusion

We tend to operate upon the assumption that stability is good and that change, simply in and for itself, is not necessarily good. Thus, in making decisions of both a personal and national nature, we demand that proposals for change be as completely justified as is possible. Unless change is so justified, we choose to remain with the way things are, we decide to maintain the present system or status quo. Those who advocate change must, therefore, shoulder the burden of proof, proving to our satisfaction that change is justified. In addition, the advocate of change must demonstrate that the status quo cannot overcome its difficulties by making modifications of its actions and structures, thereby eliminating the need to change systems. The burden of proof and the issue of inherency go hand-in-hand in forcing those who propose some type of change to rationalize making that change.

Within the structure of academic debate, upholding the burden of proof and the issue of inherency is the responsibility of those taking the affirmative position, those who desire change in the status quo. If that responsibility is not adequately upheld, then change is not justified, the status quo will be retained, and the affirmative speakers will lose that debate encounter.

Existing institutions (policies, goals, attitudes, procedures) are presumed to be good until they are proven to be insufficient, harmful or disadvantageous. All things as they now exist, everything that goes into the total makeup of the status quo, have this presumption, and we choose to retain the status quo until a change is justified. In academic debate, those supporting the status quo (negative speakers) have the responsibility to uphold presumption by both defending the status quo and by refuting the attacks of the affirmative speakers. Unless change is justified, presumption will prevail and the status quo will not be structurally affected by proposals for change.

References

1. "Homeostasis" and "balance" theories in both communication and psychology are grounded upon this notion of stability.

2. See Richard Whately, *Elements of Rhetoric*, ed. Douglas Ehninger (Carbondale, Ill.: Southern Illinois University Press, 1963), pp. 112-116.

3. Melinda Cooper and Thomas Stevenson, "Against Presidential Impoundment," an affirmative debate case. Used by permission.

4. Richard Whately, "Elements of Rhetoric," in James L. Golden, Goodwin F. Berquist, and William E. Coleman, *The Rhetoric of Western Thought* (Dubuque, Iowa: Kendall/Hunt, 1976), p. 106. For another excellent analysis of the factor of presumption, see Gary Cronkhite, "The Locus of Presumption," *Central States Speech Journal* 17 (November 1966): 270–276.

5. From the final round of the Twenty-Third National Debate Tournament, sponsored by the American Forensic Association, April 1969. Published in the *Journal of the American Forensic Association* 6 (Fall 1969): 139–147, and reprinted here with the permission of the editor of JAFA.

Practicum

1. In dealing with real-life situations, you find very quickly how powerful presumption actually is. Making changes is very difficult, especially when such changes affect actions or beliefs that have been strongly entrenched over a period of time.

Think about several recent changes you have made in your life (getting a new car, finding a new group of friends, getting your own apartment, and so on). What caused you to overcome your own life's presumption to make those changes? Did you meet the burden of proof adequately to justify the changes you made?

2. This practicum item will require some library research on your part. Find some general information concerning the proposed Panama Canal treaties and the resultant governmental and public debate about them that occurred in mid-1978. Looking upon that debate as a conflict between protreaty and antitreaty forces, answer these questions:

- Which side had the burden of proof?
- Which side had presumption?
- What major arguments were used to meet the burden of proof?
- What major arguments were used to support presumption?
- Who won this debate? Can you explain why?

Unit Three

Data Research and Analysis

Chapter 8
Researching Supporting Materials

Chapter 9
Types of Supporting Materials

Chapter 10
Fallacious Argument

Chapter 8

Researching Supporting Materials

* Initiating Research
* Finding Resource Materials
* Recording Research Information
* Filing Research Information
* Conclusion
* References
* Practicum

The importance of research to effective and meaningful argumentative communication cannot be overstated. The materials and information gathered from research serve as the virtual underpinning of the arguments and positions advanced within any argumentative setting. In formal academic debate contests, research materials are of critical importance, serving as the most noteworthy aspect of contemporary interscholastic and intercollegiate debate. Debaters spend far more time engaged in evidence research than in actual debate competition.

Because academic debate topics must serve debaters for an entire school year, September to June, they must, of necessity, be quite broad to allow for creativity and to prevent boredom during this long debate season. This necessary breadth, however, means that debaters must do a great deal of research to have the appropriate materials to cover all the possible cases and arguments that might be presented during the debate year. To be effective, arguments and counterarguments must be supported by evidence, and this supporting material can be gained only by conducting useful research.

This chapter is designed to acquaint you with the basics of research: how ideas are to be generated, how research is to be conducted efficiently and effectively, and how the information gained from your research efforts should be recorded and stored for future use.

Initiating Research

Perhaps the most difficult part of researching is getting started. Far too many debaters find themselves doing something like this:

> After the intercollegiate debate topic for the upcoming debate season was announced in mid-July, John Advocate rushed immediately to his university library and began to pull every book from the stacks that he thought might pertain to the topic. After convincing the librarian that he needed to check out sixty-seven books at one time to do his debate research, John carted this load home and began immediately to scour his materials for evidence.
>
> One week later, John had typed one thousand pieces of evidence, but he found that his information was unrelated, that it did not seem to hang together. When asked by his debate coach what he had found in his preliminary research effort, John was forced to admit, "I'm really not sure."

Other debaters find themselves in this situation:

> **After the topic was announced, Marsha D. Bater looked at the topic quickly and decided that a case dealing with wiretapping was the best affirmative case for that topic. She went immediately to her university library, pulling every book and magazine article she could find that dealt with wiretapping.**
>
> One week later, Marsha had over five hundred pieces of evidence, but she had no evidence for several prowiretapping arguments she developed at the time the topic was announced. When asked by her coach how her researching was progressing, Marsha replied that, "It'll probably take another month to find all the necessary evidence for my case."

Both preceding scenarios illustrate time-wasting methods of initiating research, but far too many debaters start their research efforts using similar methods. John ran to the library and gathered a thousand pieces of evidence, but he had absolutely no idea what he had found. He simply tried to record anything and everything that he thought pertained to the debate topic, but there was no real method to his mad dash through the library. Marsha had just the opposite problem. She constructed a case and then tried to find the evidence to support her preresearch assertions, and much of her search was unsuccessful. Both John and Marsha jumped into their research efforts too quickly; both failed to give sufficient thought to the topic before going to the library, and both wasted a lot of time in the process.

When you are asked to undertake research chores either in this class or in some other class or endeavor, you should have as your goal the accomplishment of your needed research by the most efficient and effective means possible. Going to the library takes place *after* you have devoted a great deal of thought to the task before you. Otherwise, you may wind up wasting time like John and Marsha.

In initiating research, keep the following thoughts in mind:

1. Critically examine the task before you, ascertaining its full meaning and possible components and ramifications. At this point, it is a good idea to utilize the technique of brainstorming to isolate the significant factors or issues within your research problem. Each one of the ideas generated at this point should be written down and

saved, as they will serve as the foundation for your specific library research later on.

For example, suppose you were required to research this recent interscholastic debate resolution, Resolved: that the federal government should establish a comprehensive program to increase significantly the energy independence of the United States. If you were to run to the library immediately, you probably would miss many of the important components of that topic. Instead, you ought to examine the wording of the topic, noting that it would be important to find out as much as possible about current or potential sources of energy for this country. You might develop a list of energy sources such as this:

oil
natural gas
electricity
hydroelectric power
geothermal power
wind power
solar energy
ocean-thermal gradients
nuclear fission
nuclear fusion
gasahol
coal
coal gasification
energy from solid waste (sludge)

Now you have something to work on. Unlike Marsha, you have not restricted yourself to one narrow part of the topic, nor have you run to the library without thinking as did John. You have something upon which to base your research.

2. Consider what you know already about the topic. What do you know about America's energy problem? Perhaps you have read some materials or heard something pertinent to the topic that will help you eventually to narrow your research task. Essentially, you want to avoid the research extremes exemplified by John and Marsha. John failed to examine the specifics of his topic, choosing instead to deal with it as one amorphous blob. Marsha, however, looked at only one aspect of the topic, completely overlooking the vast majority of the topic area. If you think about the components of the topic, as many of the components as you can possibly generate, you will avoid both of these extremes.

3. Now you go to the library. However, your purpose at this point is not to record all sorts of specific evidence; on the contrary, your research still must be fairly generalized so that you get a proper perspective of the topic. Using such sources as the library's card catalog and the *Reader's Guide to Periodical Literature*, you want to find materials that will provide you with a broad overview to the topic area, assisting you to develop a comprehensive viewpoint of the issues, arguments, and possible cases to be found within the debate topic. This general reading will provide thoughts and ideas for later in-depth research about particular subareas of the topic. While reading these general sources, write down those specific ideas that interest you and take note of other sources of information that are cited.

4. You might wish to construct a bibliography of sources, a listing of references you may examine in depth once you begin specific research. Not only should you include those sources consulted during your general reading, but also those sources noted in your readings' footnotes and bibliographical citations. Such a bibliography is especially useful when research assignments are given to a school's entire debate squad.

This is the proper form for recording a bibliographical entry:

> Sayer, James Edward. *Clarence Darrow: Public Advocate*. Dayton, Ohio: Wright State University Press, 1978.

5. Now you begin to sort out the important ideas and issues from the unimportant as you analyze what has been learned from your general research efforts. You are able to isolate those matters that seem to be significant, that have received considerable attention in those sources you have consulted. At this point, then, you are ready to begin specific research. You may examine one issue, such as wiretapping, in detail, finding as much information on that issue as possible. Your general research has indicated that this is an important area within the debate topic, an area that merits particular attention. Thus, you *know* before your specific research is started that the results of this effort will be worthwhile and significant.

If you will follow this five-step process in initiating your research efforts, you will find that your time will be well spent. Instead of wandering around the library in the hope that some useful evidence will turn up, you will know what you are doing because your research effort will have direction. Additionally, you will not limit your study to but one narrow part of the topic area; your study will be simultaneously comprehensive and specific, allowing you to benefit the most from your time in the library.

One final point needs to be made concerning your initial research activities. Affirmative cases are developed *after* research has reached the specific stage; that is, cases arise from the evidence gathered. Unfortunately, many debaters put the cart before the horse by developing a case and then going to the library to see if evidence exists to substantiate that case, a monumental waste of time. However, you will find your time more productively spent if you write your cases after some evidence has been gathered, because you then know that there are materials to support such an argumentative position.

Finding Resource Materials

Since books such as this are prepared for a general audience, it is not possible to deal with the specific research strengths and weaknesses that might characterize those libraries to which you have access. To a certain extent, all libraries differ in their quality and quantity of materials, overall pattern of organization, and so on. Therefore, this book can provide only general suggestions concerning the discovery of research information. For specific assistance, you should consult your reference librarian.

The Card Catalog

One of any library's reference-area cornerstones is the card catalog, the complete listing of all the books held by that particular library.[1] The card catalog should be consulted during both the general and specific stages of research, because it will be the guide to many useful sources of information. Filed within the catalog in alphabetical order, there are three types of cards to be found: subject cards, title cards, and author cards — each may be useful in your research activities.

When initiating research, the subject cards will provide your beginning sources of information. By looking for information on a given topic, you will find subject cards that list books dealing with that topic, noting the title of each specific book within the area and the book's author. In addition, subject cards list the date of publication and the specific subjects covered within the book. This information will help you decide whether the book is sufficiently contemporary and whether the book contains the particular information you seek. Subject cards should be examined carefully in developing your initial research materials.

Title cards and author cards are most useful in helping you track down incomplete information. If, for example, you know the name of a book's author but not the book's title, the author card will supply the missing information. Similarly, the title card provides the name of the book's author. Like the subject cards, both author and title cards list the book's date of publication and its major contents, additional information that will help you to decide whether the book should be examined itself.

The card catalog should be consulted often during the debate season; it should not be abandoned after initial research has been completed. As the debate season progresses, new arguments and case ideas will generate other possible avenues of research, meaning that these new research areas ought to be cross-checked through the card catalog. Since this source lists all the books held by the library, its importance is apparent and it should be utilized throughout the year.

Periodicals Listings

Perhaps the greatest disadvantage of depending too heavily upon books for debate evidence is their being inherently somewhat out of date. Books carrying a 1979 publication date, for example, may have been completed nearly two years before that time, owing to the time delay of the publication process. Obviously, a lot happened during those two years, but that book will not take note of those developments. For that reason, most of your truly contemporary evidence, especially material dealing with matters of the past year or less, will come primarily from periodicals — newsmagazines and scholarly journals and abstracts. Therefore, you need to be aware of the periodicals listings held by your library.[2]

Regardless of the size of the library and its holdings, you should be able to find two periodicals listings that will provide at least 80 percent of your periodicals-derived evidence. Again, your reference librarian can assist you with this part of your research activity.

The Reader's Guide to Periodical Literature is the best known source for periodicals and is especially useful for researching articles published in the United States in various general interest magazines, especially such news sources as *Newsweek* and *Time*. The RGPL is organized alphabetically according to topic, and articles published dealing with that topic are listed. Each listed reference will provide the title of the article, the article's author, the volume number of the magazine, the date of the magazine's publication, and the page numbers within which the article may be found. The RGPL is the best source for contemporary information in widely circulated periodicals. It, too, may be used for both general and specific research needs.

The Public Serials List notes all the periodicals held by the library. Although the PSL does not list the articles contained within the listed periodicals, the titles of many journals and pamphlets will indicate that they merit investigation for a particular debate topic. The PSL will list those obscure journals not covered by *The Reader's Guide*, so both reference sources should be consulted while conducting periodicals research.

Depending upon the library, the following additional periodicals lists may be available to you. If so, they, too, can provide helpful information and clues for your further research:

Index to Business Week
Applied Science and Technology Index
Business Periodicals Index
Human Resources Abstracts
Sociological Abstracts
Social Sciences Index
International Index
Agricultural Index
Education Index
Index to Legal Periodicals
Public Affairs Information Service
Psychological Abstracts

Government Documents

The best source for in-depth current information, and the most difficult source to research, is any library's collection of government documents.[3] These documents deal with the most significant and topical issues of our time, and every debater can profit by spending a reasonable amount of his research time in the examination of these materials.

Many debaters are overwhelmed by government documents because of their great number. A library holding even relatively few such documents will appear to be imposing, at the very least, as there is row upon row of grey, brown, and green-jacketed documents — from every conceivable corner of the legislative and executive branches of the federal government. Too many debaters simply stroll through rows of these documents, looking at one here and one there, hoping that a useful document will leap from the shelf — a great waste of time.

Instead of doing that, you should do the following:

1. Go to the reference area of your library and find the *Monthly Catalog of United States Government Publications*.

2. Within the *Monthly Catalog*, go to the subject index, the listing of topics covered within that catalog organized alphabetically much like the card catalog and the various periodicals indexes.

3. Write down all the numbers listed for each entry.

4. Turn to the catalog portion of the *Monthly Catalog* to locate the appropriate entry number, classification number, and title for the government document desired.

5. Use that information to locate the document within your library.

The *Monthly Catalog* allows you to decide what documents warrant your attention without your having to pour through every document held by the library. In a matter of minutes you will find all the recent materials you ought to research, thereby cutting your research time immeasurably.

Newspapers

The last source of current information is newspapers, and most libraries hold the most recent copies of, at the very least, those newspapers published in and around your geographic area. Larger libraries have subscriptions to faraway newspapers and newspapers of national reputation such as the *New York Times, Los Angeles Times, Washington Post, Chicago Tribune, Wall Street Journal,* and *St. Louis Post-Dispatch.*

Even if your library's holdings of newspapers is relatively limited, there is a high probability that the *New York Times Index* will be found in the reference area. That index, again arranged alphabetically by subject or topic, not only lists the important events covered by the *New York Times* and their publication dates and page numbers, but that index provides clues for researching other newspapers, too. For example, a major event covered by the *New York Times* on 17 January might be found in another newspaper on that same date or one or two days thereafter. Thus, the *New York Times Index* can be used as an indicator of potential information in all newspapers.

Before concluding this section of this chapter, brief mention should be given to the availability of external sources of debate evidence, specifically those evidence packages that may be purchased from commercial companies. At this time, you may buy literally thousands of pieces of evidence on the current debate topic, enough evidence to fill several file drawers, without your having to set foot inside a library. Not only evidence may be bought, but also affirmative case structures, negative briefs — in fact, the entire needs for a debate session can be purchased through the mail.

However, you should realize that such evidence and case packages are designed merely to stimulate and supplement your own research activities; they are not intended to replace your own efforts. If you buy such materials, use them properly. Have your own research information build and expand upon these purchased goods. Nothing can take the place of your own research; no one can do better research for you than you.

Recording Research Information

A typical intercollegiate debate team will acquire several thousands of pieces of evidence during one debate season, a plethora of information upon the debate resolution under scrutiny. Obviously, this evidence is the result of many hours of research, a task so great that care must be taken that all evidence recorded be useful now and in debates months ahead. Therefore, a consistent evidence recording system ought to be utilized.

Evidence should be recorded on index cards, preferably four inches by six inches in size. If possible, the evidence (the material taken or cited from the book, magazine, and so on) should be typed on the note card to ensure permanence and clarity. If you cannot type your evidence, make certain that you write the information clearly so you will be able to read it later. Follow this rule of thumb: write your evidence cards as if you were taking notes for someone else.

Each evidence card should contain a slug line in the upper left corner; in the upper right corner you should list the source author, the source title, the publication date, the page numbers from which you are taking evidence, and the author's qualifications. The body of the card will contain a detailed piece of evidence you gather from the source. This layout is illustrated in figure 8.1.

FIGURE 8.1

SLUG

Author
Source Title
Publication Date
Page Number
Author's Qualifications

Evidence:

Temporibud autem quinsud et aur office debit aut tum rerum necessit atib saepe eveniet ut er repudiand sint et molestia non recusand. Itaque earud rerum hic tentury sapiente spard delectus au aut prefer endis dolorib asperiore repellat. Hanc ego cum tene sententiaim quid est cur verear ne ad eam non possing accommodare nost ros quos tu paulo ante cum memorite tum etia ergat. Nos amice et nebevol, olestias access potest fier ad augendas cum conscient to factor tum poen legum odioque civiuda. Et tamen in busdam neque pecun modut est neque nonor imper ned libiding gen epular religuard cupiditat, quas nulla praid om undant. Improb pary minuit, potius inflammad ut coercend magist and et deserunt mollit anim id est laborum et dolor fuga. Et harumd dereud facilis est er expedit distinct. Nam liber tempor cum soluta nobis eligend optio congue nihil impedit doming id quod maxim placeat facer possim omnis voluptas assumenda est.

The slug should be a pencil-written crystallization of the contents of the card in several words, allowing you to know what the card contains without having to read through it. The listing of author, source, date, page, and author's qualifications is necessary for the proper presentation of the evidence within each debate round. Only one piece of evidence should be recorded per card to eliminate potential confusion.

If you record every piece of evidence according to this consistent note-taking system, you will find that you will be able to handle your evidence efficiently during the heat and pressure of a competitive debate round. Each evidence card contains the necessary information for effective argument, as well as sufficient material to support the credibility of the piece of evidence. Having a lot of evidence means absolutely nothing unless you know what your evidence says and how you should use it. A consistent note-taking scheme will help you to meet those two goals.

Filing Research Information

Once evidence has been gathered and recorded, you face one final task: filing your information so you may expeditiously locate the evidence when it is needed. Having a lot of information on subject X will be of little value if you cannot locate that information fairly quickly. In a round of competitive debate, for example, you have only a few seconds to find the evidence you need to substantiate a direct or refutational argument. Therefore, great care must be taken in storing your information. The following system of storage has been found to be quite useful for both formal and informal debate encounters.

You will need to acquire a file box to hold your four-by-six evidence cards; such file boxes are constructed of metal (fairly expensive) or reinforced cardboard (fairly inexpensive). Next, you will need file dividers, generally manila tabs that are blank on both sides. Now you are ready to file your evidence:

1. Divide your evidence into major categories. For example, if you were debating an economically oriented topic, you might have such major categories as inflation, recession, depression, unemployment, and so on.
2. For each major category, record the name or title of that category on the tab of one file divider.

3. Place the titled file divider in your file box, putting all evidence pertinent to that category *behind* that file divider (all inflation-related evidence would be filed behind the file divider labeled "inflation," for example).

4. Since many major categories have subcategories, redivide your filed evidence accordingly through the use of file dividers. Inflation is a very large category, probably containing a lot of evidence, so you might wish to subdivide your evidence into the subcategories of cost-push and demand-pull, the two major types of inflation often discussed by economists. Now your evidence within a category is more easily accessible. Continue subdividing your information until your evidence is so organized that every piece of information is easy to locate.

To assist you in refiling your evidence (putting it back into the file box after you are finished using it), consider these additional steps:

1. On the *back* side of each major category divider, begin numbering each such major category from one on.

2. On the *back* of each first-line subcategory divider, begin lettering such dividers in capital letters from A on.

3. Each further subdivision within categories can be delineated consecutively with another set of numbers and then lower-case letters.

4. On each piece of evidence, record the appropriate file code in relation to that piece of evidence's place within the file box.

Thus, at the top of the evidence card, you might see the code "3D4f." You could then turn the file box around so that the file codes on the backs of the dividers faced you and then place the piece of evidence within the proper code sequence. Such a system can be utilized for one hundred to ten thousand pieces of evidence, and you will not have to waste time reading each piece of evidence to determine where it belongs within the file. Instead, the file code shows immediately where your evidence belongs, allowing you to refile your evidence quickly and efficiently.

Conclusion

Evidence serves as the foundation for meaningful argument in both academic debate encounters and in real-life situations. Because of this importance, researching for supporting materials is both a significant and time-consuming portion of effective argumentative communication. To research well, it is essential that the researcher proceed according to a well-conceived plan, starting with preliminary thoughts through to the effective use of the resources of the library. Upon their discovery, research information should be properly recorded and filed to ensure their retention and viability for argumentative encounters in the future.

References

1. See *Using the Card Catalog* (Syracuse, N.Y.:New Readers Press, Laubach Literacy, 1971).

2. For a complete analysis of periodicals listings, see James Riley and Sharon Hobbs, "An Annotated Bibliography of Debate References," *Debate Issues* (November 1976), pp. 11–16.

3. See Marvin C. Guilfoyle, "Government Documents: A Vital Source of Information," *Debate Issues* (January 1978), pp. 14–15.

Practicum

1. To develop your research skills, go to your library and find the answers to the following questions:

- How much coal was burned in the United States in 1976?
- What was the date of the last presidential state of the union message?
- How many Americans died in automobile accidents in 1978?

Now, assess your library research technique. Do you feel that you used your time efficiently? Did you do sufficient prelibrary planning for your research venture. How would you change your research technique to improve your overall researching effectiveness?

2. You are to prepare a ten-minute oral report on this topic: "America's Energy Challenges in the 1980s." You are to cite at least seven sources of information within that report, including at least one book, one magazine, one government document, and one newspaper. You have ninety minutes to complete your research. Can you fulfill this assignment?

Chapter 9

Types of Supporting Materials

* Factual Evidence
* Opinionated Evidence
* Verbal Evidence
* The Ethics of Evidence
* Conclusion
* References
* Practicum

Having examined the sources of research information in the preceding chapters, we may now examine the kinds of materials you normally look for in conducting research for activities involving argumentative communication. In providing this examination, the kinds of supporting materials to be studied have been delineated into three segments: factual evidence, opinionated evidence, and verbal evidence. No matter how you support an argument or in what context, such support will fall within one of those three categories. Besides knowing about the types of supporting materials, it is also important that you be made aware of the proper ethical use of those materials. Accordingly, this chapter contains a significant section entitled, "The Ethics of Evidence."

Before beginning our examination of evidence types, however, it is necessary to consider the rationale for using such research materials. Perhaps you might have asked yourself this question: "Why should I find and use research information in argumentative settings?" There are two major answers to that pertinent question.

First, the discovery of information increases your own knowledge about the topic or issue being researched. Certainly, you know a great deal about many different topics, but how much do you *really know*, for example, about the specific impact of the Equal Rights Amendment, the advantages and disadvantages of the use of solar power to meet our future energy needs, and the viability of Laetrile as a cure for certain types of cancer? If you are like most people, and if you will be honest with yourself, you will admit that you know something about these three topic areas but that your information is both general in nature and limited in scope. Yes, you do know something about the ERA, solar energy, and Laetrile, but you really do not know very much. You lack specific, concrete information; you do not have comprehensive knowledge about these topics. Research, then, can overcome these deficiencies, providing you with the information needed to *know* an adequate amount about any topic. Research materials benefit your own knowledge about the social, political, and economic issues facing you.

Besides having personal benefits for you, the results of research activity also aid your persuasive attempts with others — and this is the specific reason why research support is so necessary in effective argumentative communication. Quite simply, no matter how trustworthy you may be or appear, no matter how high your reputation or image might be, your character and reputation cannot be an adequate reason why your statements should be believed and accepted. Even though your credibility may know no bounds, other people — your listeners — will demand that you prove what you say is true and accurate. Supporting materials gathered by research serve as the proof for your statements.[1]

In argumentative communication settings, you generally try to persuade others to accept or believe your arguments and conclusions. You want people to agree with you that "we should adopt the Equal Rights Amendment," for example, and the following scenario would not at all be uncommon:

Marie: We should adopt the Equal Rights Amendment.

Larry: Why?

Marie: Because, at the present time, women are being paid less for doing the same exact jobs that men do.

Larry: Is that right?

Marie: It certainly is.

Larry: Prove it!

Now if Marie can respond only, "Well, I *know* that's the way it is!" then she is not going to persuade Larry to her position. It is quite apparent by the preceding dialogue that Larry wants more than simply Marie's word that women are being paid less than men for doing the same jobs.

If, however, Marie could produce some evidence, some supporting material, to substantiate her claim, then she would increase the persuasiveness of her argument significantly. Evidence serves to support arguments, to maximize the persuasiveness of your message, and to heighten your credibility — three significant payoffs in argumentative communication settings. To make your argumentative efforts as functional and effective as possible, it is essential that you have the research evidence to support the claims of your arguments.[2]

Factual Evidence

The first type of supporting material to be examined is factual evidence, generally specific bits of information dealing with actual, real-life examples and statistical data. This is the kind of information easily found in most reference materials in any library. This is an illustration of a real-life example:

> On November 27, 1978, John Ludlow finally decided to see a doctor; he had not been feeling well for several months. The diagnosis: leukemia. Ludlow had worked at the Wambat Nuclear Power Plant for fourteen years; the doctor concluded that the radiation levels present at the plant finally had caused the disease.

In an argumentative setting, examples such as the preceding illustration are used to justify broad conclusions, such as, "The United States should stop the development of nuclear power." Specific examples are used to demonstrate concretely the problems or harms that are of concern in a particular advocacy situation. The use of such specific examples, drawn from real-world occurrences, allow the advocate to argue inductively; that is, several specific examples are melded to allow us to reach one general conclusion. By combining many specific examples, the advocate is able to demonstrate the nature of the problem under consideration, thereby strengthening her justification for some type of policy change.

The use of specific, real-life examples as supporting evidence has both advantages and disadvantages. On the positive side, those examples provide concrete proof of the contentions offered by the advocate. The general argument that people are injured by nuclear power plants is strengthened immeasurably by specific evidence documenting that harm. Now, the claimed harm or problem has been given life through the proof that that harm or problem actually has occurred. The problem no longer is merely an abstract issue; it has been given compelling concreteness through the specificity of the supporting example.

A second positive element to this type of factual evidence is that real-life examples generally deal with people, not with vague concepts or inanimate objects. Your audience is allowed to identify with the person in your example(s), perhaps being able to say to themselves, "Hey, that could have been me."[3] It is for this reason that charity campaigns use appeals based upon people, recognizing that all of us are affected in some way by what has happened to others. Therefore, specific examples are most effective in documenting argumentative claims, significantly increasing both the impact and persuasiveness of those claims.

On the less positive side of the ledger, specific examples present two major problems to the advocate and to his listeners. First, how many examples are necessary to prove your point? This is a most perplexing problem for both the sender and receiver of the argumentative message. For example, in trying to substantiate the claim that people are injured by nuclear power plants, how many examples of injuries caused by nuclear power plants would *you* demand to hear as a listener before you would accept that general contention regarding nuclear power safety? Most of us would want to hear more than one example; after all, if only one person had ever been injured, then the problem would not be seen as significant. So, how many specific examples are needed? Two? Three? Eighty-nine? Obviously, there is no absolute answer to that question. In some instances, two or three examples would be quite sufficient to prove your point, while in others many more examples might be necessary.

Generally, the answer to "how many examples are needed?" depends entirely upon your audience, specifically upon their position vis-à-vis your topic at the outset of argument. If your audience already were disposed to believe that nuclear power plants were dangerous, then only a couple of examples would be needed to substantiate the danger to that audience's satisfaction. On the other hand, a pronuclear power audience would demand many more examples to substantiate the supposed danger, again demonstrating the necessity of the advocate's knowing as much as possible about his audience before the argumentative encounter is initiated.[4]

A second problem with the use of specific examples is the typicality of those examples. Both the advocate and her audience need to be certain that the example used is typical, not atypical, that what happened in the example was not a one-in-a-million occurrence. That is why more than one example generally is needed to prove a point of contention. Two, three, or four examples tend to demonstrate that the issue under consideraton is not bizarre, that the problem is not insignificant.

Within a formal debate encounter, it is not unusual to find a myriad of competing or contradictory examples. The affirmative might present several examples detailing the dangers of nuclear power plants, and the negative might, in turn, present examples demonstrating the safety of those plants. If nothing else, that kind of situation illustrates the dynamic and interesting nature of argumentative communication. The affirmative's examples are countered by the examples presented by the negative, aptly demonstrating the give-and-take and the two-sided nature of competitive advocacy. That is why other types of evidence must be used to complement the proffered examples, why a wide array of support materials is necessary for proof in effective argumentative communication.

The second kind of factual evidence is statistical data, the kinds of materials drawn from surveys, experimental studies, field observations, and so on. Every source of information within your library will contain some amount of statistical data, often presented in raw numbers ("There are twenty million poor people in the United States"), ratios ("Eight out of ten Americans face the risk of cancer"), and percentages ("Eighteen percent of American doctors were trained in foreign medical schools"). Statistical data can be presented in the form of charts, such as that in figure 9.1, drawn from the *Report on the Energy Crisis* by the National Association of Attorneys General, or it can be presented in the form of a graph, as shown in figure 9.2, constructed from material found within the *Economic Report of the President.*

Figure 9.1

AMERICAN ENERGY (TRILLION BTUs) PROJECTIONS

	1972	1973	1974	1975	1976
Domestic production	62,785	61,964	61,409	60,885	60,233
Total use	72,091	75,259	78,565	82,017	85,621
Needed imports	9,306	13,295	17,156	21,132	25,388

Figure 9.2

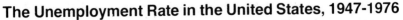

The Unemployment Rate in the United States, 1947-1976

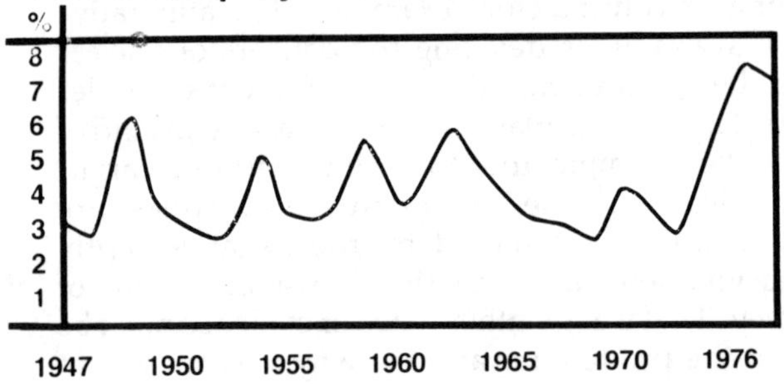

There are all sorts of visual presentations of data possible, including bar graphs, pie-shaped graphs, tabular figures, and many more, all of which are designed, at least in theory, to make the data presented more meaningful to you. As an argumentative advocate, you face the same responsibility: making statistical data relevant and meaningful to your audience.

Perhaps the greatest strength of statistics is their ability to specify and concretize proof in a short amount of time. Instead of saying that there are a lot of unemployed people in the United States — a most general and unsupported statement, statistical information allows you to say that there are "seven million" unemployed people in the United States, a specific bit of evidence in support of your overall argumentative position. Generalizations are made specific through the use of statistical data, and the impact and meaning of a situation are enhanced by such information. Figure 9.2 illustrates that unemployment dropped (or employment increased) in the United States from 1975 to 1976. That visual representation is given greater weight by the following statistically oriented statement from *The Annual Report of the Council of Economic Advisors*, 1977:

> Total civilian employment estimated from household survey data increased 3.2 percent last year over the 1975 average. The increase was widespread among demographic groups. Since the first quarter of 1975, when the trough in employment was reached, civilian employment has increased by 4.4 percent, compared to 3.9 percent in the 7

> quarters following the trough of the 1957–58 recession. Payroll employment increased 2.8 percent in 1976 over the 1975 level and 2.7 percent from the fourth quarter of 1975 to the fourth quarter of 1976. The rate of increase in jobs from the last quarter of 1975 to the last quarter of 1976 varied substantially among the sectors of the economy. Employment rose by 4.2 percent in durable goods manufacturing and in the private service-producing sectors by 2.8 percent.

With that information, the advocate would not have to contend generally that employment had increased from 1975 to 1976; instead, the advocate would have the specific statistical information to support concretely the argument that the employment picture had improved.

Although statistical data do provide specific and direct support for arguments, that data also possesses the power to confuse your opponents and your audience. If you will reread the preceding evidence from the Council of Economic Advisors, you will find that a great many statistics are used in a short space: seven percentage figures and eight year dates were presented in a piece of evidence containing just over one hundred words. Were you to read that piece of evidence aloud, many people in your audience would be confused by that great amount of data, not being able to understand exactly what has been proved by those statistics. For that reason, it is essential that statistical information be explained and clarified, telling your audience what those statistics mean and how they support your argument. Too many debaters and general advocates presume that statistical information is clear to everyone, that terms such as ***the statistical mean*** (the statistical average) are readily understood by all members of an audience. Both presumptions are false. Statistics can be quite confusing and, because of that, they need to be explained carefully by the advocate to have their maximum and desired effect.[5]

Factual evidence, then, consists of real-life examples and statistical data, materials that provide concrete support for your arguments. A significant amount of factual evidence is utilized in all argumentative encounters, both formal and informal, structured and unstructured.

Opinionated Evidence

The second type of supporting material found in argumentative communication situations is opinionated evidence, statements from experts and authorities upon the topic and issues under consideration. In contest debate encounters, this is the type of evidence that quantitatively predominates, as statements from authorities are found readily in books, magazines, newspapers, and government documents. At least 90 percent of the evidence utilized by today's interscholastic and intercollegiate debaters is of the opinionated type.

Most people write books and magazine articles to express a point of view; most people make public statements before news reporters and governmental bodies to express a point of view. In all such cases, the speaker generally attempts to persuade his listener to that point of view. Thus, an expert on nuclear power might write a book designed to convince others that nuclear power is a safe, efficient, and cost-effective means for solving the international energy crisis. Another writer, a former warden of Sing-Sing Prison, might write a magazine article detailing why capital punishment does not deter crime. A potential presidential candidate might call a news conference to tell reporters of her plans to improve the quality of life in the United States. The head of a farmers' alliance might tell a Senate investigating committee that crop support prices need to be increased to protect small family-run farms in this country. In all instances, a persuasive point of view is being expounded — an example of public argumentation.

As support materials, these statements serve to buttress the advocate's arguments. If you were concerned with the nation's unemployment problem, for example, you might take the position that present laws serve to restrict employment, contending that many status quo mechanisms actually worsen our current unemployment difficulties. At this point, your opinion is only your opinion, and most people would not be willing to accept your unsupported statement. However, with a piece of opinionated evidence as substantiation, your argument is given greater credibility. The following statement from the Committee for Economic Development's *Jobs for the Hard-to-Employ* would support your position:

> Existing laws and regulations contain numerous provisions that inhibit increased private employment for the young, old, and disadvantaged. Some, such as minimum wage laws and social security payroll taxes, reduce employers' demands for labor by increasing labor's price. Others, such as earning restrictions for social security and welfare recipients, hold back the supply of labor.

Now your position has been substantiated; now your position has greater credibility, because you have produced some proof to support your position. Opinionated evidence, then, provides viability to your argumentative positions by showing that your opinion is not only *your* opinion. Instead, experts and authorities agree with your point of view, thereby enhancing the credibility and persuasiveness of your arguments.

Since opinionated evience is so directly linked to the advocate's argumentative credibility, it is essential that the source of each piece of opinionated evidence be screened for its own credibility. Just that John Smith wrote a book about America's energy crisis does not mean inherently that John Smith is any type of energy-related expert. On the contrary, quite a few people write books without knowing much of anything about their subjects.[6] In addition, some writers are so biased and prejudiced in their viewpoints that their books and articles are very slanted and misleading. For those reasons, each source of information must be checked thoroughly as to its source's expertise (does the source really have the right to speak on that subject?) and content accuracy and objectivity. If the source of information has little or no credibility, then the opinionated evidence from that source will be of little or no value.

Verbal Evidence

The third and final type of evidence used in argumentative communication situations is verbal evidence, those materials generated by the advocate himself in the support of proffered arguments. Unlike factual and opinionated evidence, which are bits of information gathered from external sources, verbal evidence is the result of an internal process, information generated by the advocate in the substantiation of his arguments. Verbal evidence consists of three major subcategories: hypothetical examples and illustrations, analogies, and the analysis of factual and opinionated evidence. Each of these subcategories is discussed separately below.

Hypothetical Examples

There are occasions when an advocate wishes to concretize a purported harm by referring to a specific example that illustrates the problem clearly. However, what do you do if you have no specific example to use as an illustration? You may not have been able to uncover a real-life example that demonstrates the problem under consideration. In those cases, the use of hypothetical examples can fill the void caused by the lack of actual, real-life examples.

In putting together a hypothetical example, the advocate creates a virtual make-believe story that is designed to vivify and personalize a situation — the same goal one seeks in using actual examples and illustrations. Quite often, a hypothetical example looks like this:

> If John Wambat had worked in a nuclear power plant since 1965, he could be in great danger. He would face

> higher levels of radiation than we face in the outside world; he would face a greater chance of contracting leukemia than would we; his life expectancy would be much lower than ours. John would be in great danger.

Please note that that hypothetical example began with an important word, *if*, clearly indicating that the example was not real but was only hypothetical. Of course, the example could be drawn from studies indicating higher levels of leukemia in and lower life expectancies for nuclear power plant workers, but the example itself is nothing more than the creation of the advocate's imagination. That example serves to crystallize and vivify the potential harms of nuclear power plants, but "John Wambat" is a myth.

Hypothetical examples provide very little strength of proof, but they do serve to clarify a potentially confusing argument. They simplify issues for listeners, perhaps allowing them to see problems in more concrete, personal terms. Unfortunately, many competing advocates and listeners tend to take hypothetical examples at face value, reacting to them as if they were actual, real-life examples. But hypothetical examples are only hypothetical, and they should be treated as such. Hypothetical examples do clarify and vivify, but they do not really *prove* anything.

Analogies

Another kind of clarifying verbal evidence is the use of analogies, the comparison of something known to something unknown. In argumentative situations, especially in formal debate encounters that deal with the complexities of today's policy-making decisions, it would not be unusual to deal with vague and hard-to-understand concepts. Trying to explain the nature of cost-push inflation, for example, is a most difficult task when dealing with a lay audience (cost-push inflation refers to an increase in wages causing an increase in prices to offset the wage increase, which then causes another increase in wages and then prices, ad infinitum). In that type of circumstance, explaining cost-push inflation analogically to be like a cart bumping a horse might be helpful:

> As the cart rolls forward, bumping the horse from behind, the horse is nudged further ahead at a faster pace, causing the cart to bump the horse again. This back-and-forth process continues at a rapidly accelerating pace until the horse collapses in an exhausted heap.

Nearly everyone would be able to visualize that cart-and-horse analogy, seeing that each caused the other's reaction, much like the situation found in cost-push inflation. Although the analogy does not prove the existence of cost-push inflation or of its potentially harmful impact, the analogy does serve to simplify and clarify a confusing concept. Analogies generally are interesting and, because of that, people tend to like them. Analogies are an excellent clarifying device, but they, too, do not prove much of anything.

Analysis

The final type of verbal evidence is analysis, the explanation of the meaning of factual and opinionated evidence as presented. Much research information is complex and confusing to those not familiar with the topic under discussion. Thus, much evidence is meaningless gobbledygook to many listeners unless that evidence is explained by the advocate. This explanation is analysis, telling your listeners what the evidence presented means and what impact it has. The analysis of evidence consists of three steps:

1. present the evidence
2. explain the meaning of the evidence
3. demonstrate the argumentative impact of the evidence.

Too many debaters only complete step one, presuming that the evidence will speak for itself. However, without explaining and applying the evidence, its value can be lost completely, because not much evidence actually does speak for itself.

Read the following statement from *Alternative Directions in Economic Policy* by Charles K. Wilber and Kenneth P. Jameson, 1978:

> The attempt to maintain a steady full-employment expansion inevitably undermines itself. As full employment is maintained for any length of time, profits are eroded as bargaining power shifts in favor of workers and productivity declines as labor discipline weakens without the threat of unemployment.

If an advocate were to read that to her audience without explaining it, the audience might not understand the evidence at all or, even worse, a conclusion might be reached that is inconsistent with the evidence. To prevent either problem from occurring, the advocate should explain the evidence's meaning: "Thus, full employment is seen to be counterproductive, because productivity will decline without the threat of unemployment to compel workers to maximum effort." Now the advocate would show how that evidence strengthens or weakens her opponent's arguments. Now the evidence has meaning and impact — through the analysis of that evidence.

Every piece of evidence should be analyzed (reducing something to its component parts) and explained. The more complex and confusing the evidence, the more analysis and explanation will be needed to enhance argumentative communication effectiveness.

The Ethics of Evidence

Because of the importance of evidence as the supportive underpinning to arguments, it is imperative that the use of evidence be ethically based. Specifically, the unethical use of evidence, such as the use of evidence that is dishonest or has been doctored, must be considered the gravest sin in the process of argumentative communication. Using such evidence is just the same as lying under oath in a court of law, for as juries make decisions based upon the testimony they hear, argumentative communication decisions are based upon the evidence presented by the competing advocates. The unethical use of evidence cannot be tolerated, and the three following unethical evidence practices must be circumscribed.[7]

1. *Fabrication*. It is completely unethical to assert the existence of a piece of evidence that does not, in fact, exist. For example, if an advocate were to say that "the Secretary of the Treasury has forecast a deep recession for next year" when no such forecast had been made, that would be evidence fabrication. This is the most serious of the three unethical practices in the use of evidence.

The relatively humorous thing about evidence fabrication is that it is completely unnecessary. An advocate might be tempted to fabricate to fill in a hole that exists in his stockpile of evidence or to support an argument that, at the moment, stands unsupported by evidence whatsoever. That advocate has done an insufficient amount of research, because, quite honestly, every bizarre idea you can imagine already has been written about, already has been advanced by some author in print. All you need to do is dig out the research material. There is, in fact, absolutely no need to fabricate evidence, because the specific evidence sought exists already.

Fabrication is the same as an out-and-out lie. It cannot be countenanced.

2. *Misrepresentation*. It is unethical to misrepresent evidence, to give a meaning to a piece of evidence that was not intended by the source of that evidence. This problem generally occurs during the analysis of evidence stage of argumentative communication when the advocate explains what a particular piece of evidence means to her listeners. A study of several thousand New Englanders, for example, might be misrepresented as a nationwide study, one that examined all elements of America's diverse population. That would clearly be a case of misrepresentation.

Evidence tends to be misrepresented in the heat of argument in an attempt to make the evidence stronger and of greater import than it actually is. Much misrepresentation often is the result of error (the advocate does not fully understand his own evidence) or of a mistake in judgment. Regardless of the reason, this type of unethical practice cannot be justified or excused.

3. *Distortion*. It is unethical to distort evidence physically — specifically, to cite a piece of evidence out of context. To delete *not* from this quotation would completely distort the quotation: "Wage and price controls will *not* serve to control the cost-push inflationary spiral." The misimpression created by such distortion is obvious. Similarly, the failure to cite qualifying phrases and sentence parts often results in evidence distortion:

> *Full citation*: Communists should be allowed to teach in our public schools, unless they disqualify themselves by using the classroom for propaganda purposes.
>
> *Distorted citation*: Communists should be allowed to teach in our public schools.

Obviously, the failure to cite the qualifier ("unless they disqualify. . . .") completely changes the meaning of the statement and distorts the evidence.[8]

Advocates must be extremely careful in gathering, recording, and using evidence, because evidence distortion is the easiest unethical practice to commit by accident. In the fervor to find just "that right piece of evidence," it is very easy to take a statement out of context, to distort the intended meaning of the evidence. That is why a reasonable amount of time should be given to evidence gathering; the more hurried the research, the more likely that evidence distortion will occur.

Whether your argumentative communication encounters be formal or informal, structured or unstructured, you must be constantly aware of the need for the ethical use of evidence. There exists no justification for the fabrication, misrepresentation, or distortion of evidence, because such unethical practices strike directly at the foundation of reasoned argumentative discourse.

Conclusion

Evidence serves as the structural underpinning of arguments, providing the materials for the differentiation between sound argument and weak assertion. There are three major types of evidence: factual, which emphasizes the use of real-life examples and statistical data; opinionated, the conclusionary statements from experts and authorities in the topic area; and verbal, information generated by the advocate through the use of hypothetical examples, analogies and analysis.

Regardless of the types of evidence utilized in argumentative communication, such evidence must be used ethically. The fabrication, misrepresentation, and distortion of evidence cannot be tolerated.

References

1. See William R. Dresser, "The Impact of Evidence on Decision Making," *The Journal of the American Forensic Association* 3 (May 1966): 43–47; and James C. McCroskey, "The Effects of Evidence in Persuasive Communication," *Western Speech* 31 (Summer 1967): 189–199.

2. The concept of proof in argumentative communication generally coincides with the Aristotelian notion of nonartistic proofs — materials gathered by the advocate and not created by him. Research, then, often is considered to be an external search for materials, not an internal process of reflection.

3. The importance of identification is stressed by all contemporary persuasion theorists and rhetorical scholars. The whole notion of coactive persuasion is based upon identification. See Herbert W. Simons, *Persuasion: Understanding, Practice, and Analysis* (Reading, Mass.: Addison-Wesley, 1976), pp. 134–138.

4. The significance of audience analysis to effective and functional communication is explored by Theodore Clevenger, Jr., *Audience Analysis* (Indianapolis: Bobbs-Merrill, 1966).

5. Clarence Darrow, famous American trial attorney and public advocate, felt that statistical data often were misleading and confusing. In addition, he believed that statistics could be twisted to prove practically anything, a point exemplified by his statement during a public debate on 26 October 1924: "I will guarantee to take any set of statistics and take a little time to it and prove they mean directly the opposite for what is claimed."

6. There exist so-called subsidy publishers in the United States, firms who will publish virtually anything you want if you provide the funds to subsidize the publication, generally several thousands of dollars. Thus, anyone, with the right amount of money, can publish a book.

7. For an interesting discussion concerning ethics and evidence, see James Edward Sayer, "The Ethics of Evidence," and Dale Hample and Judy Hample, "Evidence Credibility," *Debate Issues* 12 (October 1978): 2–5.

8. That was the exact type of distortion utilized so often by the infamous Senator Joseph McCarthy of Wisconsin. See James Edward Sayer, "The Rhetoric of Distortion of Joseph R. McCarthy," masters thesis (University of Arizona, 1969), pp. 28–29.

Practicum

1. Unethical practices in the use of evidence are not limited to public statements by political leaders and other advocates dealing with social, political, or economic issues. One of the most prevalent and constant forms of public argument is mass communication advertising: television and radio sales pitches, newspaper and magazine ads, and so on. Examine several of these advertisements, oral and written, carefully. Then answer these questions:

- How often were sources of evidence cited in the advertisements?
- What types of evidence were found in those advertisements?
- Was the evidence cited clearly and with apparent care for accuracy?
- Was enough of the evidence presented in support of the advertisements' claims?
- Overall, how would you assess the ethical use of evidence in the advertisements you examined?

2. The following is an excerpt of one of the most interesting speeches of argument presented in American history. In 1872, Susan B. Anthony, one of the pioneers in the women's rights movement, voted in the presidential elction of that year — in direct violation of the law. She was arrested, tried, and fined $100 for this act, calling forth the following speech in justification of women's voting privileges.

In putting together her argument, Anthony used a variety of evidentiary sources to substantiate her position. Which type of evidence predominated? Which type of evidence did you find to be the most persuasive? How would you rate the argumentative quality of the one hundred-plus-year-old speech?

> Friends and fellow-citizens: I stand before you to-night, under indictment for the alleged crime of having voted at the last Presidential election, without having a lawful right to vote. It shall be my work this evening to prove to you that in thus voting, I not only committed no crime, but, instead, simply exercised my *citizen's rights*, guaranteed to me and all United States citizens by the National Constitution, beyond the power of any State to deny....

The preamble of the Federal Constitution says:

"We, the people of the United States, in order to form a more perfect union, establish justice, insure *domestic* tranquillity, provide for the common defence, promote the general welfare, and secure the blessings of liberty to ourselves and our posterity, do ordain and establish this Constitution for the United States of America."

It was we, the people; not we, the white male citizens; nor yet we, the male citizen; but we, the whole people, who formed the Union. And we formed it, not to give the blessings of liberty, but to secure them; not to the half of ourselves and the half of our posterity, but to the whole people — women as well as men. And it is a downright mockery to talk to women of their enjoyment of the blessings of liberty while they are denied the use of the only means of securing them provided by this democratic-republican government — the ballot.

The early journals of Congress show that when the committee reported to that body the original articles of confederation, the very first article which became the subject of discussion was that respecting equality of suffrage. Article IV said: "The better to secure and perpetuate mutual friendship and intercourse between the people of the different States of the Union, the free inhabitants of each of the States (paupers, vagabonds and fugitives from justice excepted), shall be entitled to all the privileges and immunities of the free citizens of the several States."

Thus, at the very beginning, did the fathers see the necessity of the universal application of the great principle of equal rights to all; in order to produce the desired result — a harmonious union and a homogeneous people. . . .

B. Gratz Brown, of Missouri, in the three days' discussion in the United States Senate in 1866, on Senator Cowan's motion to strike the word male from the District of Columbia suffrage bill, said:

"Mr. President, I say here on the floor of the American Senate, I stand for universal suffrage; and, as a matter of fundamental principle, do not recognize the right of society to limit it on any ground of race or sex. . . ."

Charles Sumner, in his brave protests against the fourteenth and fifteenth amendments, insisted that, so soon as by the thirteenth amendment the slaves became free men, the original powers of the United States Constitution guaranteed to them equal rights — the right to vote and to be voted for. . . .

Article I of the New York State Constitution says:

"No member of this State shall be disfranchised or

deprived of the rights or privileges secured to any citizen thereof, unless by the law of the land or the judgment of his peers."

And so carefully guarded is the citizen's right to vote that the Constitution makes special mention of all who may be excluded. It says:

"Laws may be passed excluding from the right of suffrage all persons who have been or may be convicted of bribery, larceny or any infamous crime." . . .

"The law of the land" is the United States Constitution, and there is no provision in that document that can be fairly construed into a permission to the States to deprive any class of their citizens of their right to vote. Hence, New York can get no power from that source to disfranchise one entire half of her members. Nor has "the judgment of their peers" been pronounced against women exercising their right to vote; no disfranchised person is allowed to be judge or juror, and none but disfranchised persons can be women's peers; nor has the Legislature passed laws excluding them on account of idiocy or lunacy; nor yet the courts convicted them of bribery, larceny or any infamous crime. Clearly, then, there is no constitutional ground for the exclusion of women from the ballot-box in the State of New York. No barriers whatever stand to-day between women and the exercise of their right to vote save those of precedent and prejudice. . . .

For any State to make sex a qualification that must ever result in the disfranchisement of one entire half of the people is to pass a bill of attainder, or an *ex post facto* law, and is therefore a violation of the supreme law of the land. By it the blessings of liberty are forever withheld from women and their female posterity. To them this government has no just powers derived from the consent of the governed. To them this government is not a democracy. It is not a republic. It is an odious aristocracy; a hateful oligarchy of sex; the most hateful aristocracy ever established on the face of the globe; an oligarchy of wealth, where the rich govern the poor. An oligarchy of learning, where the educated govern the ignorant, or even an oligarchy of race, where the Saxon rules the African, might be endured; but this oligarchy of sex, which makes father, brothers, husband, sons the oligarchs over the mother and sisters, the wife and daughters of every household; which ordains all men sovereigns, all women subjects; carries dissension, discord and rebellion into every home of the nation. . . .

Webster, Worcester and Bouvier all define a citizen to

be a person in the United States, entitled to vote and hold office.

The only question left to be settled now is: Are women persons? And I hardly believe any of our opponents will have the hardihood to say they are not. Being persons, then, women are citizens, and no State has a right to make any law, or to enforce any old law, that shall abridge their privileges or immunities. Hence, every discrimination against women in the constitutions and laws of the several States is to-day null and void, precisely as in every one against negroes.

Chapter 10

Fallacious Argument

* The Meaning of Fallacious Argument
* Prevalent Fallacies in Argumentative Communication
* Fallacious Argument: A Case Study
* Conclusion
* References
* Practicum

We conclude our third unit with the study of fallacious argument, especially as it relates to the *structure* of arguments used in various communicative transactions. This chapter should be read eventually in conjunction with chapter 14, "Refutation," and its analysis of arguments made weak by inadequate supporting evidence. This chapter, however, is not concerned with the nature of evidentiary support; on the contrary, the study of fallacious argument principally is concerned with the form in which an argument is presented or how (as in the case of mass advertising) it is packaged. Since it was noted in the preceding chapter that evidence can be found to substantiate even the most bizarre of arguments, it is very important that the advocate be quite careful about how her arguments are structured — and this is doubly important for the consumer of those arguments.

Besides detailing the most prevalent fallacies found within argumentative communication, this chapter also presents a case study analysis of fallacious argument, something you should find to be both interesting and humorous. If all arguments and argumentative positions were critically examined in a similar manner, the quality of contemporary argumentative communication would be improved dramatically.

The Meaning of Fallacious Argument

The nature of fallacious argumentative structure is much akin to the notions of validity and invalidity as taught by formal logicians, meaning that the very structure of an argument makes that argument untenable. Hence, the study of syllogisms, Venn diagrams, and the other tools of the formal logician is designed to ferret out the nonviable argumentative structure.

Although all fallacious arguments analyzed here certainly are invalid because of their structure (as the logician would view them), we are more concerned with the irrational nature of their fallaciousness. In argumentative communication, a fallacious argument is one whose structure is so irrational or incomplete as to make its value minimal to a reasonable person.[1] Although it is possible to agree intuitively or emotionally with many fallacious arguments, since we tend not to operate on a logical level at all times, it is imperative at the very least that we recognize the inherent irrationality of these arguments. Then we do not delude ourselves about the actual worth of such arguments and conclusions drawn from those arguments.

Perhaps the greatest danger posed by fallacious arguments is their impact upon us as consumers of information. As such, we may find ourselves persuaded by fallacious reasons — persuaded to vote for certain candidates, to buy certain products and services, and to lead our lives in certain ways — all because of fallacious, irrational arguments. Since rhetorical reasoning is such a large part of our daily lives, and since we make many decisions based upon our reasoning processes, it is essential that we try to minimize the incidence of fallacious arguments impacting upon the decision-making process.

Prevalent Fallacies in Argumentative Communication

Many texts dealing with argumentative communication contain impressive, if not overwhelming, lists of fallacious arguments, the kinds of arguments to be avoided in argumentative transactions. Often expressed in their original Latin terms (such as *post hoc ergo propter hoc* — the fallacy in causal reasoning), such taxonomies tend to present many kinds of fallacious arguments not found in normal argumentative communication situations. This section details the eight most prevalent argumentative fallacies, plus the seven major propaganda devices isolated by persuasion theorists. These most prevalent fallacies can be observed in daily personal encounters, television commercials, election campaigns — the full range of human communication activity.

Faulty Assumptions

A faulty assumption means that an argument or an entire chain of reasoning is based upon an irrational or unsupported theoretical or conceptual foundation. As any dictionary definition might tell us, an assumption is the taking for granted of something as true, correct, accurate, or good. As effective practitioners of functional argumentative communication, we must be very careful in dealing with the assumptions that underlie most arguments.

A *faulty* assumption, then, is one that is presumed to be true, correct, accurate, or good, but of which the verity has not been proven. For example, if you were to hear the statement, "Lavoris is not a good mouthwash, because it does not prevent its user from catching the flu," you would hear an excellent example of a faulty assumption. What makes that argument fallacious is that Lavoris was not designed to prevent its users from contracting the flu, a cold, or any other type of illness. That mouthwash product only was designed to improve the scent of one's breath. That faulty assumption, then, inappropriately condemns a product for not doing what it not was supposed to do.

Faulty assumptions are dangerous rhetorically because they cause us to reach inaccurate and inappropriate conclusions, completely skewing the overall decision-making process. As practitioners and consumers of argument, we need to examine the assumptions upon which arguments are based very carefully. Faulty assumptions lead to faulty conclusions — a complete chain of fallacious argument.

Question Begging

Somewhat similar to the faulty assumption, the fallacy of question begging leads to a conclusion that is essentially the same as the assumption upon which the conclusion is based. For this reason, question begging often is termed "argument in a circle":

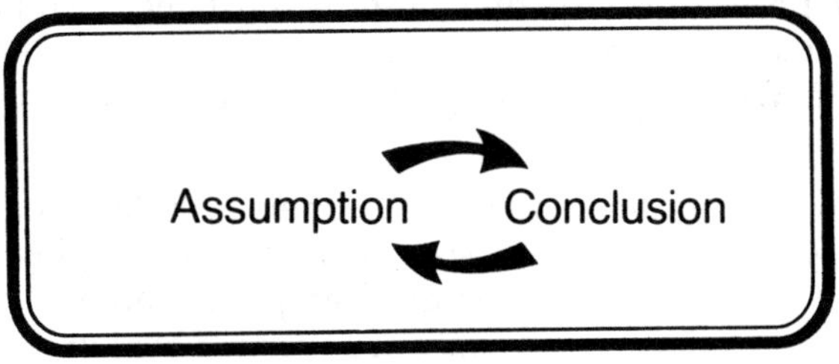

The following exemplifies the fallacy of begging the question:

> If a speaker is attempting to prove the cause of high unemployment rates, and claims that unemployment rates are high because so many people are out of work, the speaker has begged the question. Unemployment rates quantify the number of people out of work and looking for jobs; the speaker has offered no causal explanation of high unemployment rates.[2]

Faulty Causality

One of the most prevalent argumentative fallacies found in day-to-day communication is that of faulty causality, literally the assumption that X caused Y. Faulty causality occurs when we assume a direct causal relationship between two observable phenomena. As a very simple example, let us suppose that right after Manfred walked into the classroom, the lights in that room went out. Someone might exemplify faulty causality by asserting, "Because Manfred walked into the room, the lights went out," and that statement could be shown like this:

Manfred enters room ——→ lights in room go out.

This demonstrates the direct linear relationship of cause claimed by that statement; that is, Manfred is *the cause* for the lights going out in the classroom; but, of course, no proof has been offered to support such a statement.

Perhaps the most difficult task found in the decision-making process is the establishment of direct causal relationships. Since all systems are the products of many input factors, it is exceedingly difficult to demonstrate a one-to-one relationship between a system's input and output stages. Professor Dan DeStephen has noted the necessary requisites for the proper, nonfallacious establishment of causality:

> A causal relationship between two variables (x and y) implies that: (1) y precedes x in time; and, (2) y is a necessary and sufficient condition for the existence of x. To prove causality, then, a study must demonstrate that ***each*** time y occurs, x follows. Moreover, if x occurs without y occurring first, a causal relationship does not exist.[3]

To demonstrate causality viably, DeStephen's conditions must be met. Thus, when we hear such statements as, "Unemployment is the cause of poverty," we hear an example of faulty causality, because there are many other causes of poverty (poor job skills, lack of an adequate education, low motivation to work, and so on) besides unemployment.

Causal relationships must be subjected to careful scrutiny because of the complex nature of most systems. Complex outputs generally result from complex inputs; very few systems, policies, or events come from single, simple causes.

Hasty Generalization

A hasty generalization is a fallacious argument that generally asserts the allness or completeness of a situation: "Today's young people do not respect their fellowmen. The actions of such groups as the Hell's Angels prove this lack of respect." This argument is fallacious, because it takes one example (the motorcycle group known as Hell's Angels) and draws a conclusion about an entire class (today's young people). Many daily arguments illustrate this type of argumentative fallacy, because we tend to deal in generalizations. Such statements as, "Everyone wants to reduce taxes," or, "Everybody thinks our government is too big for our own good," exemplify hasty generalizations — broad argumentative conclusions based upon a relatively small or minor amount of data for support.

Personal Attack

This fallacy is often described by the Latin term *ad hominem*, meaning "against the men," an argument directed against the source of a statement and not to the viability of the statement itself. Unfortunately found quite often in political campaigns, a personal attack diverts our attention away from that which should be the argumentative focus. Consider this example:

Argument: To combat the spiraling cost of health care, we need to implement a system of socialized medicine.

Response: Only an idiot who wears hair that long would advocate socialized medicine.

Please note that the merits and demerits of socialized medicine have become secondary in the response. In the response, the central issue of concern is the length of hair worn by the advocate of socialized medicine, and the viability of the health care proposal has been pushed into the background. The advocate's hair is totally irrelevant to the viability of socialized medicine, but the fallacious response of a personal attack has caused our attention to be diverted away from that significantly more important issue.

Straw Man

The straw man fallacy is the presentation and refutation of an argument either very peripheral or completely irrelevant to the major issue under consideration. Much like the fallacy of the personal attack, the straw man diverts our attention away from the main point being discussed. Consider this example:

> The United States should not return the Panama Canal to the Panamanians. After all, if we do make such a mistake, then our Latin American neighbors will move north in an attempt to take control of our governmental processes. And I say that America ought to be run by Americans!

You should see that the primary issue of returning the Panama Canal to the Panamanians has been pushed into the background by the straw man issue of having our governmental processes taken over by our Latin American neighbors. Although we might agree that "America ought to be run by Americans," we reach that emotional statement via an argument grounded upon a straw man, something completely irrelevant to the general Panàma Canal question.[4]

Irrelevant Reason

The irrelevant reason, known by the Latin term *non sequitur*, is the argumentative fallacy of reaching a conclusion that does not follow from the information or data upon which that conclusion is based. The following exemplifies the fallacy of the irrelevant reason:

Reason: Nuclear power is a financially expensive alternative energy source.

Conclusion: Nuclear power is dangerous to human lives.

The irrelevant reason is the most elemental of all argumentative fallacies, yet it exists surprisingly more often than you might imagine. Arguments thrown together quickly and without a great deal of thought often fall prey to this type of fallacy. No reasonable individual should accept any conclusion predicated upon such a fallacious rationale.

Slippery Slope

The slippery slope might be considered the fallacy of inevitability — the notion that once some action is begun its consequences are unavoidable. Many youngsters might have heard this example of the slippery slope fallacy from their parents:

> "Once you begin to smoke cigarettes, that is the beginning of the end. Next you'll take to drinking and staying out late and running around with a bunch of wild people. You'll lose your job and your family, and you'll end up as a skid-row bum with nothing to show for your life."

Yes, you will end up on skid row because you started to smoke cigarettes — if you believe that fallacious line of reasoning.[5]

Major Propaganda Devices

We end this section of this chapter with a brief consideration of the seven major propaganda devices as originally isolated more than forty years ago. In the late 1930s, the Institute for Propaganda Analysis was formed as "a nonprofit corporation organized for scientific research in methods used by propagandists in influencing public opinion."[6] At that time, there was widespread thought that World War I had been caused by propagandists and that public exposure of propaganda methods might prevent another world-wide conflagration. The IPA went out of existence with the onset of World War II.

Although the public exposure of the methods of propaganda did not prevent World War II, the seven major propaganda devices isolated by the IPA merit continued study by students of contemporary argumentative communication. Political campaigns, mass advertising, and all other forms of mass persuasion utilize the tools of the propagandist, and those tools are as follows:

1. *Name calling.* The propagandist gives "bad names" to ideas, policies, and people that he wants us to condemn and reject.
2. *Glittering generalities.* The propagandist tries to identify her ideas with so-called virtue words such as freedom, honor, and justice.
3. *Transfer.* The propagandist tries to transfer the respect of something or someone we have to that which he wants us to accept.
4. *Testimonial.* The propagandist uses the testimonials of people we respect to support the ideas that she wants us to accept.
5. *Plain folks.* The propagandist tries to win our confidence by showing that he or the idea espoused is "of the people."

6. *Card stacking.* The propagandist presents only that information that supports his ideas.
7. *Bandwagon.* The propagandist urges the support of his idea because "everyone agrees with it."[7]

And what is the danger of these seven propaganda devices — of propaganda itself? The IPA had this answer: "It appeals to emotion, and decisions made under stress of emotion often lead to disaster when the emotion crowds out cool, dispassionate thought."[8]

Thus, like the eight major fallacies of argumentative reasoning, the seven propaganda devices are irrational in nature, causing us to accept unsupported and unreasonable conclusions.

Fallacious Argument: A Case Study

In chapter 3 (page 55), a copy of an article, "Why I'm Against Younger Voting Age," by Don MacLean, was presented as an example of public argumentation. If you read that article carefully, you probably found yourself disagreeing with many of the claims made within it. There are ten significant examples of fallacious argument within that article, and we will detail the argumentative shortcomings of that article. The article is reprinted again, with the sections italicized and numbered to correspond to the analysis following the article.

Why I'm Against Younger Voting Age

There's a lot of talk about lowering the voting age — from 21 to 18. The young people are yelling for it and *many politicians are going along with them because, well, because that's where the votes are, baby.* (1)

This doesn't mean any sensible politician really thinks an 18-year-old is old enough to vote. Not for a minute. *It just means he hopes that when the kids do vote — be it 18 or 21 — they'll remember he was for them.* (2.)

Should the voting age be lowered, *it'll amuse me to see that the kids, far from voting for kindly old Senator Whoosis, will instead vote for the current rock'n'roll star or protest singer.* (3.) The kids almost deserve somebody like that as President, but the rest of us don't, and that's why I'm against lowering the voting age.

In fact, I think it should be raised — to about 25. While it is difficult to peg any particular age as that which most persons reach maturity, *at least the age 25 suggests that the individual will have read something besides comic books and viewed something on television other than "Teen-Age Dance Party."* (4.)

Yet we have people like Senator Alan Bible (D., Nevada) who has introduced a bill to lower the voting age to 18 by amending the Constitution. He says things like, "If you're old enough to be a soldier, you're old enough to vote."

Well, bully for him, but I think the Senator (and anyone else who parrots that idiotic line) ignores certain facts. For one thing, while many kids are old enough to be soldiers, *many of them are not old enough to take it in good grace. Otherwise, they would not be burning draft cards, having anti-draft rallies and running off to Canada.* (5.)

Responsibility, i.e., responding to the draft when your number is called, is one test of maturity. So many of our youngsters have failed this test I'd be afraid to trust them with the vote. (6.) *Besides, they's just vote for any candidate who promised to keep their dear little necks out of the service.* (7.)

I remembered when I was 18 (it wasn't that long ago). On the day that I registered for the draft, *I wasn't any more qualified to vote for President than I was to pilot a 707 over the North Pole.* (8.) Old enough to fight, old enough to vote? *Let's face it, an 11-year-old can fight: does that mean he should vote?* (9.)

Remember, *it was youngsters who propelled Senator Eugene McCarthy into prominence.* (10.) To me, this alone signifies that, as a group, the 18-year-olds are not ready for self government.

1. The statement that politicians supported the lowering of the voting age to eighteen because "that's where the votes are, baby" exemplifies the fallacy of argument from a faulty assumption. The writer completely assumes that the only reason a politician would support lowering the voting age would be to gain some type of partisan advantage, and absolutely no proof is offered in support of that position.

2. The same faulty assumption is continued in the article's second paragraph, as the writer attributes a base motive to politicians' actions — again with no support for that position. This argument eventually begs the question

as it assumes that the politicians are motivated by political reasons to support the conclusion that the politicians are motivated by political reasons.

3. The notion that eighteen-year-old voters will vote "for the current rock'n'roll star or protest singer" also is a faulty assumption unsupported by proof and leads to fallacy number four.

4. It is a hasty generalization that most young people do nothing more than read comic books and watch dance shows on television. Although it probably is true that some individuals do only read and watch such materials, the accusation is generally applied most fallaciously to all people of a certain age.

5. Another hasty generalization centers upon the Vietnam war protesters who burned their draft cards, held antidraft rallies, and fled to Canada to avoid the draft. Again, the actions of a few thousand individuals have been generalized to typify the actions of millions.

6. The concern that an antidraft, anti-Vietnam war position will lead to disasterous voting habits exemplifies both the fallacies of the irrelevant reason (opposing a war is no reason why poor voting habits should result) and the slippery slope (that opposing the war will inevitably lead to poor voting habits).

7. The faulty assumption of vote motivation is repeated.

8. Just because the writer wasn't qualified to vote at the age of eighteen does not mean that all people at that age are similarly afflicted. To assert that argument is to offer a fallacious position built upon yet another hasty generalization — a *very* hasty generalization.

9. Denying the argument of "old enough to fight, old enough to vote" by responding that "an 11-year-old can fight: does that mean he should vote?" is an irrelevant and absurd reason. Certainly, an eleven-year-old person can fight, but that is not the same idea of fighting as applied to eighteen-year-olds and the war in Vietnam. The writer offered a non sequitur game of semantics on that point.

10. The article concludes with a straw-man argument dealing with former Senator Eugene McCarthy. The support of many young people of that politician's campaign for the presidency has absolutely no relevance to the central issue at hand: should the voting age be lowered to eighteen?

The MacLean article presents an excellent illustration of contemporary fallacious argumentative communication. Practically the entire position offered by that writer was based upon fallacious reasoning. Each argument that you offer and have offered to you should be examined as critically and carefully as we did the MacLean article, thereby allowing you to assess the relative value and strength of those arguments and how you should respond to them.

Conclusion

There are many possible fallacious arguments to be found in human communication situations, arguments that are irrational or incomplete so as to make their value minimal to a reasonable person. However, in most argumentative communication encounters, eight primary fallacious arguments stand out: (1) faulty assumptions; (2) question begging; (3) faulty causality; (4) hasty generalizations; (5) personal attacks; (6) straw men; (7) irrelevant reasons; and (8) the slippery slope. Arguments should be examined critically to ferret out such fallacies and to prevent conclusions from being reached by such irrational means.

In addition, because we live in a mass communication society with its mass television political and advertising campaigns, we need to be aware of the seven major propaganda devices that might cause us to reach irrational decisions: (1) name calling; (2) glittering generalities; (3) transfer; (4) testimonial; (5) plain folks; (6) card stacking; and (7) bandwagon.

References

1. See Howard Kahane, *Logic and Contemporary Rhetoric* (Belmont, Calif.: Wadsworth, 1971), pp. 1–2.

2. Richard C. Huseman and James I. Luck, editors, *Bicentennial Youth Debates Participant Guide* (Washington, D.C.: Bicentennial Youth Debates, 1975), p. 52.

3. Dan DeStephen, "Analyzing Study Evidence," *Debate Issues* (November 1978), p. 6.

4. Unfortunately, a great many arguments in the political arena, especially those that are emotionalized for vote-getting purposes, are full of straw men.

5. A most interesting example of the slippery slope fallacy may be found in the "Trouble" soliloquy from "*The Music Man*" by Meredith Wilson.

6. *Propaganda Analysis* 1 (October 1937): 1.

7. "How to Detect Propaganda," *Propaganda Analysis* 1 (October 1937): 3.

Practicum

Both components of this chapter's "Practicum" ask you to examine materials for fallacious arguments. Studying fallacies in a vacuum is of minimal practical value, and for that reason two widely divergent kinds of argumentative materials are presented for your scrutiny. Study both carefully; both actually were used to persuade others to a desired point of view.

1. Near the start of the twentieth century, an important issue within this country and others was imperialism and the question of America's undertaking a policy of territorial acquisition. One of the supporters of American expansionism was United States Senator Albert J. Beveridge of Indiana, and a portion of his speech on behalf of that position is printed here. Examine his arguments carefully. Beveridge wanted the United States to expand its influence in such places as Cuba and the Phillipines. Were his arguments supported adequately or was his position based on fallacious reasoning?

The Republic Never Retreats

The Republic never retreats. Why should it retreat? The Republic is the highest form of civilization, and civilization must advance. The Republic's young men are the most virile and unwasted of the world, and they pant for enterprise worthy of their power. The Republic's preparation has been the self-discipline of a century, and that preparedness has found its task. The Republic's opportunity is as noble as its strength, and that opportunity is here. The Republic's duty is as sacred as its opportunity is real, and Americans never desert their duty.

The Republic could not retreat if it would; whatever its destiny it must proceed. For the American Republic is a part of the movement of a race — the most masterful race of history — and race movements are not to be stayed by the hand of man. They are mighty answers to Divine commands. Their leaders are not only statesmen of peoples — they are prophets of God. The inherent tendencies of a race are its highest law. They precede and survive all statutes, all constitutions. The first question real statesmanship asks is: What are the abiding characteristics of my people? From that basis all reasoning may be natural and true. From any other basis all reasoning must be artificial and false.

The sovereign tendencies of our race are organization and government. We govern so well that we govern ourselves. We organize by instinct. Under the flag of England our race builds an empire out of the ends of earth. In Australia it is today erecting a nation out of fragments. In America it wove out of segregated settlements that complex and wonderful organization, called the American Republic. Everywhere it builds. Everywhere it governs. Everywhere it administers order and law. Everywhere it is the spirit of regulated liberty. Everywhere it obeys that voice not to be denied which bids us strive and rest not, makes of us our brother's keeper and appoints us steward under God of the civilization of the world.

Organization means growth. Government means administration. When Washington pleaded with the States to organize into a consolidated people, he was the advocate of perpetual growth. When Abraham Lincoln argued for the indivisibility of the Republic he became the prophet of the Greater Republic. And when they did both, they were but the interpreters of the tendencies of the race. . . .

What of England? England's immortal glory is not Agincourt or Waterloo. It is not her merchandise or commerce. It is Australia, New Zealand and Africa reclaimed. It is India redeemed. It is Egypt, mummy of the nations, throttling the plague in Calcutta. English law administering order in Bombay. English energy planting an industrial civilization from Cairo to the Cape, and English discipline creating soldiers, men and finally citizens, perhaps even out of the fellaheen of the dead land of the Pharaohs. And yet the liberties of the Englishmen were never so secure as now. And that which is England's undying fame has also been her infinite profit, so sure is duty golden in the end.

And what of America? With the twentieth century the real task and true life of the Republic begins. And we are prepared. We have learned restraint from a hundred years of self-control. We are instructed by the experience of others. We are advised and inspired by present example. And our work awaits us.

The dominant notes in American history have thus far been self-government and internal improvement. But these were not ends only, they were means also. They were modes of preparation. The dominant notes in American life henceforth will be not only self-government and internal

> development, but also administration and world improvement. It is the arduous but splendid mission of our race. It is ours to govern in the name of civilized liberty. It is our to administer order and law in the name of human progress. It is ours to chasten that we may be kind, it is ours to cleanse that we may save, it is ours to build that free institutions may finally enter and abide. It is ours to bear the torch of Christianity where midnight has reigned a thousand years. It is ours to reinforce that thin red line which constitutes the outposts of civilization all around the world.

2. Of course, not all argumentative communication is oral; a great deal of it is in written form. The following is a handbill that was distributed in the mid-1970's in opposition to the Equal Rights Amendment. How would you evaluate the argumentative worth of this piece of argumentative communication? Is the reasoning sound or fallacious?

THE FRAUD CALLED THE EQUAL RIGHTS AMENDMENT

WOMEN: EQUAL RIGHTS WITH MEN MEANS EQUAL RESPONSIBILITY AND EQUAL TREATMENT WITH MEN IN EVERY AREA OF LIFE.

IF THE EQUAL RIGHTS AMENDMENT PASSES:

1.
Women will be drafted and will fight in combat units on the front lines in the event the U.S. becomes involved in any type of war or conflict.

All girls at the age of 18 will register for the draft. Being married or having children will not defer women from the draft. If men have to fight in wars, so will women and girls have to fight in wars. This is the meaning of EQUAL RIGHTS FOR WOMEN.

2.
Women will compete with men on an equal basis for all jobs that are available in the U.S.

3.
Men will no longer be primarily responsible to support the family. This pertains to every family whether the family is intact, or following a separation or divorce action.

When Federal Day Care Centers exist in a community, (such as in Marietta), or when children are in school, wives could be forced to share an equal responsibility to support the family. A husband would not necessarily have to pay more support to maintain the family than what his wife could earn. This would also pertain where a separation or divorce has occurred.

Professor Paul Freund of Harvard Law School, the most distinguished authority on Constitutional Law in the United States, has made clear that if the E.R.A. is passed every wife and mother will lose the right to be supported by her husband.

No more radical piece of legislation could have been devised to force women out of the home.

4.
Where a separation or divorce has occurred, all existing support payments and property arrangements that have been made can be altered and renegotiated if it can be shown that the settlement favors the woman in any way.

5.
The Equal Rights Amendment could legalize homosexual marriages.

The E.R.A. indicates that no legal distinctions between the sexes will be allowed under the law. The pro-lesbian Women's Liberation Movement insists on the passage of the E.R.A. They demand that the E.R.A. be construed "absolute" and that there shall be no legal differentiation whatsoever, between men and women. The National Organization of Women - (N.O.W.), which boasts a 10 Percent lesbian membership, demands passage of the E.R.A.

6.
The Equal Rights Amendment can require that men and women use the same public restroom facilities.

The legal concept of "Separate but Equal" was reversed and held invalid by the 1954 Supreme Court decision of Brown vs. The Board of Education. There are many sex-integrated public restrooms in Europe and Asia. We don't want sex-integrated public restrooms in the United States.

7.
The Constitutional concept of a right to privacy based on sex could be invalidated by the E.R.A. because: EVERY NEW AMENDMENT TAKES PRECEDENCE OVER EVERY OTHER AMENDMENT OR CONSTITUTIONAL ARTICLE WITH WHICH IT IS INCONSISTENT.

The E.R.A. could mean that all available jobs in the U.S., all public restrooms, all prisons and prison cells, all public and private schools, all professional and amateur athletic teams, etc. will be open to both men and women alike, with no distinction made.

8.
For women in industry, the E.R.A. will mean absolute equality of treatment between men and women. Special privileges for women and protective labor legislation for women alone will no longer be allowed.

Under the E.R.A., if a woman isn't capable of doing a job that a man can do, she will be discharged and become ineligible for unemployment compensation. No female protective labor legislation will be written into any labor contract unless the same protection is given to all men. LOTS OF LUCK! The E.R.A., will in fact, usher in a new era of actual female exploitation in industry. Women in industry will no longer be protected, and they can thank the Women's Liberation Movement for that!

9.
The Yale Law Journal states that the E.R.A. will wipe out all laws against prostitution that pertain to women only, and all laws against rape that pertain to men only. The E.R.A. will strike down all laws that apply to one sex only.

THE E.R.A. WILL CONTINUE TO ERODE THE PRIVILEGES THAT CIVILIZED FREE COUNTRIES HAVE ALWAYS AFFORDED WORKING WOMEN AND MOTHERS IN ORDER TO PRESERVE THE FAMILY UNIT AS THE BASIC INSTITUTION OF A HEALTHY SOCIETY.

EQUAL PAY for EQUAL WORK can now be obtained through existing legislation.
Women are already protected against discrimination by the Equal Pay Act, the Civil Rights Acts of '64 and '68, the Equal Opportunity Employment Act of 1972, and the 5th, 14th and 19th Amendments!

Unit Four

Concepts of Formal Debate

Chapter 11

The Debate Proposition

* Types of Propositions
* Examples of Debate Propositions
* Requirements of a Debate Proposition
* Defining the Proposition's Terms
* Conclusion
* References
* Practicum

Having laid the basic theoretical groundwork for the study of argumentative communication, we can begin to examine our topic from a more pragmatic viewpoint. Unit 4, "Concepts of Formal Debate," focuses on contemporary academic debate practices, providing observations and suggestions for effective competitive debating. We begin our examination of academic debate by examining the debate proposition, the topic about which the debate encounter takes place. Since effective oral communication requires that both speaker and listener deal with the same subject for discussion, academic debate requires its debaters to deal with the same proposition or topic within a given debate. This requirement, then, guarantees that the arguments, counterarguments, and so on offered by all debaters will pertain to the same general topic area, thereby maximizing effective communication interchange.

Types of Propositions

In looking at all the possible topics that people could debate about, three general categories or types of propositions or topics emerge: propositions of *fact*, *value*, and *policy*.[1] Each type of proposition merits brief explanation, although academic debate generally employs propositions of policy.

A *proposition of fact* asserts that something is true or factual. For example, "Resolved: that people in the United States bought more coffee in 1973 than in 1976" is a proposition of fact. If such a topic were to be debated, those on the affirmative would contend that that statement was true — yes, people did buy more coffee in 1973 than they did in 1976. Those on the negative, however, would contend that that statement was not true, that people did not buy more coffee in 1973 than in 1976. Theoretically, propositions of fact are easily settled because of the inherent nature of the proposition. Something is either true or false, and the determination of the question of fact quickly resolves the dispute. Practically, however, propositions of fact are not that easy to settle, because (a) there is a wide divergence of opinion as to what actually constitutes a fact and (b) there would be greatly conflicting bits of evidence presented by the debaters to support their particular position on the topic. The listener would have to decide which facts presented were better than other facts presented; that is, which facts were more accurate than other facts — a very difficult kind of decision. For that major reason, and because most factual topics are relatively boring (do you really care how much coffee was bought by Americans in *any* year?), propositions of fact are rarely used in academic debate.

A ***proposition of value*** asserts some type of judgment or worth statement about something. "Resolved: that the Equal Rights Amendment is detrimental to the cause of true womanhood" exemplifies a proposition of value, a statement that presents some kind of evaluative judgment. In many of our everyday decisions, we make many kinds of value judgments much akin to a proposition of value, and our own experiences document how difficult it often is to deal with such items. Your parents didn't want you hanging around with Fred because he was a "bad boy"; you went to a certain college because it had a "pleasant environment"; you take classes you don't like because your adviser assures that "they are good for you." Okay, now what do those various statements mean? What is a *bad* boy? What is a *pleasant* environment? And what is *good* for you? Those questions exemplify the difficulty presented by a proposition of value. Since all of us are different, our personal systems of value are going to differ, making it very difficult for us to agree upon a common criterion for evaluation. The topic dealing with the ERA illustrates this point.

Values and the ERA

Resolved: that the Equal Rights Amendment is detrimental to the cause of true womanhood.

Abner: I agree with that statement. After all, women should be home cooking, not running around burning their underwear.

Louise: Hey, very few women have done that. Get real, and besides, the ERA allows us to be the full human beings with full potential that we have the right to be.

Abner: Women have been complete human beings ever since the beginning, but now they're losing their femininity.

Louise: You know, you're a sexist, that's all. What is femininity, anyway?

Abner: It means wearing dresses, keeping quiet, and walking two steps behind men!

Louise: I'm surprised you don't live in a cave. You, Tarzan; me, Jane!

Abner and Louise did not agree upon what was true womanhood, so they found it impossible to carry on a meaningful dialogue about the ERA being potentially detrimental to the cause of true womanhood. They had divergent concepts of what a woman was and should be, causing them to be unable to deal with the same type of value configuration. Abner and Louise could talk on for hours, but they never would really debate that topic, because they would not be talking about the same things. This demonstrates the difficulties posed for debaters in dealing with propositions of value.[2]

Because of problems with both propositions of fact and value, most academic debates utilize the *proposition of policy*, a statement that suggests some action should or should not be taken. A recent interscholastic debate topic illustrates the proposition of policy — Resolved: that the federal government should guarantee a minimum annual income for each family unit. Within a proposition of policy, a specific action is urged, and those on the affirmative advocate the adoption of the resolution. In this case, the affirmative would support the notion that the federal government should guarantee a minimum income yearly to each family unit. Conversely, those upholding the negative position would oppose the institution of any guaranteed annual scheme.

You should note that a proposition of policy not only contains an element of action (somebody should do something), but it also contains elements of the propositions of fact and value. Quite literally, issues that are pertinent to both a proposition of fact and a proposition of value will be found to be pertinent to broader propositions of policy. This can be exemplified by examining what would happen in a debate centering upon the guaranteed annual income resolution.

First, the affirmative advocates would have to justify implementing some type of guaranteed income scheme. They would have to demonstrate some kind of *need* for having a guaranteed annual income. How would this need be demonstrated? In all probability, the affirmative advocates would contend (*a*) that poverty exists in the United States, (*b*) that poverty is harmful, (*c*) that the status quo antipoverty measures are ineffective, and, therefore, (*d*) that a new system of a guaranteed annual income is needed to eliminate the problem of poverty. To demonstrate specifically *a*, *b*, and *c*, the affirmative would gather and present specific, factual evidence that proves the existence of poverty, its harm, and the ineffectiveness of current antipoverty programs. Thus, facts would be assembled to justify the adoption of a guaranteed income policy — the same types of materials that form the underpinning of a proposition of fact.

Second, a proposition of policy contains elements of a proposition of value, because both the affirmative and negative will issue arguments that relate to our own value systems. For example, the affirmative might argue that "eight million people in this country are slowly dying from malnutrition and improper diets" in the presentation of a need for a guaranteed annual income. The affirmative argument assumes that the listeners would agree internally that having people die from malnutrition and the like was bad, that it is not good to have people die needlessly and unnecessarily. The affirmative argument assumes that the value inherent in that argument will align itself with one of our own personal values. Similarly, the negative might contend that "a guaranteed income should not be implemented because billions of our tax dollars would be wasted," thereby assuming that our value system abhors the wasting of hard-earned money. So, the impact of both the overall positions and the specific arguments of the affirmative and negative advocates is based on various value judgments, indicating that any proposition of policy contains materials inherent in any proposition of value.

Because propositions of policy contain elements of fact and value, and because propositions of policy provide the competing advocates the greatest amount of latitude in the construction of specific arguments and overall argumentative positions, academic debates generally use propositons of policy for their topics. Since both high school and college debate activities cover the major part of the academic year (at least from September through late April), it is necessary to have topics that are broad enough to allow the debaters to deal with those topics meaningfully for that long period of time.

Examples of Debate Propositions

Since competitive academic debate continues throughout most of the academic year, it is necessary that the policy propositions used be of interest and breadth to maintain effective and lively argumentative encounters for that length of time. In addition, so that tournaments can be held wherein debaters from different schools can compete against one another, one national topic is used for most competitive academic debates.[3] The following is the list of the official intercollegiate debate resolutions from 1969–1970 through 1979–1980; notice the varied topics that these resolutions cover:

1969–1970 — Resolved: that the federal government should grant annually a specific percentage of its income tax revenue to the state governments.

1970–1971 — Resolved: that the federal government should adopt a program of compulsory wage and price controls.

1971–1972 — Resolved: that greater controls should be imposed on the gathering and utilization of information about United States citizens by government agencies.

1972–1973 — Resolved: that the federal government should provide a program of comprehensive medical care for all citizens.

1973–1974 — Resolved: that the federal government should control the supply and utilization of energy in the United States.

1974–1975 — Resolved: that the power of the presidency should be significantly curtailed.

1975–1976 — Resolved: that the federal government should adopt a comprehensive program to control land use in the United States.

1976–1977 — Resolved: that the federal government should significantly strengthen the guarantee of consumer product safety required of manufacturers.

1977–1978 — Resolved: that law enforcement agencies in the United States should be given significantly greater freedom in the investigation and/or prosecution of felony crimes.

1978–1979 — Resolved: that the federal government should implement a program which guarantees employment opportunites for all U. S. citizens in the labor force.

1979–1980 — Resolved: that the federal government should significantly strengthen the regulation of mass media communication in the United States.

The last four intercollegiate debate topics were subject to a recent development in the use of a national debate topic at the college level. For a number of years, and increasingly since the late 1960s, many communication teachers and theorists have complained about the interpretation of the national intercollegiate debate proposition.[4] Specifically, many have become upset with the way in which affirmative advocates put together debate cases to justify the adoption of the resolution; many felt that the justifications presented were, at best, only marginally related to the actual topic area implied within the debate resolution. This unhappiness reached its peak during the 1975–1976 academic year's debates on the control of land use, when some affirmative teams attempted to justify the resolution (Resolved: that the federal government should adopt a comprehensive program to control land use in the United States) by considering such apparently irrelevant issues as the legalization of prostitution, the growing of marijuana, and the legalization of homosexuality. Thus, since 1976, a "parameter statement" has been issued along with the resolution designed to define more clearly the intended interpretation of the resolution. So, the following is the complete statement of both resolution and parameter for the intercollegiate debate topics from 1976 through 1980:

1976–1977 — Resolved: that the federal government should significantly strengthen the guarantee of consumer product safety required of manufacturers.

Parameter: this policy proposition calls for the expansion of existing requirements or adoption of additional requirements to reduce the risk to purchasers of manufactured items.

1977–1978 — Resolved: that law enforcement agencies in the United States should be given significantly greater freedom in the investigation and/or prosecution of felony crimes.

Parameter: this policy proposition calls for legitimizing investigative and/or prosecutorial procedures (prior to conviction) currently disallowed by court decisions or prohibited by law, for one or more of the following law enforcement agencies: state and local police, FBI, and/or the offices of the district attorney, state attorney general, and the U.S. attorney general.

1978–1979 — Resolved: that the federal government should implement a program which guarantees employment opportunities for all U.S. citizens in the labor force.

Parameter: this policy proposition calls for the federal government to provide employment opportunities, directly or indirectly, through the public and/or private sectors, for all U.S. citizens who are willing and able to work.

1979–1980 — Resolved: that the federal government should significantly strengthen the regulation of mass media communication in the United States.

Parameter: this policy proposition calls for federal control over television, radio, print, and/or film industries to be substantially increased.

National debate topics at both the high school and college levels reflect issues of current national importance. Issues of war and peace, the economy, justice, social equality, governmental surveillance, and many others have been debated by this country's college debaters during the past ten years. The topics alone suggest that competitive debating is a most interesting and challenging activity.

Requirements of a Debate Proposition

Putting together a good debate proposition is a more difficult task than it might initially appear. To be considered good, a proposition should meet the following eight criteria, which are applicable to debate propositions for club meetings, political gatherings, and the academic debate contest:

1. The proposition should clearly have two sides with each having fairly equal amounts of supportive evidence available for use by the speakers. A proposition, for example, that called for the legalization of murder would not meet this test, because it would be nearly impossible to support reasonably the affirmative position. Our moral, ethical, and legal constructs are such that to advocate the legalization of murder would be a ridiculous, impossible persuasive attempt.

2. The proposition must deal with an item of current interest that will not, in all probability, be solved or eliminated during the course of the debates. Certainly, the item must be of interest, otherwise debates would be mere exercises of technique with a minimal amount of relevant

substance. To debate an out-of-date item would be a waste of time. Also, great care must be taken to select a topic that will not have its legitimacy eliminated during the course of debates upon that topic. For example, during the 1964-1965 debate season, the college debate topic was "Resolved: that the federal government should establish a national program of public work for the unemployed." Unfortunately, midway through the academic year, the United States achieved full employment, thereby eliminating the major justification for the adoption of the resolution.

3. The proposition must be definite and clear, completely free of ambiguous terms — a task much easier stated than accomplished. What is clear and unambiguous to me might be very unclear and confusing to you. That is why the specific wording of the proposition is of such importance. Occasionally, of course, propositions will not be worded appropriately, exemplified at the college level in the 1971–1972 academic year, when the Speech Communication Association's Committee on Intercollegiate Discussion and Debate had to reword the national college debate proposition in midyear to eliminate confusion created by the improper wording of the initial resolution. The use of parameter statements also is designed to improve clarity and to reduce ambiguity.

4. The proposition (following "Resolved: that . . .") must be a complete sentence that is stated in the affirmative. Incomplete sentences, of course, would create constant confusion regarding the intent and interpretation of the proposition, and a negatively stated resolution (Resolved: that the United States should *not* adopt a guaranteed annual income) would be confusing and would reverse the traditional roles of the affirmative and negative advocates. You will note that the college topics listed are complete sentences and that all are stated most definitely in the affirmative — that somebody *should do* something.

5. The proposition must specifically propose a definite, concrete course of action to be followed. A proposition that said we should consider doing something or we should think about doing something would be of minimal value. We can, in fact, consider or think about nearly anything we choose, but only specific courses of action are applicable to reasonable and realistic decision making.

6. The proposition must encompass only one central idea. For example, debating a topic that had two or more ideas (Resolved: that the United States should adopt a guaranteed annual income and legalize prostitution) would be an argumentative nightmare. Which idea would you give greater emphasis to? Could you relate those two ideas to each other? Which idea is of greater significance? You will note that the sample debate propositions are limited to one major idea each.

7. The proposition must place the burden of proof on the advocates of the affirmative, and they must call for some sort of change within the status quo. To affirm the resolution means to advocate change; therefore, the proposition must be so worded as to force the affirmative to justify some type of change.

8. Finally, the proposition must place the burden of presumption upon the advocates of the negative, causing them to support in some manner or another the status quo. The proposition must be worded so that the negative advocates oppose the change supported by the affirmative advocates.

As you can see, wording an effective debate proposition is a difficult and time-consuming task; it is not something that can be done lightly and quickly. Great deals of thought and research go into the topic selection process for academic debate encounters at both the high school and the college levels.

Defining the Proposition's Terms

Even the most clearly worded and well-phrased debate proposition will require some definitions by those who debate that proposition. Since all of us are different individuals, and since language itself is an imprecise medium of thought transmission, it is essential that the terms of the resolution be clearly defined to ensure that all debaters agree upon what is meant by the proposition's phraseology. It is the specific burden of the affirmative advocates to define the terms within the resolution, and the negative advocates have the right to accept those definitions or to oppose the affirmative's definitions and propose alternative definitions. In any case, three rules for defining debate propositions ought to be followed, regardless of the context in which a debate takes place.

First, debaters should define only those terms within a resolution that appear to be unclear and might be confusing; you do not need to define every word within the debate proposition. Imagine how absurd it would be to define *that*, *the*, and *a* within the proposition, Resolved: that the United States should implement a guaranteed annual income.

Second, it is not necessary to define terms that are commonly defined in standard language usage. Thus, it is unnecessary to define such terms as *the United States* or *the federal government*, because all of us consensually agree beforehand what those terms are intended to mean. To take the time to define such obvious terms is to waste time.

Third, all propositions of policy, the standard proposition type for both high school and college academic debates, contain the word *should* within the wording of the proposition. You will discover that every other proposition of policy listed within this chapter says that somebody *should* do something. By common agreement for many, many years, "should" is defined within debate encounters as "ought to be but not necessarily will be," meaning that the affirmative advocates need only argue that their proposed changes *ought to be* implemented but that they do not have the responsibility of proving that their proposed changes *will be* implemented. Since all propositions of policy call for future action, it would be impossible for any affirmative team to prove that something will happen in the future; at best, all they can do is argue that it ought to happen in the future.

After deciding what terms within a proposition merit definition, you need to decide how you will define them. You have to select a method for defining those terms. Contrary to a popular misconception, you may define words other than by simply going to the nearest dictionary and looking them up; in fact, there are six major methods for defining terms:

1. by usage — how the word or term is generally used within society
2. by derivation — how the word came to be defined from its roots in such other languages as Latin and Greek
3. By comparison — how the word or term is closely related to or is similar to another word or term
4. By contrast — how the word or term is diametrically different from another word or term

5. by authority — how the word or term is defined or used by experts in the topic-related area
6. by dictionary — how the word or term is defined according to a standard reference dictionary such as *Webster's* or *Black's Law*.[5]

Because how the proposition's terms are defined will play an important role in both the substance and quality of all debate encounters, it is imperative that you allocate sufficient time and study to a thorough definition of terms. To give you an idea of how a full-blown definitional analysis might look, consider a sample of such an analysis as prepared by this writer for a group of high school debaters in 1977. Those debaters had just completed a year's debates on the topic of penal reform; now they were preparing to debate a topic dealing with the system of health care in the United States. As you read this sample definitional analysis, you should be able to note that quite a bit of thought and research must go into the effective definition of terms.

Topic

Resolved: that the federal government should establish a comprehensive program to regulate the health care system in the United States.

Sample Definitional Analysis

In looking at this topic, the first item of business is to define all unclear or confusing words or terms within the resolution. A quick glance indicates that there are several such items within this topic. Those of you who have debated extensively on this year's topic of penal reform will see immediately that another "comprehensive program" is mandated within the structure of next year's resolution, just the same as the penal reform topic. Those of you who had endless haggles over what a comprehensive program was will have another year of similar struggles. The topic contains three terms that require definitional examination: *comprehensive program*, *to regulate*, and *health care system*, and each term is considered below.

A *comprehensive program* means a plan or proposal that either includes much or deals with all or many of the relevant details (see *Webster's* or *Black's Law* for fuller citations of this and other definitional notes). The significance of this term lies not so much with its inherent definition but with its placement within the wording of the resolution. As with the wording of the penal reform topic, the new topic does *not* require the affirmative to propose comprehensive health care; the topic requires a "comprehensive *program*" that will regulate the health care system in the United States. This is an important distinction that must be made and kept clear by the debaters. Far too many debates have been muddled this year by the failure of both debaters and their coaches and judges to recognize the difference created by the simple location of *comprehensive* in relation to the other terms within the topic.

The required comprehensive program must be widespread; that is, it must cover many, if not most, of the items involved in the creation and implementation of that program. It may not deal with only one minor aspect of any program; it must be comprehensive in the establishment of that program. Thus, the affirmative has the same responsibility as a federal government policymaker: the complete range of program inception, establishment, and implementation falls within the advocate's prerogative. However, as with any academic debate topic, the affirmative, unless presenting a case based upon attitudinal inherency, does not have to guarantee that the proposal will be adopted. The affirmative has only the responsibility to show that it should ("ought to, but not necessarily will") be adopted.

To regulate has several definitions, and these differences may prove to be important in examining the affirmative's burden in upholding the requirements of the resolution. For example, *to regulate* may mean "to control, direct, or govern," which implies that the federal government would serve as a virtual overseer of the comprehensive program. Thus, the affirmative easily could suggest the creation of another federal-level regulatory body that would direct a national program, merely another cog in the vast machinery of the federal bureaucracy. On the other hand, *to regulate* may mean "to make uniform, methodical, orderly," and this places greater responsibilities upon the affirmative advocate. Under this type of definition, the affirmative case must be considerably more detailed in creating a uniform program of health care service. Since the responsibilities vary significantly, it would be wise to define this term carefully, either overtly or operationally, with a great deal of thought.

Health care system will prove, however, to be the real killer in next year's topic. It is a killer because of its expansive breadth and difficulty to understand. David Mechanic, in *Public Expectations and Health Care*, pages 24–25, has seen this definitional problem:

> It is not easy to sketch out the broad outline of the health care system in the United States. The health sector is extremely large, complex, and varied; and there are few studies that provide broad descriptive information on even one locality, much less the vast range of variations in different geographic areas. . . .
>
> The three major components of the health services system are manpower, facilities, and technologies. About 3.5 million people work in the health sector, encompassing a wide range of skill levels and competence. Although the most attention is given to physicians and nurses, they are only a minority of all health workers and, in recent decades, there has been a great proliferation of new technical jobs relevant to the delivery of health services. . . .
>
> Facilities refer to all physical locations in which patients are treated or which provide ancillary assistance or support in their treatment. The most basic facility, of course, is the hospital; but also included within this concept are physicians' premises, research and clinical laboratories, nursing and convalescent homes, locations for the training of health manpower and the like. . . .
>
> The concept of technology — perhaps the most difficult and most important of the three components — refers to any set of operations that is believed to be instrumental in the recognition, treatment or prevention of disease or disability. These operations may be encompassed within a set of technical facilities such as computers, laboratory tests, diagnostic instruments, or drugs. But technologies also include physical, psychological, and social theories that direct the approach of health workers toward their clients. Technologies thus include such varied operations as x-ray, prescription of insulin, psychotherapy, the

> social organization of the hospital ward, and so on. . . .
>
> The health care sector, of course, is not a tight little island; it is closely interwoven with other aspects of the economy and social life, and these relationships must be grasped to appreciate the whole picture.

Therefore, Mechanic's lengthy description of this country's health care system points out one clear fact: *health care system* is even more complex and involved than was *penal reform*, encompassing large numbers of personnel, activities, services, and physical and psychological hardware and processes. It is such complexity that will make *health care system* the critical term in the resolution.

Simply recognizing that the term is varied and complex, however, does not eliminate the need for definition. After all, if confusion exists as to what *health care system* means, how can a meaningful debate be carried on? A concern for proper definition and a precise definition must be manifested by the debater if a reasonable clash of ideas and arguments is to result. Moreover, the complexity of this term demonstrates that simple dictionary definitions may not prove to be completely helpful in clarifying meaning.

By turning to *Webster's*, we would find the following definitions of the words that compose *health care system*:

> *health*: dealing with physical or mental well-being
>
> *care*: charge, protection, custody; a responsibility
>
> *system*: a series of things related or connected to form a whole.

Putting this together, we might define *health care system* as "a series of items that provide for the protection of an individual's physical and mental well-being." Isn't that helpful? Not really — that definition is so broad and vague as to be almost without debatable value. Instead of approaching that term's definition in that manner, you may wish to cite authorities' operational definitions to enhance clarity and specificity. For example, several parts of the previously quoted section from Mechanic's *Public Expectations and Health Care* could serve very nicely as your definitional base of health care system. There are, of course, other such experts and definitions. Sobel's *Health Care* (page 1) provides a more statistically oriented and hardware-oriented definition:

> The U.S. health-care system comprises some 325,000 doctors, 750,000 nurses, 7,000 hospitals, 3 million beds in hospitals or other inpatient facilities, 4.4 million workers in a variety of health-related occupations and an annual expenditure estimated at more than $105 billion, about 8% of the gross national product, or at least $500 for every American.

Before rushing into *your* definition of *health care system*, it would be a beneficial idea to read pages 4 through 9 in Andreano and Weisbrod's *American Health Policy*. Those few pages provide some interesting insights into answering the question, what is the health system?[6]

Defining the propositions' terms is an important part of effective debating; it is something that must be done skillfully and completely. As the preceding definitional analysis demonstrated, there is more than one way to define what a word or term means; you need to be aware of all possible definitions and not rely exclusively upon simple dictionary definitions.

Conclusion

Debates may use either propositions of fact, value, or policy; most academic debates use propositions of policy because they are broader, more interesting, and better suited to the give-and-take process of argumentative communication. The debate proposition serves as the foundation for clash within the debate; its proper wording delineates the positions and responsibilities of both the affirmative and the negative advocates. Because of its central importance, the specific wording of the proposition should be studied carefully, and sufficient time and energy should be devoted to the effective definition of the proposition's possible meanings and interpretations.

References

1. Some debate theorists claim there is a fourth propositional type: the proposition of definition. This is not covered within the text, because (*a*) few, if any, debates have been held using that type of topic and (*b*) arguments over definitions occur within the other propositions of fact, value, and policy. Other theorists prefer the classifications of "judgment" and "policy" as advocated by Terris. See Walter F. Terris, "The Classification of the Argumentative Proposition," *Quarterly Journal of Speech* 49 (October 1963): 266–273. The traditional classifications of fact, value, and policy can be subsumed in Terris's two-part classification.

2. It should be noted that since about 1975 there has been an increased interest in the possible use of propositions of value at the intercollegiate debate level. The 1976 Bicentennial Youth Debates, a national competitive activity created to celebrate America's two-hundreth birthday, did utilize propositions of value with apparent success. CEDA, the Cross-Examination Debate Association, has been experimenting with value propositions — again with apparent success.

3. At the high school level, two national organizations, the National Forensic League (NFL) and the National University Extension Association (NUEA) issue national high school debate topics after polling their respective memberships as to topic preference. In most cases, the NFL and the NUEA select the exact same topic; however, in 1977, although both organizations had topics within the same general area of health care, the wordings of their respective topics differed significantly.

At the college level, the Speech Communication Association Committee on Intercollegiate Discussion and Debate issues the national college debate topic after polling the country's college and university forensic directors.

4. See, for example, David W. Shepard, "Burden of What?" *Journal of the American Forensic Association* 9 (Winter 1973): 362; John Baird, "The President's Message," *The Forensic* 6 (May 1975): 26; and Evan Ulrey, "The President's Message," *The Forensic* 61 (January 1976): 3.

5. It should be noted that, in the past several years, there has been an increase in the use of operational definitions of terms at the interscolastic and intercollegiate debate levels, meaning that the resolution's terms are operationally defined by the specific components of the affirmative's particularized proposal for change. This notion is discussed in chapter 13.

6. From "Examining Health Care," *Debate Issues* (May 1977). Reprinted with the permission of James E. Sayer, editor of *Debate Issues*.

Practicum

1. To see the prevalence of deeply held values in debate encounters, do some research to discover the differing viewpoints regarding the Equal Rights Amendment (ERA). Find a position statement from the National Organization for Women (NOW); then find an anti-ERA statement by that proposal's leading opponent, Phyllis Schlafly. Not only will you note a significant difference of opinion concerning the ERA itself, you also should note significantly differing value systems underlying those positions.

Now can you see the importance of carefully wording the debate proposition? Given the different values, attitudes, and opinions all of us possess, it is essential that we, at the very least, debate the same topic to hold miscommunication to a minimum.

2. Not all debate topics have to deal with foreign policy, domestic woes, and other such heavy topics. On the contrary, topics should be modified to meet the circumstances surrounding the debate. For example, to have students enjoy debating for the sheer sake of debating, this writer has used such "fun" topics as, Resolved: that the horse is smarter than the pig — a proposition of fact that has hilarious overtones —and, Resolved: that women should walk two steps behind men — a proposition of policy loaded with many value judgments.

Try constructing debate propositions for the following groups:

- a men's business club that meets twice a month
- a women's club that meets weekly
- a religious conference that meets once a year
- the annual meeting of the American Medical Association

Do your proposed topics adhere to the eight criteria noted within this chapter?

Chapter 12

Formal Debate Burdens

Many people believe there exists a set of formal, official rules for intercollegiate and interscholastic debate, an equivalent of the Ten Commandments for formal argumentative encounters. Unfortunately, this is a mistaken belief, as there are no official rules for debate as such. Instead, debate encounters proceed today in accord with customs and traditions developed over the passage of many years. With the possible exception of the requirement that the affirmative advocates support the proposition in one way or another and the negative advocate opposes it, there are no hard and fast rules for debate. Everything else is merely custom or tradition; most of debate's procedures are not chiseled in stone.

In this chapter, we examine several of these traditional procedures, which have been used in competitive debate encounters for many decades. Although these debate burdens were not carried from Mount Sinai by Moses, they do serve like rules, because debate practitioners and critics expect the competing advocates to uphold their respective burdens within every debate encounter. These various burdens then are translated into the particular speaking responsibilities to be met by both the affirmative and negative advocates, a topic to be addressed in the following chapter. We shall begin our examination of the seven major debate burdens by first examining the overall structure of competitive debate.

Debate as Equalizer

Unlike most daily argumentative encounters, wherein either you or the other person commands a majority of the speaking time, competitive debate, at both the college and high school levels, provides an equalizing opportunity for the presentation and refutation of argument. That does not mean, of course, that all arguments carry equal weight or that the affirmative advocates' position is inherently argumentatively equal to the position advanced by the negative advocates. Instead, debate serves as the great equalizer of time; both sides have an equal amount of time for the presentation of their own arguments and for the refutation of their opponents' arguments. Unlike your daily argumentative encounters, no one side predominates timewise in formal debate encounters.

Examine again the structure of a typical Oxford-style intercollegiate debate:

First affirmative constructive speech	10 minutes
First negative constructive speech	10 minutes
Second affirmative constructive speech	10 minutes
Second negative constructive speech	10 minutes
First negative rebuttal speech	5 minutes
First affirmative rebuttal speech	5 minutes
Second negative rebuttal speech	5 minutes
Second affirmative rebuttal speech	5 minutes

You will note that both the affirmative and negative teams have an equal amount of speaking time, thirty minutes per team; each advocate of both the affirmative and the negative has an equal fifteen-minute speaking time allotment (one ten-minute constructive speech and one five minute rebuttal speech). The very structure of competitive debate does equalize time availability for the presentation and refutation of arguments.

However, as you examined the structure of a typical college debate, you might have observed that the affirmative both begins and ends the debate; the first affirmative constructive speech opens the debate, and the second affirmative rebuttal speech closes the debate. At first, that might appear to give the affirmative a tremendous advantage in that argumentative confrontation. After all, the structure of debate does give the affirmative both the first and last word. Therefore, the debate structure does give the affirmative an advantage, doesn't it?

The answer to that question is no, as many experienced affirmative advocates would be willing to attest. While the affirmative does gain some advantage by beginning and ending the debate, this advantage is sufficiently offset by the *negative block*, the fifteen-minute chunk of negative speaking time composed of the second negative constructive speech and the first negative rebuttal speech. As you can see by looking at the debate's structure, this fifteen-minute negative tme block is followed by a five-minute affirmative speech, the first affirmative rebuttal. Thus, the three to one time advantage of the negative block versus the first affirmative rebuttal speech serves to counterbalance the affirmative's advantage of opening and closing the debate. The affirmative's advantage is, therefore, offset by the negative's advantage, resulting in an equalized situation.

The prerogatives of the competing advocates also demonstrate the equalizing nature of contest debate. Although the affirmative has the advantage of picking virtually any reasons to support the debate propositon, the negative has the equivalent advantage of selecting a variety of responses to the affirmative arguments. That is, although the affirmative advocates do have the advantage of knowing what their arguments in support of the proposition will be, they do not know how the negative will respond to those arguments. Conversely, although the negative does not know beforehand the particulars of the affirmative's argumentative case, the negative does have a broad arsenal of possible responses, plus the negative always possesses the potent argument of inherency. Again, the affirmative's advantage is offset by the negative's advantage, and the very structure of debate serves to equalize the strengths and weaknesses of the competing advocates.

Thus, unlike everyday argumentative encounters, one of contest debate's primary strengths is its equalization provided to competing arguments, issues, and positions. Neither the affirmative nor the negative has a structural advantage over the other. Both have an equal opportunity to present and refute arguments, to gain a favorable decision. If nothing else, academic debate epitomizes the philosophy of free speech so fundamental to our nation; academic debate guarantees that both sides will have an equal opportunity to be heard and that no one side or argument is given an unfair advantage over another. Decisions, therefore, can be based on a one-to-one comparison and contrast of arguments; decisions will not be influenced by a preponderance of time or by a weighted structure that favors one side of the competing advocates. Contest debate is the finest equalizer of conflicting arguments.[1] Thus, contest debate provides an excellent vehicle for the honing of argumentative skills to be used in real-life argumentative encounters.

Traditional Debate Burdens

In maintaining this sense of equilibrium, custom and tradition have given us seven major responsibilities or burdens that debaters must uphold in traditional academic debate. Three of these burdens rest with the affirmative advocates; two rest with the negative advocates; and two are shared by both the affirmative and negative. We shall examine these burdens as they are appropriately grouped.

Affirmative Burdens

Because the affirmative advocates have the responsibility of initiating the debate encounter in their support of the debate proposition, it is logical that the three main affirmative burdens reflect this responsibility.

1. *The Burden of Proof.* As previewed in chapter 7, the affirmative advocates have to uphold the burden of proof; they must demonstrate why some type of change is justified, why the proposition should be adopted. Each academic debate resolution forces the affirmative to advocate some type of change, and the affirmative, to uphold the burden of proof, must justify making this change. For example, during the 1978-1979 academic year, the intercollegiate debate topic was, Resolved: that the federal government should implement a program which guarnatees employment opportunities for all U.S. citizens in the labor force. By the wording of that proposition, the affirmative had to devise some type of system whereby the federal government somehow guaranteed employment opportunities, and that proposed system, a most definite change from the status quo, had to be completely justified by the affirmative speakers. Those advocating change have the burden of proof to provide a reasonable rationale for change, as well as a reasonable proposal for effectuating the desired change.

If the affirmative fails to uphold its burden of proof, if the affirmative fails to show why the desired change is warranted, then the debate decision must be awarded to the negative advocates, those who defend the status quo. As in a court of law, the status quo is presumed innocent until proven guilty, and the affirmative must substantiate their arguments to make their indictments stick. Without a reasonable and justified rationale for change, no change can be made, and the status quo will be retained.[2]

2. *Burden of Definition.* Because the affirmative initiates the debate encounter by supporting the proposition, it is the affirmative's burden to define the words and terms within the debate proposition so that meaningful argument can proceed. Regardless of how the terms are defined, the affirmative has the primary responsibility of defining them so that argumentative clarity is ensured from the onset of the debate. Of course, the negative has the right to challenge affirmative definitions, providing justified substitute definitions in their place, but the initial responsibility of term definition rests with the affirmative.

Not too many years ago, it was common practice to have affirmative teams define nearly every word or term within the debate proposition and then have the proposition restated in terms of its various definitions. Thankfully, this practice is no longer followed, as it consumed a great deal of time and the practical necessity of defining such terms as *United States* and *federal govemment* was nonexistent. Today, only those terms that are unclear or that might cause confusion need to be defined, and it is the responsibility of the affirmative to offer appropriate definitions for such terms.

One final note should be added concerning the burden of definition. Not only must the affirmative define terms to ensure argumentative clarity, but all definitions so offered must be of a sane and reasonable nature. Occasionally, affirmative speakers attempt to gain an advantage by defining terms outrageously (defining *land use* as prostitution, for example) in the hope that the negative speakers will not be able to combat an affirmative case built upon such a weird definition of terms. Remember, the negative does have the right to object to such unjustified definitions, because the purpose of debate is not to have the affirmative so define terms as to make its position undebatable, nor are definitions to be countenanced that make a mockery of argumentative discourse.[3]

3. *Burden of Prima Facie Case.* The final exclusive affirmative debate burden is to present a *prima facie* case, with *case* being defined as the total position or collection of arguments offered in support of the proposition. A *prima facie* case is sufficiently strong to uphold the burden of proof prior to negative refutation. That is, the affirmative must present a *prima facie* case during the first affirmative constructive speech; there must be sufficient justification presented at that time that, if no negative speech were presented, the listener would have no choice but to decide in favor of the affirmative's position. This burden is put on the affirmative for two reasons.

First, since the affirmative generally advocates change in the status quo, it has the responsibility to initiate the debate encounter by supporting the proposition. If the affirmative did not present a *prima facie* case, the very impression of which apparently justified the desired change, then there would be no need to continue with the debate. This same responsibility rests with the prosecution in a court of law. If the prosecution fails to present a *prima facie* case against the defendant, then the trial is immediately canceled and the defendant is released.

Second, the affirmative is forced to present a *prima facie* case to prevent an unfair use of the debate's structure. Because the affirmative gets both to start and to close every academic debate encounter, without the *prima facie* requirement, affirmative teams might say little of value during the first three affirmative speeches (first affirmative constructive speech; second affirmative constructive speech; first affirmative rebuttal) and save the best arguments and evidence for the last speech, the second affirmative rebuttal, which has no negative speech following it, thereby precluding negative refutation of the affirmative's true position. The *prima facie* requirement prevents such an unethical practice.

Therefore, in pushing its indictments against the present system, the affirmative must offer sufficient justification for change during the inital affirmative presentation. Without a *prima facie* case, the debate decision must be awarded to the negative.[4]

Negative Burdens

The negative advocates have two major burdens to support, which counterbalance the responsibilities placed upon the affirmative.

1. *Burden of Presumption*. The negative upholds the burden of presumption; to deny the need or justification for change as offered by the affirmative and to support, in one way or another, the workings of the status quo. Since change is not seen to be a good in and of itself, there must be those in the practice of argumentative communication who closely and carefully examine and question the need for proposed changes. In academic debate, this responsibility falls to the negative advocates.

Presumption actually serves as the negative's great advantage, especially since the potent argument of inherency generally acts as the foundation of presumption. The status quo is so large and all-encompassing (after all, it is the sum total of all policies and practices that currently exist) that affirmatives are hard-pressed to find an inherent flaw within the present system that warrants change. Thus, by holding to presumption and strong inherency arguments, the negative forces that affirmative to justify change completely. The methods to be used in upholding presumption are discussed in the following chapter.[5]

2. *Burden of Rebuttal.* This second negative burden often confuses people because of its name. Perhaps it would be better to refer to it as the burden of clash, because it requires the negative to clash directly with the arguments and evidence as offered by the affirmative. The negative cannot develop its own case (again defined as the total position or collection of arguments) irrespective of the affirmative's case.

Public debates of several decades ago exemplified the problems created when the negative was not compelled to shoulder the burden of clash. The affirmative would present a case dealing with topic X and the negative would present its previously prepared case on topic X. Although both cases would, of course, be different because of the contradictory perspectives of the competing advocates, the speakers would not necessarily deal with the same issues. Thus, in discussing the American economy, the affirmative might be concerned about inflation and the negative might deal mainly with employment practices; then there would be little interaction over the same issues. In such a situation, it would be impossible for an observer to render a reasoned decision, because there would be little, if any, debate over the same issues. To eliminate such an occurrence, today's negative advocates must clash directly with the specifics of the affirmative case.

For a negative debate team to fail to uphold this burden guarantees a loss for the negative. Just as the affirmative must present a *prima facie* case that upholds the burden of proof to be able to win any debate encounter, so the negative must uphold the burden of clash. If the negative fails to deal directly with the affirmative case, then the debate decision must be awarded to the affirmative.

Shared Burdens

The final two major academic debate burdens are shared by the affirmative and negative advocates. Both have the responsibility to uphold these burdens in addition to their more particularized individual burdens.

1. *A Burden of Proof.* Whereas the affirmative must uphold *the* burden of proof, both teams must uphold *a* burden of proof, meaning that both debate teams must document and support all arguments presented within their respective cases. You must

remember that there is a difference between an *argument* and an *assertion*. An argument is a well-supported line of reasoning, and an assertion is nothing but unsubstantiated conjecture. Since academic debate mirrors the critical decision-making process, it is essential that decisions be based upon solid and supported reasons. Thus, both teams must document their arguments, giving evidence supporting their positions, to warrant the receipt of the debate's decision. Because a supported argument is infinitely superior to an unsupported assertion, both teams must uphold a burden of proof, exemplifying the age-old dictum of debate that he who asserts must prove — a primary requirement for advocacy in the court of law.

2. *Burden of Progression*. Both the affirmative and the negative have the responsibility to advance the arguments and evidence offered within the debate, constantly extending and building upon preceding arguments and evidence. The structure of debate is such that, theoretically, the eight speeches (four constructive speeches and four rebuttal speeches) allow an observer to see how arguments are refuted and defended, thereby allowing him to render a well-thought-out and tested decision at the conclusion of the debate encounter. If, however, the debaters do not build upon prior arguments and evidence, if the speeches are nothing more than repetitions of past speeches, then the debate stagnates and the eventual decision is not as sound as is desired. Both teams must build upon the arguments of the other.

Conclusion

Academic debate provides a system of equality for the presentation and refutation of arguments. Unlike daily argumentative situations, debate guarantees that all views will be heard and that no one side or position is given an unfair advantage over the other. Debate is the great equalizer of public argument.

In supporting this notion of equality, there are seven major burdens that must be upheld by the competing advocates within each debate encounter. The burdens of proof, of definition, and of *prima facie* case rest with the affirmative. The burdens of presumption and of rebuttal rest with the negative. Both affirmative and negative are responsible for a burden of proof and the burden of progression. See figure 12.1. If the affirmative upholds its three burdens, if the negative upholds its two burdens, and if both teams uphold their shared burdens, then the debate will be lively, interesting, and of significant value to the decision-making process.

Figure 12.1

DEBATE BURDENS		
	AFFIRMATIVE	NEGATIVE
BURDEN OF PROOF (THE)	X	
BURDEN OF DEFINITION	X	
BURDEN OF PRIMA FACIE CASE	X	
BURDEN OF PRESUMPTION		X
BURDEN OF REBUTTAL		X
BURDEN OF PROOF (A)	X	X
BURDEN OF PROGRESSION	X	X

References

1. It was because of the structure of debate, with its competing arguments over significant public issues, that President John Kennedy referred to debate as "the tool of democracy."

2. See Robert P. Newman, "The Inherent and Compelling Need," *The Journal of the American Forensic Association* 2 (May 1965) : 66–71.

3. See David W. Shepard, "Stipulation Definitions and Elementary Logic," *Central States Speech Journal* 24 (Summer 1973): 131–136.

4. See Robert L. Scott, "On the Meaning of the Term *Prima Facie* in Argumentation," *Central States Speech Journal* 12 (Autumn 1960): 33–37.

5. See J. W. Patterson, "The Obligations of the Negative in a Policy Debate," *The Speech Teacher* 11 (September 1962): 208–213.

Practicum

1. Go to your local courthouse while a trial is in session. Try to get there before the actual trial begins; that is, before the arguments and evidence have been presented. Listen carefully to the first attorney's presentation (she will be known either as the prosecutor if this is a criminal trial or as the attorney for the plaintiff if this is a civil procedure). Now, answer these questions:

- Did she present a ***prima facie*** case in your estimation?
- What information or arguments tended to make you accept the prosecution's case?
- Did she adequately uphold the burden of proof to overcome presumption?
- Did the other attorney (attorney for the defense or respondent) charge that a ***prima facie*** case had not been presented?
- Which attorney did the better job of upholding his respective argumentative burdens?

2. Reread the sample debate speeches presented in chapter 7. You should note that the major debate burdens are covered in the main by the arguments and evidence in the two sample speeches. Did the affirmative speaker provide a sufficient rationale for change? Did the negative speaker directly counter that rationale? Which speaker better upheld the argumentative burdens for which he was responsible?

Chapter 13

Duties of Advocacy Speaking

*** Duties of the Affirmative**
*** Types of Affirmative Cases**
*** Duties of the Negative**
*** Types of Negative Cases**
*** The Negative Block and the Affirmative Response**
*** Conclusion**
*** References**
*** Practicum**

Now that we have analyzed the major burdens that must be met by the competing advocates within the structure of formal debate, we may turn our attention to the specific speaking responsibilities of contest debaters. Again, although there are no formal rules that must be followed in academic debate advocacy, custom and tradition do dictate certain procedures and actions. Therefore, the materials presented within this chapter are in accord with time-honored and long-established methods for competing effectively within formal debate encounters.

It must be noted, moreover, that because academic debate is part of the argumentation process debate activity is in a constant state of change and development. Approaches to issues, case structures, and types of acceptable arguments undergo constant change. Specifically at the intercollegiate debate level, there have been more changes in contest debate activity during the past fifteen years than in the preceding several decades. Therefore, you should be aware that, to a certain extent, textbooks on debate theory and practice are inherently out of date. New theories and practices come along so quickly that it is impossible for textbook writers to keep pace. You need to stay attuned to the nuances in debate theory so that your own debate encounters will reflect current thinking and practice. This chapter presents materials pertinent to academic debate through the late 1970s; modifications certainly will occur in the future. Nevertheless, the basics of argumentative advocacy do have permanence, and their viability and effectiveness are equally as important in nonformal argumentative encounters, as well.

Duties of the Affirmative

In examining the functional responsibilities of affirmative advocates in contest debates, it is essential that a difference be delineated between the overall argumentive responsibilities of the affirmative team and the specific responsibilities of the two particular speakers. Accordingly, this section dealing with the duties of the affirmative is divided into two subsections to analyze affirmative team responsibilities and then the particular responsibilities of both affirmative advocates.

Expectations of the Affirmative Team

Overall, the affirmative has the major responsibility of upholding the debate proposition and justifying the desired changes from the status quo in propositions of policy calling for a change in the present system. Specifically, by applying the analysis of the four stock issues, the affirmative must demonstrate some type of need for a change, offer a plan for effecting that change, and show that the plan is not an infeasible approach to the problem under consideration and will accrue additional advantages — or that it will not, at the very least, create disadvantages so large as to negate the beneficial impact of its implementation.[1] In presenting an affirmative case that meets the four stock issues, other particular expectations must be met by the affirmative advocates, and each of these expectations are discussed individually below.

Definitions. The affirmative has the initial responsibility to define the terms of the debate proposition so that both the negative team members and the critic or judge will understand the argumentative intentions of the affirmative. Only those terms that might be confusing if left undefined should be defined, and this is a responsibility of the affirmative team.

In recent years at the intercollegiate debate level, more and more teams have opted for the use of operational definitions, meaning that the specific components of the affirmative plan serve as the virtual definitions of the debate proposition. Although this is an acceptable practice in most instances, operational definitions do not give the affirmative the right to define unfairly or too narrowly the terms of the proposition. Of course, regardless of the type of definition offered, the negative always has the right to challenge any and all definitions they consider to be in error or unjustified.

Significance. Regardless of the wording of the debate proposition or of the particular justification used by the affirmative to call for a change in policy, the rationale for change presented must be significant. That is, the justification for change must be shown to be compelling, in that the problem to be solved or the advantage to be obtained is of such significance that the proposed change must be adopted. In the making of rational, thoughtful decisions, this requirement of significance is most certainly commonsensical. We would not choose to change things unless the issue demanding change were significant; we would not change policies, actions, or attitudes because of some insignificant or trivial item.

In most debate contexts, significance is demonstrated quantitatively though the use of statistics. We are told that a "guaranteed annual income is needed in the United States because more than twenty million people are suffering from the deprivations of poverty." We are told that "the federal government should employ all those currently unemployed because hundreds of thousands of children are virtually starving in households where parents have no jobs." We are told that "the United States must develop a new energy policy because billions of dollars have been lost in paying the high price for oil demanded by the OPEC nations." Twenty million people, hundreds of thousands of children, and billions of dollars — examples of quantified significance in justifications for change. Significance often is an issue of people or dollars.

However, significance is not limited merely to the recitation of statistical data. On the contrary, significance is an important value judgment in all our lives, and affirmative advocates can take advantage of this factor. For example, if the debate propositionn were, Resolved: that the United States should abolish the use of capital punishment, the affirmative might attempt to build a justification for the proposition by contending that capital punishment may take the lives of innocent victims. Such an argument has been offered for years by the opponents to the death penalty, pointing out that capital punishment is irreversible; if a mistake is made, there is no way to correct it because the innocent party, unfortunately, now is dead. That particular argument makes a great deal of sense and appears to be fairly solid until you try to quantify its significance. See how many innocent people have been executed erroneously in the United States, and you will find that you cannot discover millions or even thousands. At most, no more than a handful of innocent people have been executed by error. In that instance, the affirmative would have to base its justification for change upon *qualitative* or *philosophical* significance since there are insufficient numbers to demonstrate quantitative significance. Taking the value-laden position that every human life is sacred, the affirmative would argue that any system that mistakenly takes a life needs to be changed, that no system that erroneously violates the sanctity of human life should be allowed to continue. Although it certainly is easier to develop a justification for change upon quantitative significance, there are topics where quantitative significance is nearly impossible to find. In such situations, the affirmative may demonstrate significance qualitatively or philosophically, and such an argumentative approach, though difficult, is tenable.

Inherency. One of the primary responsibilities of the affirmative is to demonstrate that the rationale for change is inherent, that the status quo cannot overcome the problem or gain the advantage as desired by the affirmative. Quite simply, if the affirmative fails to demonstrate that the rationale for change is inherent, then the negative advocates will contend that there is no need to make a change. After all, they will argue, if the status quo can solve its own shortcomings, there is no justification for changing policy systems. Unlike most other major issues, inherency can determine alone the eventual outcome of a debate. Should the affirmative lose the issue of inherency, then the affirmative will lose that debate — period. While the affirmative might be able to hedge on other issues (justifying a case that is only marginally significant, for example), there is no such latitude for the issue of inherency. It is *the* paramount issue within any debate encounter.

In advancing an inherency indictment, the affirmative has three major types of inherency arguments from which to choose: structural, gap, and attitudinal. The particular type selected should depend upon the nature of the debate proposition and the kind of indictment lodged against the status quo in putting forth the justification for change.[2]

Structural inherency, the type of inherency indictment found most often within academic debate encounters, contends that some problem or flaw exists within the very structure of the *status quo* and prevents that system from eliminating the problem isolated by the affirmative (the stock issue of need) or from gaining the advantage desired by the affirmative. Essentially, structural inherency contends that there is a structural blockage between the status quo and the goal.Thus, the affirmative contends that, since the *status quo* is structurally prevented from solving the problem or accruing the advantage, a new policy system is justified for the desired goal (the elimination of the problem or the accrual of the advantage) to be reached.

In most academic debate situations, the structural blockage isolated by the affirmative is an existent law, regulation, or court decision that, theoretically at least, prevents the status quo from doing what the affirmative contends ought to be done. Guaranteed income proposals were justified, for example, on the grounds that current welfare regulations prevented certain poor people from rising above the government-established poverty line. Thus, the affirmative advocates argued, because the very structure of the status quo prvented the elimination of the poverty problem by those various welfare regulations, a guaranteed income was justified to do that which the status quo was structurally precluded from doing.

The second type of inherency indictment is termed *gap inherency* or *priority inherency*, an indictment based upon the position that the status quo has no policy or concern for the problem under discussion. That is, the issue isolated by the affirmative is said to be outside the purview of the present system's goals, policies, and actions.

The affirmative would attempt to demonstrate that the status quo was unable to deal with the problems under discussion because it lacked appropriate programs and policies for dealing with that specific problem. Therefore, to overcome this deficiency or gap, a new policy as advocated by the affirmative wold be justified to deal with this untouched problem. Gap inherency appears to exist in areas directly affected by new technological developments, an area in which consumer protection legislation and other various safeguards have lagged behind recent technological development.

The final type of inherency, attitudinal inherency, is the most difficult of the three to argue and sustain within an academic debate round. Basically, the affirmative would argue that it is *not* the structure of the status quo that allows or causes the problem to exist, nor that there is a deficiency in status quo coverage in dealing with the problem. Instead, the affirmative would contend that it is the prevalent attitude of the status quo and of its decision makers and policy makers that has either created the problem or allowed it to continue. Even if the status quo has a program or policy designed to deal with the problem, the attitudinal difficulties are so severe that the program or policy is rendered completely ineffective. In this situation, it is an attitude that acts as a roadblock to the progress of the status quo in reaching the goal. The thrust of attitundinal inherency was summed up best by David Ling and Robert Seltzer in *The Journal of the American Forsenic Association:*

> *The present system's inability to achieve a given goal is a function of that system's control by a group of men who are attitudinally opposed to that goal or who find other conflicting goals more desirable.*[3]

Thus, in pressing an attitudinal inherency indictment, the affirmative advocates would attempt to demonstrate that, regardless of the new or modified programs instituted by the status quo, the problem would not be solved because of the countervailing attitude against the solution of the problem. It was argued, for example, that welfare programs would not eliminate poverty, no matter how they might be modified and improved, because many top-level decision makers held the attitude that the poor were lazy and shiftless. With that kind of attitude, it would be impossible for welfare programs to work effectively; therefore, a new policy system was justified to overcome this crippling attitude.

Although the theory of attitudinal inherency makes a great deal of sense and is based upon proven psychosociological constructs (all of us have our actions controlled to some degree by our conscious and unconscious attitudes), it is a most difficult argument to support and defend within the rigors of academic debate. For example, how do you discover the existent attitudes of our policy and decision makers? Can you assume that their actions directly exhibit their attitudes on any given issue? Can you further assume that their public statements really and accurately mirror their unexpressed attitudes (please remember Richard Nixon and his public statements versus his private expressions concerning Watergate)? More importantly, even if the affirmative is able to establish concretely the presence of these negative attitudes, it is the further responsibility of the affirmative to assure us completely that similar negative attitudes will not overwhelm their proposed plan of change. In short, the affirmative must be able to guarantee specifically that negative attitudes will not render their proposal ineffective, and, of course, it is most difficult to be able to ensure things in the future.

Regardless of the type of inherency indictment selected, it is imperative that the affirmative carry the issue of inherency within the debate encounter. The affirmative must be able to demonstrate that the status quo cannot overcome the problem or accrue the advantage as desired by the affirmative to justify the need for change. Again, inherency is so critical an issue that the negative can lose every other issue, but if it wins inherency, then the negative should be awarded the debate decision.

Plan. Besides presenting justification for change, the affirmative also must explicate how a change is to be effectuated, a plan for a change in policy must be presented. The specific wording of the resolution will dictate the major thrust of the plan itself. For example, in the debate resolution, Resolved: that the federal government should implement a program which guarantees employment opportunities for all U.S. citizens in the labor force, the basic requirements of the affirmative plan have been mandated clearly: the affirmative must put together some type of proposal wherein the federal government guarantees employment opportunities. In meeting the requirements of the resolution, the affirmative must indicate fairly specifically such items as (*a*) how the plan is to be put into operation, (*b*) who will control or oversee the plan, (*c*) how the plan is to be financed, and (*d*) how the plan will be enforced — the very issues facing real-life decision makers. Importantly, the affirmative does *not* have to prove that its proposal *will* be adopted; the affirmative has only the responsibility to advocate that it *should* be adopted. Since the affirmative cannot be expected to foretell the future (unless, of course, the case is based upon an attitudinal inherency indictment), it has the responsibility to argue only that the plan ought to be adopted.

Constructing plans to fit affirmative cases is a most difficult chore and should be approached with great care. Far too often debaters spend the majority of their time developing rationales for change and then devote inadequate thought and time to putting together how that change is to be made. The justification for change and the plan must go hand-in-hand; the two areas must fit together neatly to present a credible and functional overall affirmative position. A brilliant justification for change can be scuttled completely by a poorly thought-out and ill-considered plan for effectuating that change.

Solvency. The basic expectation of the affirmative plan is that it be solvent; that is, the plan must deal with the problem or advantage cited by the affirmative advocates within the justification for change. For example, if you were to contend that poverty is a major problem in this country, which warrants our adopting a guaranteed annual income, then your plan for such a guaranteed income *must* eliminate the problem of poverty that you utilized in your justification for change preceding the affirmative plan. In short, the plan must solve the problem isolated by the affirmative or accrue the advantage desired by the affirmative. Without meeting this requirement for solvency, then the entire affirmative proposal is doomed to failure. It makes absolutely no sense to change policy systems to overcome a problem when the new policy system will not solve the problem or do any better than the status quo.

Feasibility. Although the affirmative does not have to prove that its proposal will be adopted in the future, the affirmative must demonstrate that its proposed plan is, in fact, a workable and practical approach to the problem under consideration. Many plans that are solvent simply are impractical, much too impractical, to be implemented. Consider the following:

PROBLEM: Poverty exists in the United States.

PLAN: Kill all people earning less than five thousand dollars per year.

SOLVENCY: Plan solves the problem of poverty by killing all the poor.

Although killing all the poor people certainly would eliminate the structural problem of poverty (there cannot be poverty if all the poor are dead), that is not a very practical approach to problem solving. Aside from the obvious humanitarian objections, that solution provides no long-term relief for the problem. The poor will again be with us in the future; the root causes of poverty have not been affected by that approach.

Affirmative plans must present realistic approaches to the solution of significant societal problems. Although the affirmative is given great latitude by having to argue that its proposal should be adopted but not having to prove that it will be adopted in the future, such latitude does not give the affirmative license to create absurd plans for change. The requirement that plans be practical and workable forces the affirmative to make its policy system consistent with the real world.

Having briefly examined the major expectations of the affirmative team in putting together a complete rationale for change, you now may examine a sample affirmative case. The desired expectations have been noted in the margin to help you visualize how these responsibilities are met by the affirmative advocates.

Sample Affirmative Case

Secretary of Transportation William Coleman observed in Hearings on Railroad Revitalization last summer that "if we are to attain the goal of energy independence, if we are to serve shippers and consumers, we need to rebuild our railroads and rebuild them now."

In agreeing with the secretary of transportation and in response to the question of "How should the U.S. best improve its rail service system?" we are most pleased to offer our proposal based on the following in-depth analysis of rail service in the U.S. today.

Observation I. Rail Service Is a Vital Part of U.S. Transportation

The essential character of American railroads is seen through two lines of analysis:

(A) *Rails Are a significant mover of freight*

Secretary Coleman tells us that "despite many years of decline, the railroads still carry nearly as much freight as motor carriers and inland waterways combined." The dependence such volume creates is illustrated by Massachusetts Lieutenant Govenor O'Neill who attests that ". . .nearly half the jobs in Massachusetts depend on rail service. . . ." Rails, therefore, are a significant mover of freight which American Industry depends on. The reasons for this dependence are seen in

(B) *Railroads Are Economically and Socially Desirable*

Rails are desirable because they are both a cleaner and more efficient form of transportation. Again, Lieutenant Governor O'Neill gives documentation: ". . .railroads are four times more energy efficient than are trucks, and sixty times more efficient than aircraft. At the same time they contribute less pollution than does any other form of transportation. . . ." Thus, railroads are economically desirable because they conserve energy, and are socially desirable as they pollute less.

For these reasons, then, conclude our first observation that railroads are a vital part of U.S. transportation.

Observation II. American Railroads Are Beset by Difficulties

Despite their essential character, railroads in the U.S. are beset by crippling difficulties. We document these problems in three areas:

(A) *Financial Difficulties*

Secretary Coleman detailed these problems in hearings last summer as, "Nine railroads in this country are now in bankruptcy and several others are very weak. Even in good years, if there is such for the railroad industry, return on investment averages less than 4 percent. Low profits do not attract investment capital. But railroads do need additional funds now if they are to begin to repair the past neglect. . . ." American railroads have financial problems. We examine the results of these problems in

(B) *Dangerous Physical Conditions Exist*

Fred Rooney, Chairman of the House Commerce Committee, describes the situation as ". . .the place is going ramshackle . . .safety is taking a licking; injuries, loss, and damage are running high; railroad service is poor." At the same hearings, J. Raymond McLaughlin, of the National Railroad Laborer's Association, presented documentation showing 438 injuries and deaths in 1974 alone due to defects in or improper maintenance of ways and structures. A more graphic example is offered by William Coleman: "Last year there were in excess of 7,900 derailments. Roadbeds are in such bad condition that we have even had derailments of *standing* trains."

Poor tracks have another harm as seen in

(C) *Inefficient Operations and Service Result*

Again, Secretary Coleman tells us, ". . .great segments of our railroad system are just barely functioning . . .it is not uncommon to have trains operating on mainline tracks at only ten miles per hour." John Ingram, president of the Chicago, Rock Island, and Pacific Railroads summarizes the predicament as, "We are not providing the shipper with competitive service — again, because our tracks cannot sustain the speeds necessary to move the nation's commerce effectively."

Overall, we can see that railroads have financial problems that have resulted in poor maintenance of track. This means danger and risk runs high, while service and efficiency are at all time lows. The root cause of these problems is examined in

Observation III. Present Policies Toward Transportation Rights-of-Way Discriminate Against Railroads

(A) *Only Railroads Must Operate on Private Rights-of-Way*

Lieutenant Govenor O'Neill elaborates on these policies by stating: "While railroads and their customers risk passage on private rights-of-way, most of which are taxed with other railroad property, trucks roll on publicly built and maintained highways; barges float on public canals; and aircraft fly through public space to land at public terminals." The effect of this unfair policy is to disguise railroads' natural efficiencies and make other modes appear cheaper than they really are. Thus we see,

(B) *Dollar Subsidies Will Not Solve the Problem*

The Conference of States in 1975 tells us that "even a massive infusion of government cash does not solve the underlying problems of the rail industry throughout the nation. Rather, it simply masks the symptoms where they are most obvious. The inescapable fact is that we require our rail system to carry the burden of a high capital investment in fixed plant while we subsidize nearly all of the corresponding facilities of other modes." Clearly, what is needed is a basic structural change in the nature of railroading in the United States today.

The Conference of States summarizes with, "The rail mode must be placed on parity with other modes if it is to compete. The railroads cannot continue to be the only mode that pays the full cost of its right-of-way." In view of the preceding in-depth analysis, and in agreeing with the Conference of States, we present the following four-plank affirmative proposal:

1. The federal government shall purchase the interstate railroad right-of-way and track through use of future lease rights.
2. Creation of the Interstate Rail System to rehabilitate and maintain roadbeds and track financed by a rail users surcharge trust fund.
3. All current railroads shall retain and operate their rolling stock.
4. The affirmative plan shall be enacted by all necessary means and with all deliberate speed.

Stephen Ailes, president of the American Association of Railroads, testified in 1975 that "the plain fact that government subsidization of the modes of transportation with which the rails compete is far and away the most important single cause — the root cause — of the railroad problem." Today, we offer you the chance to remedy this root cause and put railroads back in a competitive position. With this philosophy in mind, we ask for concurrence with the affirmative posture.[4]

As you can see, the preceding case does meet the major requirements expected of an affirmative presentation; it is a *prima facie* case that stands by itself and presents sufficient information and argument to warrent a policy change. In addition, a plan was presented to effectuate the desired change and, at this point, it appears that the proposed plan would handle those evils isolated earlier by the affirmative in its justification for change. Of course, subsequent negative refutation might cause us to change our opinion concerning the viability of the affirmative's lines of argument, but, at this point, a sufficient justification for change has been presented to merit our full consideration of the affirmative case and its desired changes.

Expectations of the Affirmative Speakers

Although the particular responsibilities of the two affirmative speakers will vary according to the type of affirmative case presented (see "Types of Affirmative Cases" immediately following this section) and to the style of refutation offered by the negative, certain broad speaker responsibilities may be indicated for effective affirmative advocacy. The most efficient method for examining these expectations is to do so by considering the four affirmative speeches within a formal debate encounter.

First Affirmative Constructive Speech. This speech initiates the debate, setting forth the major lines of argument and organization that will be developed throughout the debate by both the affirmative and negative speakers. The first affirmative constructive speaker or speech, whom or which we will refer to hereafter as 1AC, has several responsibilities that need to be met to start the debate effectively:

1. She must present an introduction to the affirmative case position that essentially establishes the affirmative philosophy in the debate. This usually is accomplished by presenting a piece of evidence that crystallizes the major concerns covered by the affirmative case. This introduction serves the same purpose of any introduction to any speech: it prepares the listener for that which is to come.

2. She must state the resolution ("Resolved: that the federal government should establish a comprehensive program to significantly increase the energy independence of the United States"); this

guarantees that everyone in the debate will be dealing with the same topic and ensures the debaters that the critic-judge will know what is being discussed.

3. She must give definitions of terms pertinent to debating effectively the particular resolution. Such definitions should be offered early within the 1AC to maximize shared meanings and clear understanding regarding the forthcoming arguments.

4. She must present the basic components of the affirmative case, including the justification for change and the proposal for effectuating that change. Remember, the case must be *prima facie*, it must be able to stand completely by itself prior to negative refutation; so the full rationale for change should be presented by the 1AC.

5. Finally, she should offer a summary of the major points in the total rationale for change to make the affirmative's position as clear as possible to the critic-judge. This serves the same purpose as the traditional conclusion within a public speech.

The example of a sample affirmative case was the speech of a 1AC speaker; reread that speech to see exactly how each of the 1AC responsibilities were upheld.

Second Affirmative Constructive Speech. Known as 2AC, this speech follows the refutation offered by the first negative constructive speaker. Because of that, the major responsibility of 2AC is to support the position and arguments outlined by 1AC through the substantive refutation of the arguments presented by the preceding negative speaker. Thus, the structure of the 2AC speech is mainly dependent upon the organization of the case offered in the 1AC speech, and the 2AC proceeds down through the affirmative case, refuting the first negative's arguments. The 2AC should retain the argumentative organization presented in 1AC in refuting the first negative speaker's arguments. Moreover, since this *is* a speech, the 2AC speaker should develop an introduction, previewing what he will do within this speech, and a conclusion, summarizing how the 2AC refutation demonstrates that the affirmative rationale for change remains viable.

First Affirmative Rebuttal Speech. The 1AR is the most difficult and the most important speech within any debate round. It is a difficult speech because it follows the negative block — the back-to-back speeches of the second negative constructive and the first negative rebuttal. Thus, the 1AR speaker has but five minutes to deal with the arguments offered in fifteen minutes of negative speaking time (2NC is ten minutes; 1NR is five minutes). At a minimum, it is the responsibility of the 1AR to handle completely the major issues presented by the second negative constructive speaker; all such arguments not refuted by the 1AR will stand against the affirmative case position. Additionally, the 1AR should deal with as many of the arguments offered by the first negative rebuttalist as time permits. In short, the more arguments within the negative block that can be handled by the 1AR, the better will be the overall strategic position of the total affirmative position.

Because of this extreme time pressure (five minutes to refute fifteen-minutes' worth of arguments), it is essential that the 1AR speaker utilize word economy in responding to the negative arguments, making his arguments as precise and clear as possible. Since this is such an important speech, either affirmative speaker may fill the 1AR slot. That is, either the 1AC *or* the 2AC speaker may present the 1AR speech, the only time within an academic debate when speakers may switch speaking positions, allowing, for example, the 2AC speaker to also give the 1AR speech. Debaters should carefully consider who should present the 1AR, because in many debates it is *this* speech that will determine the eventual outcome of the debate.

Second Affirmative Rebuttal Speech. The 2AR speech concludes the debate, bringing together all the major arguments that will influence greatly the critic-judge's final decision. The 2AR speaker has but two major responsibilities: (1) to refute those arguments presented by the preceding second negative rebuttalist (who will crystallize all the main negative arguments), justifying why the critic-judge should vote to adopt the resolution. It is important that the 2AR serve as a salesman, attempting to compel the critic-judge to vote for the affirmative team. By maximizing what has been proven by the affirmative, the 2AR speaker should attempt to use her final speech as the ultimate in persuasion.

Types of Affirmative Cases

Perhaps nothing more has exemplified the many changes in formal debate over the past fifteen years than the development of many types of possible and, to a large extent, acceptable case structures to present the affirmative rationale for change.[5] Until the early 1960's, there was but one case structure: the need-plan-advantage or so-called stock issues case. Since that time, many more case types have appeared, with some having greater use and acceptability than others. At the beginning of this chapter, a caveat was issued that asked you to recognize that no textbook on argumentation and debate can be completely up to date, that development in theory and practice occur so rapidly that textbook writers always will be one step behind the very latest developments. The types of affirmative cases exemplify that warning. Most assuredly, new case forms will be forthcoming as we head into the 1980s; thus, you must keep abreast of those latest developments. Texts always will lag somewhat behind.

The seven major affirmative case types outlined within this section are the major case structures prevalent in intercollegiate and interscholastic debate competition today. The nature of the particular debate topic, as well as the types of arguments to be presented, should dictate the type of case structure you select. There is no perfect case structure; each has its own advantages and disadvantages. As a functional rule, you should remember that the best type of affirmative case structure is one that can be supported and defended well by you and your colleague. Even the most basic structure will do the job nicely if you can ably defend it.

Need-Plan-Advantage Case

The oldest affirmative case form, often referred to as the stock issues approach by veteran debate coaches, is the need-plan-advantage type of structure. This case type literally deals with the four stock issues of need, plan, feasibility, and advantage directly through the structure of the case presented by the affirmative speakers. It would contain these elements:

Need. The evils of the present system are disclosed and the need for change is made clear.

Plan. The procedure for implementing the proposed policy change is spelled out, the plan's details are stated and the application of the plan to the need area is shown.

Advantage. Additional advantages stemming from the adoption of the plan are presented.

The stock issues case is the most straight forward approach to dealing with a question of policy. The case structure is, quite simply, a direct problem-solving format. The need area presents the problems to be considered, the plan presents the resolution-based method for eliminating the problems, and the advantage or advantages note the additional benefits to be achieved if the affirmative plan is adopted. Two points should be remembered, moreover, concerning the area of additional advantages.

First, the advantages cannot be simple restatements of the problems cited within the need area of the affirmative case structure. For example, if you attempted to justify the implementation of a guaranteed annual income as a solution to the problem of poverty in the United States, you could not claim the elimination of poverty as an extra advantage to the adoption of the plan. To be solvent, your plan would have to eliminate poverty to justify completely the adoption of your guaranteed income proposal. Instead, advantages must deal with items outside the need area.

Second, advantages must be substantiated with evidence, remembering that there is a great difference between argument (which is supported by evidence in one manner or another) and assertion (which is simply unsupported conjecture on the part of the advocate). Although it is difficult to prove something willl happen in the future if your plan is put into effect, you can secure sufficient probability evidence to substantiate adequately your claim of future benefits. Some years ago, for example, it was claimed that the reduction of American armed forces stationed in Europe would not only reduce the dangers of nuclear confrontation with the Soviet Union (need area) but would also provide the additional benefit of reducing our balance of payments deficit by slowing the flow of American dollars out of the country (advantage).

Need-Plan Case

Because of the difficulty involved in substantiating significant advantages in the stock issues case approach, many affirmative teams have adopted a modification of that case structure: the need-plan case. In addition, as more arguments and evidence have been utilized in contest debate rounds during the past decade than ever before, many affirmative advocates found it impossible to defend adequately all three parts of the stock issues case. So, the advantage area was dropped. The thrust of the need-plan case, therefore, is exactly the same as the stock issues case (problem-solution structure); the only difference is that no additional benefits are claimed for proposal adoption in the need-plan affirmative case structure.

Comparative Advantage Case

Up through the early 1960s, the need-plan-advantage case and its need-plan half-brother served as *the* case structure for affirmative advocates, and then the process of case structure development began. The first major alternative to the stock issues case was the comparative advantage case, an argumentative structure that has its roots in Aristotelian rhetorical theory.[6] This variation from the time-honored stock issues approach created open hostility in many academic debate circles, causing the publication of a series of articles dealing with the concept and validity of this new avenue of affirmative analysis.[7] Despite this early opposition, the comparative advantage case has survived, becoming the paramount structure in case construction on the intercollegiate debate circuit by the mid-1970s.

The comparative advantage case contends that the proposed change from the status quo is justified because the new policy will create significant advantages superior to those created by present system policies. Thus, the comparative advantage case takes the philosophy that "we can deal with issue **X** better than the present system" in providing a rationale for policy change:

Plan. The procedure for implementing the proposed policy change is spelled out: the plan's details are stated and the application of the plan to the advantages is shown.

Advantage. Each advantage of the plan is demonstrated:

- showing why the status quo cannot accrue the advantage
- showing why the plan can accrue the advantage
- showing the actual advantage of the advantage

The reason why many affirmative case builders switched to the comparative advantage structure was that they found this case format easier to defend than the stock issues case. For example, if the problem of poverty in the United States were used to justify a guaranteed income proposal under the stock issues approach, the affirmative would be expected to be able to prove that their plan would completely eliminate the problem of poverty — a most difficult burden to shoulder. However, using the comparative advantage structure, the affirmative would contend that the proposed guaranteed income would garner the advantage of reducing the problem of poverty in the United States. Please note that there is not the burden to eliminate poverty totally, only to reduce the problem of poverty significantly, demonstrating that the new policy will do a more advantageous job than the status quo.

Despite the fact that there is a structural difference between the stock issues case and the comparative advantage case, many similarities do exist. Both cases *must* present significant and inherent rationales for change; the stock issues case must deal with a compelling problem that cannot be solved by the present system and the comparative advantage case must present a compelling advantage that cannot be gained by the present system. Any stock issues case can be revamped very simply to fit into the comparative advantage structure, and doing so makes it somewhat easier to defend.

Modified Affirmative Case

Following the development of the comparative advantage case, some debaters began to use a case that was a hybrid of need-plan and comparative advantage: the modified affirmative case. In its basic form as developed in the mid-1960s, the modified affirmative case was structured as follows:

Observation. The philosophy upon which the rationale for change is based is presented; difficulties found to exist within the status quo dealing with the topic under discussion are explored.

Plan. The procedure for implementing the proposed policy change is spelled out: the plan's details are stated and the application of the plan to the advantages is shown.

Advantage. Each advantage of the plan is demonstrated:

- showing why the status quo cannot accrue the advantage
- showing why the plan can accrue the advantage
- showing the actual advantage of the advantage

Although the modified affirmative is designed to function and be defended like the comparative advantage case because the rationale for change is provided by the affirmative advantage area, many negative speakers were unsure as to what to do with the observation. Some negatives treated the observation as a reworded need statement and attacked the case as if it were a need-plan-advantage case; other negative speakers decided to overlook the observation area altogether. Both approaches proved to be dysfunctional.

Because the general rationale for this affirmative case is presented within the opening observations, negative speakers must deal with that area; refutation to the observation area is highly essential. However, the justification for change does rest within the advantage area, so the preponderance of negative refutation should be offered at that segment of the modified affirmative case structure. Although the use of this case format has declined, it does present the affirmative with the advantage of spreading out the negative refutation and making concentrated negative attack more difficult; and it continues to confuse novice negative debaters. Aside from those two slim benefits, the modified affirmative is nothing more than a modest modification of the traditional comparative advantage case.

Goals Case

There are debate topics in which the status quo is committed to gaining or maintaining certain goals or desired ends. In such circumstances, the goals case is an excellent affirmative case structure to be considered. This case justifies a change in policy by contending that the new policy will do a better job of achieving the goals than the status quo:

Goal. The goals of the status quo are presented and substantiated.

Plan. The procedure for implementing the proposed policy change is spelled out; the plan's details are stated and the application of the plan to the goals area is shown.

Advantage. The advantage of meeting the goals is demonstrated:

- showing that the status quo cannot achieve the goals
- showing why the plan can achieve the goals
- showing the benefit of achieving the goals

The goals case is defended exactly like the comparative advantage case. For example, in dealing with, Resolved: that the federal government should implement a program to guarantee employment opportunities to all U.S. citizens in the labor force, many affirmatives utilized the status quo goal of full employment as stated in the Employment Act of 1946 as the goal to be achieved. Then it was argued that the affirmative plan would do a much better job of meeting the goal of full employment than current status quo programs, thereby providing an advantage to this new policy system and justifying the change. The final debate decision would rest upon the determination as to which system better met the stated goal.

Criteria Case

Very similar to the goals case is the criteria case:

Criteria. The criteria for dealing with a problem are established and substantiated.

Plan. The procedure for implementing the proposed policy change is spelled out; the plan's details are stated and the applications of the plan to the criteria are shown.

Advantage. The advantage of meeting the criteria is demonstrated

- showing that the status quo cannot meet the criteria
- showing why the plan meets the criteria
- showing the benefits of meeting the criteria

As with the goals case, this case justifies change by demonstrating that the affirmative better meets the established criteria than the status quo mechanisms. Of course, experienced negative advocates will be most hesitant to accept the criteria offered by the affirmative, preferring instead to deny the validity of the criteria or to offer alternative criteria by which to decide viable policy options. That is why the affirmative must present reasonable, almost banal criteria so that negatives might be willing to accept such material at the onset of the debate. For example, in dealing with the problem of poverty, the affirmative might contend that the functionality of antipoverty mechanisms should be determined in relation to their efficiency and flexibility. Thus, efficiency and flexibility would serve as the criteria. If the negative accepted this statement, the debate's outcome would rest largely upon the determination of which system, the affirmative plan or the status quo, better met the criteria in dealing with the problem of poverty.

Modular Affirmative Case

The most recent affirmative case development has been the modular affirmative case structure, often known as the alternate-justification case or even the mini affirmative. The modular case can take any other affirmative case form and turn traditional approaches to affirmative advocacy into this new case structure. Essentially, the modular case presents two or three separate cases in one, offering two or three separate justifications for change within the structure of one affirmative case. This case format may be examined for the topic, as follows:

Resolved: that the federal government should implement a program to guarantee employment opportunities to all U.S. citizens in the labor force.

Need I. To eliminate illegal Mexican immigration.
Plan I. Issue identification cards to all illegal aliens, and so on.

Need II. To reduce discriminatory hiring practices.
Plan II. Mandate racial quotas in all interstate businesses, and so on.

Need III. To reduce the spiraling cost of living.
Plan III. Implement mandatory wage and price controls, and so on.

Affirmative advocates justify the structure of the modular affirmative by contending that they only have to provide a rationale for change. Therefore they argue, if only one of the three separate proposals and justifications for change carry throughout the debate, then the critic-judge must vote for the affirmative. Of course, this case structure puts a great deal of pressure on the negative, because three separate reasons for change must be defeated, not just one.

Strategically, the modular affirmative does provide its users with a significant advantage. By the time of the second affirmative rebuttal speech, that speaker can examine all the previous arguments offered by both sides in the debate and then make the decision as to which of the three mini cases retains the greatest strength. And that would be the case advocated almost exclusively in that final speech.

Many individuals, including this writer, question the ethical nature of this newest case format. Instead of taking one clear and direct position, the modular case takes several positions, and it is not until the last speech that you know what the affirmative wants you to believe or do. In addition, to many of us, competitive debate never was designed to be a "hare and hound" game, wherein the affirmative kept hopping around from one mini case to another until the negative had no more chances to offer refutation. At this time, very few affirmative teams at either the interscholastic or intercollegiate level present modular cases; it is to be hoped that that trend continues.

Duties of the Negative

As we did in our examination of the responsibilities of affirmative advocacy, we shall look at negative speaking responsibilities from both general and specific perspectives. As an overview, negative speakers can take all issues developed in the "Duties of the Affirmative" section and simply invert them to gain an understanding of negative responsibilities. Many of the particular activities of the negative advocates will be covered in the following chapter, "Refutation."

Expectations of the Negative Team

Overall, the negative has the main responsibility of opposing the affirmative's case (burden of rebuttal or direct clash) in attempting to deny the offered justification for change (burden of presumption). Whereas the affirmative wants to change policy systems, the negative wants to retain the status quo, or, at least, to deny the viability of the affirmative proposal. In so doing, the negative will consider the following matters of argument.

Definitions. Whereas the affirmative has the responsibility to define terms within the resolution, the negative has the right to accept or to object to those definitions. Importantly, if the negative opposes a definition offered by the first affirmative constructive speaker, then it is the responsibility of the first negative constructive speaker to (*a*) directly state the objection to the affirmative's definition, (*b*) specifically explain why the affirmative's definition is unfair or erroneous, and, most importantly, (c) present an alternative definition that is reasonably substantiated to demonstrate its superiority over the affirmative definition. In dealing with definitions, then, the negative must do more than simply object to the affirmative's definitions. The reasons for the objection must be established, and a substitute definition must be offered.

Significance. In opposing the affirmative's justification for change, one of the most important negative arguments is to challenge the significance of the affirmative indictment. Since we do not make changes capriciously, we demand that a significant reason be given to justify any and all changes in policy. Therefore, the negative should examine very carefully all the reasons offered by the affirmative to justify change, attempting to minimize the problems isolated by the affirmative or to minimize the significance of the advantages claimed by the affirmative.

If the negative is able to deny the significance of the affirmative's justification for change, the negative will be able to deny adoption of the affirmative proposal. The affirmative must be able to demonstrate that its proposal is significant, and if it is unable to do so, the negative should be awarded the debate decision.

Inherency. The issue of inherency is the single most important issue within any formal policy debate, and it is for this reason that negative speakers, principally the first negative speaker, should concentrate a great deal of both their research and speaking time on the issue of inherency. The reason for the importance of inherency is simple: if the negative is able to show that the status quo can solve the problems or accrue the advantages as desired by the affirmative, then there is absolutely no reason at all to change policy systems. If, for example, the negative can prove that our current welfare programs can eliminate the problem of poverty, then there is no justification for the adoption of the affirmative's guaranteed annual income scheme and that proposal will be rejected. Inherency is *the* foundation upon which policy decisions are based.

Because of this issue's great importance, negative advocates need to become familiar with the total operations of the status quo concerning the topic area as possible. The negative advocates need to be aware of every existent program that functions at every level; in short, they must become virtual subject-matter experts regarding the present system and the topic discussed. Having such complete knowledge and information allows the negative to be able to demonstrate exactly how the status quo can eliminate the problem or gain the advantage desired by the affirmative. As noted before, even if the affirmative wins every other issue within the debate, if the negative wins the issue of inherency, the negative wins the debate.

Causality. The negative advocates also must examine the nature of causality, examining and questioning the causal connections offered by the affirmative in dealing with those issues justifying change. Very few problems have simple causes; most of our national social ills stem from many causes, exemplifying the concept of "multiple causality." This is an important concept to remember, because an affirmative case developed on an inaccurate or too simplistic concept of causality will be an unrealistic and nonviable approach to decision making, and both the affirmative's justification for change and plan for effectuating change may be shown to be inappropriate.

For example, if the affirmative attempted to justify the implementation of a guaranteed income because people lacked adequate money to meet their needs, claiming that poverty was caused by the lack of money, the negative could attack the causal connection stated therein. By proving the lack of adequate education, job training, job skills, motivation, and other factors, the negative could demonstrate that the plan would not deal with the other causes of poverty, meaning that the plan would not be solvent in eliminating the poverty problem. The issue of causality, then, is an important issue that must be considered by the negative advocates.

Topicality. The negative must make certain that the affirmative's proposal is topical, that it meets the requirements stated within the debate resolution. For example, if the topic called for the federal government to guarantee an annual cash income to all citizens, then the affirmative's plan must provide a guarantee of money to all people within the United States, probably enough to ensure that each person would be lifted above the poverty line as established yearly by the federal government. The negative should examine critically the specifics of the affirmative plan to make certain that the mechanism is topical, that all the resolution's requirements are met. The following example should demonstrate how a topicality argument comes into play.

Some years ago, when the intercollegiate topic dealt with a guaranteed income proposal, affirmative advocates often attempted to justify such a scheme on the grounds that people were suffering from malnutrition because they did not have enough money to buy adequate amounts of food; therefore, the plan was offered to have the federal government give them the necessary money. However, negative advocates countered this proposal with the argument that simply giving people money would not ensure good nutrition. After all, they argued with supporting evidence, if the people used the money to buy "junk food" or starchy foods, their nutrition level would not be improved. So, to preempt this argument, affirmatives began to insert the requirement into their plans that the people had to use their money to purchase only certain kinds of food. Therefore, the negative claimed that the solution of malnutrition problem was nontopical, because it came not from the provision of a guaranteed income but from the nontopical requirement that people spend their money in a certain way.

Actually there are two major types of nontopicality arguments. Nontopicality refers to an affirmative proposal that does not meet the requirements stated within the wording of the debate resolution. *Extratopicality* refers specifically to the kind of situation found in the preceding example: when something outside the stated resolution is included within the affirmative plan to assist in the elimination of a problem or in the accrual of a desired advantage. Very few affirmative proposals are nontopical, but quite a few actually are extratopical. To prevent possible negative plan attacks, many affirmatives include extraneous elements within their plan details. Negative advocates should watch for such items and be prepared to offer extratopicality objections. The affirmative has the responsibility to meet the topic; the negative should not allow affirmative plans either to fall short (nontopicality) or go beyond (extratopicality) that topic.

Solvency. The negative must determine whether or not the affirmative plan will meet the justification for change by solving the indicated problem or by gaining the desired advantage. The negative must check to see that the plan is solvent. An excellent solvency argument is circumvention, the idea that the affirmative plan's details may be circumvented, thereby allowing the problem to continue to exist or preventing the accrual of an advantage. The negative should examine the specifics of the plan for loopholes, small matters that would prevent the plan from working as desired. Although very few cases are so sloppily constructed as to fail to meet the justification for change, practically every plan can be circumvented to some degree or another. Often, the possibility of circumvention is suggested by the affirmative's own evidence documenting the significance of the problem or advantage, and negative speakers should be willing to use that evidence as support for their circumvention objections.

Disadvantage. The final major negative argumentative responsibility is the area of potential disadvantages to the affirmative plan. Recognizing that all policies are examples of systems theory, all changes in policy will have many different effects. Some of these effects are beneficial and would be desired by the affirmative advocates (a guaranteed income would reduce poverty); some of these effects would be undesirable (pumping billions of dollars into the economy would exacerbate the inflationary spiral). The negative should search for these nonbeneficial effects, arguing that these disadvantages outweigh the benefits of the affirmative proposal. Essentially, negative disadvantage arguments utilize a cost-benefits analysis in examining the affirmative plan, and if the costs (disadvantages) outweigh the benefits (solution of the problem or accrual of the advantage), then the negative should try to persuade the critic-judge to reject the affirmative proposal.

Expectations of the Negative Speakers

As with the affirmative advocates, the specific actions of the negative speakers will be dependent upon the type of affirmative case presented. Moreover, since one of the main negative responsibilities is to deal directly with the affirmative case and the argumentative structure as presented, the negative speaker's actions will be very highly dependent upon the actions of the affirmative. Despite this variability, certain responsibilities may be isolated for all four negative speeches within a formal debate.

First Negative Constructive Speech. This speech, referred to as 1NC, presents the first negative arguments against the affirmative case, establishing the lines of argument and argumentative philosophy that will be carried by the negative throughtout the debate. The 1NC speaker should:

1. Start the speech with an introduction, often through the use of a piece of evidence, that crystallizes the basic negative position to be taken in the debate and outlines the types of attacks to be lodged against the affirmative case.

2. Accept or reject those definitions or terms offered by the 1AC speaker. Acceptance does not have to be stated, but a rejection of affirmative definitions must be explained and counter definitions must be offered and justified.

3. Directly clash with the affirmative's justification for change, be it in the need area within a stock issues case or the advantage area within the comparative advantage case. Importantly, the 1NC

speaker *does not* consider the affirmative plan; the 1NC speaker limits his refutation to the affirmative's justification for change.

4. Summarize the arguments at the conclusion of the speech, reemphasizing the fact that those arguments deny the justification for change, persuading the critic-judge not to accept the affirmative position.

Second Negative Constructive Speech. The 2NC speaker concentrates his arguments exclusively upon the affirmative plan, pushing the arguments of topicality, solvency, and disadvantage (the only exception to this would be if the affirmative offered a need-plan-advantage case; then, the 2NC would also contend with the extra advantages claimed by the affirmative). Although it is inviting to cover the areas covered by the 1NC, the 2NC must not accept that invitation. The 2NC speaker must limit refutation to the plan; this tight limitation will be explained later in this chapter under "The Negative Block and the Affirmative Response."

First Negative Rebuttal Speech. The 1NR speaker immediately follows the 2NC speaker on the floor; there is no intervening affirmative speech. Therefore, since the affirmative has not yet had an opportunity to respond to the 2NC's plan arguments, it would be a complete waste of time to reiterate them in the 1NR speech. Instead, the 1NR speaker should return to those arguments she initially presented within the 1NR speech and resupport them by providing new evidence and by refuting the responses given by the second affirmative constructive speaker. Thus, the 1NR speaker emphasizes exclusively those arguments dealing with the affirmative's justification for change.

Second Negative Rebuttal Speech. This is the last negative speech in the debate, so the 2NR speaker has one major responsibility: to crystallize *all* the major negative arguments against adoption of the affirmative proposal. The 2NR speaker must reiterate all the major indictments against the affirmative's justification for change and all the major objections against the affirmative plan. It is this speech that maximizes all the reasons why the critic-judge should not accept the affirmative case, so the 2NR speaker emphasizes all those major reasons why the vote should go to the negative team.

Types of Negative Cases

Although negative speakers do not have a case in the same sense that the affirmative has a case (after all, the negative can do nothing until the affirmative case has been presented), the strategic approaches taken by the negative are considered cases, because they bring together the negative arguments to the affirmative position. In approaching the many possible kinds of affirmative cases upon a plethora of issues, negative advocates have four major avenues of argument (cases) from which to choose.

Straight Refutation

The straight refutation approach requires that the negative attempt to deny or refute every argument offered by the affirmative. In most situations, this is a most difficult, if not untenable, posture, because it is virtually impossible to refute every argument or contention presented by the affirmative speakers — for two reasons.

First, to be able to refute every argument would require that the negative have counter evidence to everything presented by the affirmative. Even the best researched negative team will, from time to time, find some affirmative arguments for which they have no counterevidence, arguments they have never considered and are not prepared to handle. It is impossible for the negative to be so prepared as to be able to refute with evidence every possible affirmative argument.

Second, there are simply some arguments that would make the negative speakers look foolish if they did try to refute them directly. For example, if the affirmative contended that poverty exists in the United States, the negative would be hard pressed to assert that poverty does not exist in the United States with a straight face. Even though there are bizarre sources of evidence that might allow you to support such an argument, that position is so absurd on its face that it would be a total waste of time for the negative even to consider such a position.

There are certain issues, generally referred to as admitted issues, that are virtually truisms, and for the negative to attempt to refute these issues directly would be strategically counterproductive.

For those two reasons, the straight refutation approach is not the best approach for the negative speakers to adopt. It presumes that every affirmative position can be refuted adequately, but that is a presumption that does not exist.

Defense of the Status Quo

A second possible negative case, which is not much better than straight refutation, is a complete point-by-point defense of the status quo. This extreme position essentially contends that the present system can do no wrong, that things are in pretty good shape all the way around. That philosophy forces the negative speakers to attempt to minimize the significance of all the indictments and arguments lodged by the affirmative, which is, at the very least, a most difficult chore.

Academic debate often is criticized as being too "ivory-towerish" or too unrealistic, in that many arguments and points of contention found in academic debate would be laughed out of existence in the "real world." The straight defense of the status quo exemplifies this complaint by its presumption of error-free actions by the present system. Since this negative case is both philosophically unrealistic and strategically indefensible, very few negative teams utilize this approach in attacking the affirmative cases.

Status Quo with Repairs

The most used and most easily defended negative approach is the defense of the status quo with repairs, the approach that combines the two preceding negative cases with the all important issue of inherency. Certainly, the negative attempts to directly refute those affirmative arguments that can be directly refuted; certainly, the negative tries to defend the actions, philosophies, and policies of the present system. However, and most importantly, this approach utilizes the issue of inherency as its structural backbone, contending that certain minor repairs within existent policies can solve the problem or accrue the advantage as desired by the affirmative. It is this approach that allows the negative to use all the status quo programs, and nonstructural changes in those programs, as vehicles to deny the affirmative's justification for change. By demonstrating that the present system is able to accomplish the affirmative's goals, the negative denies the rationale for the implementation of a new policy system.

Because there are so many status quo programs that deal with every possible debate topic, it is not surprising to find the defense of the status quo with repairs as the most prevalent negative strategy. The affirmative has the subsequent responsibility to respond to all programs offered by the negative, demonstrating why these programs are inadequate and why the rationale for change still exists. Of course, this puts a great deal of pressure upon the affirmative, as many negative teams attempt to bury the affirmative advocates in a plethora of status quo programs and modifications of those programs.

One final point needs to be made concerning this particular negative case. The negative is given great latitude in arguing the defense of the status quo with repairs; truly, the full and complete range of present system policies and actions are available for use to deny the affirmative warrant for change. However, the negative does not have the latitude to make structural changes in status quo programs; the negative cannot alter the basic shape of existent policies and procedures. The following two examples should illustrates what the negative can and cannot do in repairing or modifying the status quo.

An Acceptable Nonstructural Change

Problem: Affirmative contends that poor people have inadequate money for food, clothing, and shelter.

Response: Negative contends that the present system has various welfare programs to give money to the poor.

Response: Affirmative responds by saying that the welfare programs do not provide enough money, giving only one-half the amount needed by the poor for a minimum standard of living.

Response: Negative responds that all the status quo has to do is double the amount of money to the poor provided by the welfare programs, thereby eliminating the affirmative's inherency indictment.

The negative is well within the limits of acceptable status quo modifications in this preceding example. Why? The present system is committed to the financial support of the poor, a point granted by both the affirmative and negative teams. Therefore, simply increasing the amount of money given by welfare programs does not affect the structure or policy of the status quo; the negative's minor repair only affects something that exists within the policy.

An Unacceptable Structural Change

Problem: Affirmative contends that many poor people suffer from the lack of adequate food, clothing, and shelter.

Response: Negative contends that the status quo has welfare programs to meet the needs of the poor.

Response: Affirmative says that these programs cannot do the job, because existing eligibility requirements preclude many poor people from being able to receive the services and benefits of these welfare programs.

Response: Negative contends that all the status quo has to do is toss out those eligibility requirements, thereby eliminating the affirmative's inherency indictment.

This example illustrates a negative team violating the latitude of the status quo with repairs approach. Since eligibility requirements are part of the present system's welfare program structure, the proposal to drop those requirements must be considered a change in the status quo structure, and the negative is not permitted to go that far in denying the affirmative's inherency position. The negative may offer all sorts of modifications of present system programs only so long as those modifications stay within the structure of the present system; the negative cannot change the structure of the status quo. And, it should be added, negative repairs cannot go so far that the negative essentially adopts the resolution. The negative may not adopt the total affirmative position.

Counterplan

The final major negative case is the counterplan, the most extreme strategy that the negative case can take in attempting to deny the affirmative's case. The counterplan is extreme because in this approach the negative *does not* defend the status quo at all; in fact, the negative agrees that the present system cannot solve the problem or accrue the advantage but additionally contends that the affirmative's proposal will not get the job done very well either. Therefore, the negative presents a counterplan, a proposal that is different than the plan offered by the affirmative, although both are designed to replace the status quo. Essentially, with the presentation of a counterplan, the present system is not much of a factor in the debate as the policy decision now rests in comparison and contrast of the affirmative's plan versus the negative's plan.

To run a viable counterplan, the negative must remember four very important points:

1. The plan must lie entirely outside the terms of the debate resolution. *Counterplan* means, "in opposition to the resolution," so the negative may not do anything as specified within the terms of the resolution. For example, if the topic called for the federal

government to halt inflation through wage and price controls, the negative's counterplan could not have the federal government implementing wage and price controls. Some other way of halting inflation would have to be presented by the negative.

2. The plan must do a better job of meeting the affirmative's goals than the affirmative plan. The philosophy of the counterplan is that the negative's proposal will do a job superior to that of the affirmative proposal, so the counterplan must be found to be better — more efficient, more effective, less costly, or whatever.

3. The plan must be as detailed and supported as that expected of the affirmative plan. The counterplan must be solvent, workable, practical, and free from crippling disadvantages — the same requirements to be met by the affirmative proposal.

4. The plan must be competitive. The counterplan must compete directly with the components, objectives, and goals of the affirmative plan. It must be in the ring with the affirmative plan, competing for policy adoption.

Because of the complex nature of recent contest debate topics, the use of the counterplan has increased during the past few years. Therefore, debaters should become well acquainted with this negative strategy.

The Negative Block and the Affirmative Response

Before closing this chapter on the duties of advocacy speaking, some last words are warranted concerning the all-important negative block.

It must be remembered that academic debate brings together two overall strategies of argument and refutation in attempting to persuade a critic-judge as to what should or should not be done. Every advantage or strategy possessed by one team is offset by an advantage or strategy of the other team. While it is obvious that the affirmative benefits from opening and closing the debate, the negative has an equalizer: the negative block. By properly utilizing the combined time period of the second negative construction and the first negative rebuttal speeches, the affirmative advantage of speaking first and last will disappear under the combined negative onslaught of case and plan arguments.

In using the negative block to its fullest, the 2NC speaker limits her arguments exclusively to the affirmative plan; the 2NC speaker does not consider those areas and points covered by the first negative construction speaker. 2NC must limit her analysis to plan-oriented concerns such as topicality, solvency, workability, practicality, and disadvantages. The 2NC speaker does not deal with those areas covered by 1NC, because that speaker immediately follows 2NC to the podium to deliver the first negative rebuttal speech.

The 1NR speaker then has the responsibility to limit his arguments to those areas covered within the affirmative's justification for change; the 1NR speaker does not issue arguments against the plan. Obviously it would be a waste of time to reconsider the plan, because his colleague has just spent ten minutes doing exactly that and there has been no intervening affirmative speech. Besides, even if the 1NR speaker developed a plan objection that the 2NC speaker had not presented, it would go uncounted as no new issues may be presented within the rebuttal periods (new evidence may be presented, but not new issues). Thus, 1NR concentrates upon those arguments he initially developed within the first negative construction speech, expanding his analysis to include refutational arguments offered by the second affirmative construction speaker.

By looking at the 2NC and 1NR speeches, we can see the advantages provided by the structure of the negative block. There are ten minutes of plan argument followed immediately by five minutes of case arguments, a solid fifteen-minute period of direct negative refutation without the presence of an intervening affirmative speech. After the negative block, the first affirmative rebuttalist has only a five minute speech to counter the negative arguments raised in the block. Thus, the 1AR speaker is at a three-to-one time disadvantage (fifteen minutes versus five minutes), thereby making the 1AR speech the most difficult speaking assignment in any academic debate encounter.

In responding to the negative block, the 1AR speaker must (*a*) refute every plan objection offered by the 2NC speaker and (*b*), with whatever time remains, refute as many of the major 1NR arguments as possible. It is imperative, however, that all the 2NC plan objections be covered by this speaker; that is his minimum responsibility. If the 1AR speaker is able to handle most of the arguments within the negative block, then the affirmative has an excellent chance to win the debate. Quite simply, the more of the block that can be refuted by the 1AR speaker, the more the affirmative has a chance to win the debate round.

Because of the importance of the negative block and the immediately-following first affirmative rebuttal speech, debaters ought to take the time to practice their techniques in handling these three speeches. A well-constructed negative block can, by itself, win the debate for the negative; a well-constructed 1AR speech can tip the scales to the affirmative. Those three successive speeches can determine the final outcome of most formal debates.

Conclusion

Despite the fact that there are few formal rules for competitive debate advocacy, practice and tradition have resulted in a number of responsibilities and expectations that debaters are virtually required to uphold. This chapter has presented those major expectations, examining them from both the affirmative and negative perspectives. To facilitate your understanding of many of the duties of advocacy speaking, figures 13.1 and 13.2 crystalize the speaking responsibilities of contest debaters in typical debate clashes. By looking at the actions of all speakers in two debate situations (a need-plan case and a comparative advantage case), you will have a better understanding of what will be expected of you.

Figure 13.2. Duties of the speakers: comparative advantage case.

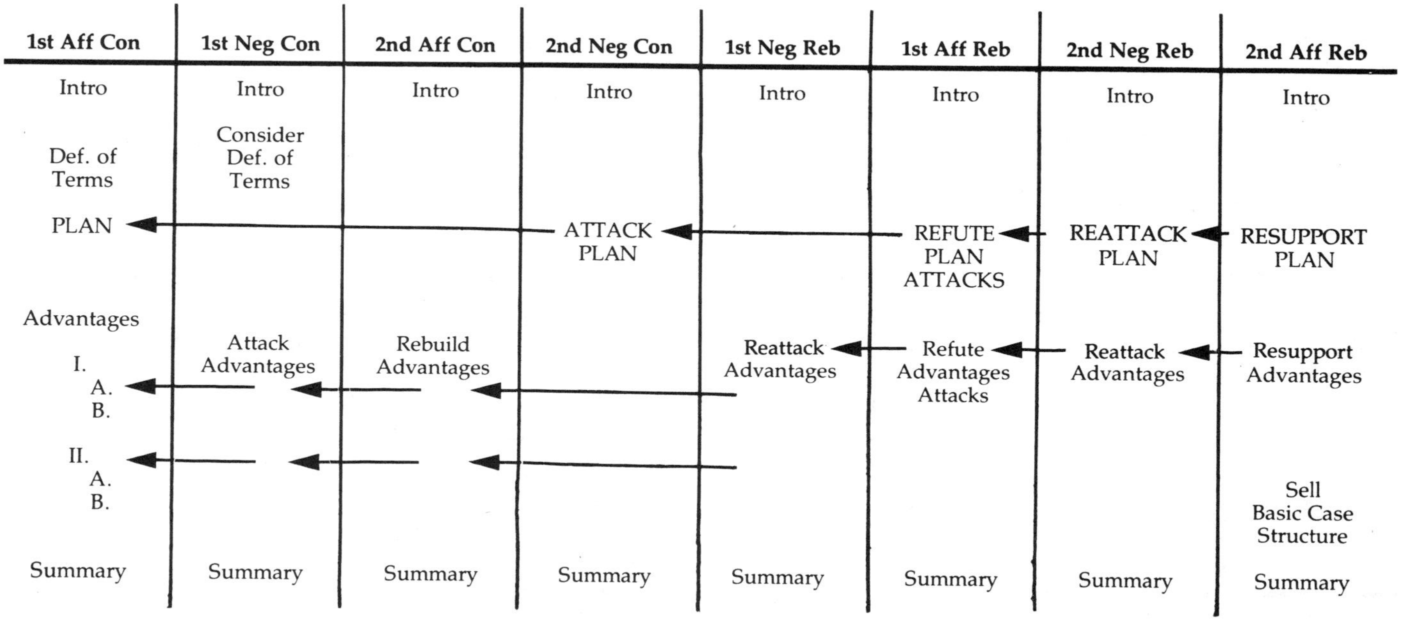
1st Aff Con
1st Neg Con
2nd Aff Con
2nd Neg Con
1st Neg Reb
1st Aff Reb
2nd Neg Reb
2nd Aff Reb
Intro
Def. of Terms
PLAN
Advantages
I. A. B.
II. A. B.
Summary
Consider Def. of Terms
Attack Advantages
Rebuild Advantages
ATTACK PLAN
Reattack Advantages
REFUTE PLAN ATTACKS
Refute Advantages Attacks
REATTACK PLAN
Reattack Advantages
RESUPPORT PLAN
Resupport Advantages
Sell Basic Case Structure

Figure 13.1 Duties of the speakers: need-plan case.

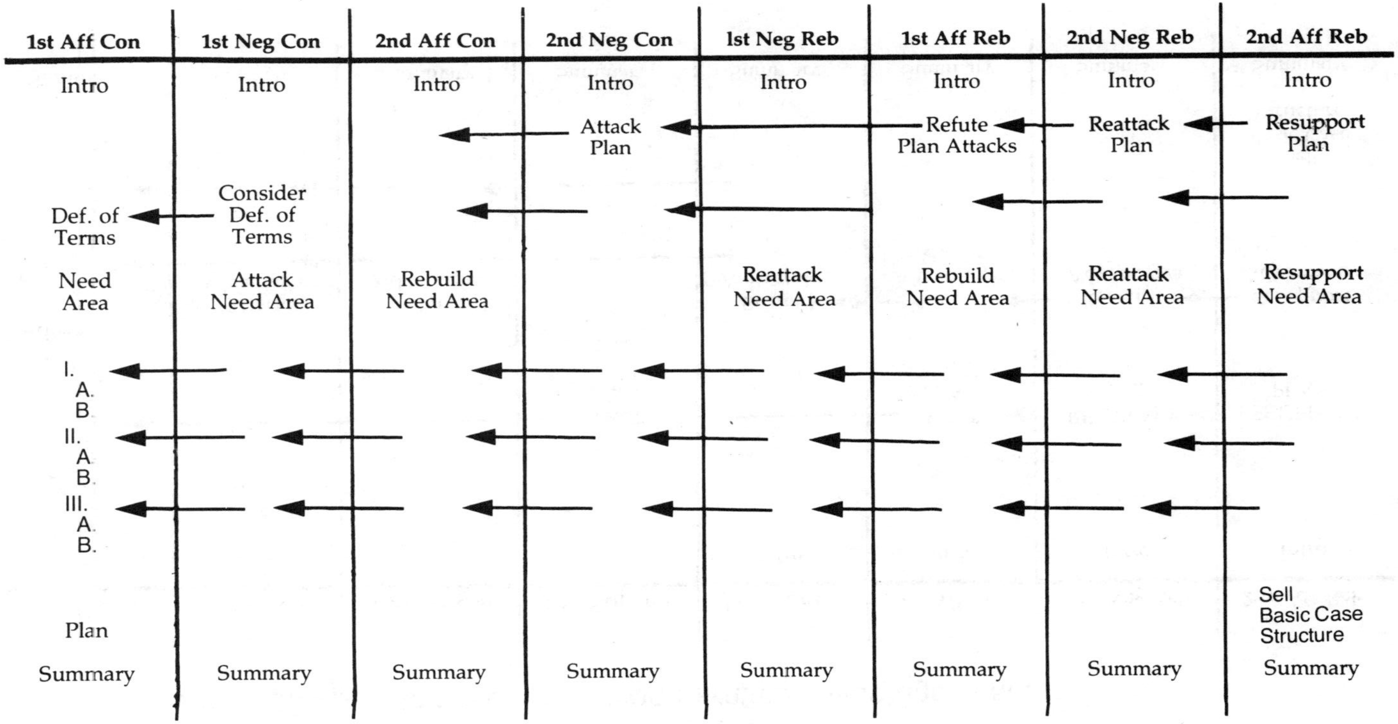
1st Aff Con
1st Neg Con
2nd Aff Con
2nd Neg Con
1st Neg Reb
1st Aff Reb
2nd Neg Reb
2nd Aff Reb
Intro
Intro
Intro
Intro
Intro
Intro
Intro
Intro
Attack Plan
Refute Plan Attacks
Reattack Plan
Resupport Plan
Def. of Terms
Consider Def. of Terms
Need Area
Attack Need Area
Rebuild Need Area
Reattack Need Area
Rebuild Need Area
Reattack Need Area
Resupport Need Area
I.
A.
B.
II.
A.
B.
III.
A.
B.
Plan
Sell Basic Case Structure
Summary
Summary
Summary
Summary
Summary
Summary
Summary
Summary

References

1. For a traditional view of the responsibilities of affirmative advocates, see Glenn R. Capp, Robert Huber, and Wayne C. Eubank, "Duties of Affirmative Speakers — A Symposium," *The Speech Teacher* 8 (March 1959):139-149.

2. See M. Gordon Widenhouse and L. Dean Fadely, "The Historical Development of Inherency," *Debate Issues* (October 1977): 8-16.

3. David Ling and Robert V. Seltzer, "The Role of Attitudinal Inherency in Contemporary Debate," *The Journal of the American Forensic Association* 7 (Spring 1971): 278-279. The best article published to date concerning the strategic factors involved in arguing attitudinal inherency is Jack Rhodes, "Attitudinal Inherency: Handle with Care," in *Proceedings of the National Conference on Argumentation*, ed. James I. Luck (Fort Worth, Tex.: Texas Christian University, 1973), pp. 78-85.

4. Sample affirmative case prepared by David Brimm and James Luke. Used by permission.

5. These changes can best be exemplified by comparing the analysis in the article by Capp, Huber, and Eubank with the analysis of affirmative cases in this chapter.

6. See Austin J. Freeley, *Argumentation and Debate*, 3rd ed. (Blemont, Calif.: Wadsworth, 1971), pp. 207-208. Freeley cites Aristotle's "Universal Topoi" as substantiation for this claim.

7. This series of articles includes Arthur Kruger, "The Comparative Advantages Case — A Disadvantage," *The Journal of the American Forensic Association* 3 (Spetember 1966): 104-111; Bernard L. Brock, "The Comparative Advantages Case," *The Speech Teacher* 16 (March 1967): 118-123; L. Dean Fadely, "The Validity of the Comparative Advantages Case," *The Journal of the American Forensic Association* 4 (Winter 1967): 28-35; Vernon E. Cronen, "Comparative Advantage: A Classification," *Central States Speech Journal* 19 (Winter 1968): 243-249; James W. Chesebro, "The Comparative Advantages Case," *The Journal of the American Forensic Association* 5 (Spring 1968): 57-63; Sharla Barber, "In Defense of a Deficiency," *The Forensic* 54 (January 1969): 8-9; and David Zarefsky, "The 'Traditional Case' — 'Comparative Advantages Case' Dichotomy:Another Look," *The Journal of the American Forensic Association* 6 (Winter 1969): 12-20.

Practicum

1. Here is a sample debate proposition — Resolved: that the use of passive euthanasia should be legalized. Just from what you know about mercy killing and "death with dignity," compose a brief affirmative case outlines

- in the need-plan format
- in the comparative advantage format

Which format did you find it easier to work with? That is how affirmative cases should be developed: case structure is selected ***after*** evidence and arguments have been assembled.

2. The following speech, presented to the Senate on 10 February 1978 by United States Senator Frank Church (Idaho), presents what essentially could be called an affirmative case for the development of gasohol to aid in our country's energy problem. Read this case very carefully and critically. Does the senator's proposal meet the requirements for a good affirmative case? What negative arguments come to your mind that might serve to refute the senator's case?

GASOHOL: Let's Grow Some of Our Energy

Senator Frank Church

Mr. President, today I am introducing the Gasohol Motor Fuel Act of 1978, legislation designed to establish a national requirement to mix alcohol produced from renewable resources with gasoline, in a 10 percent alcohol–90 percent gasoline blend. Such blends are popularly known as "gasohol."

Our nation's appetite for costly imported oil continues to grow unabated. It is shocking to realize that our dependence on foreign oil has now reached almost one-half of our daily consumption of petroleum. Last year we paid about $45 billion for foreign oil. Not only does this leave us increasingly vulnerable to potential embargoes, but we are daily drained of our financial strength, resulting in a record balance of trade deficit.

The bulk of the foreign oil we import is consumed as gasoline. Motor vehicles in our country use over 40 percent of all the energy we consume yearly. Thus we have a vast transportation network which is dependent on petroleum. Dwindling supplies of petroleum and the spectre of still higher prices in the future make it imperative that we develop renewable sources of liquid fuel. Energy Secretary Schlesinger recently stated:

> The principal oil exporting countries are likely to have severe difficulties in supplying all the increases in demand expected to occur in the U.S. and other countries throughout the 1980s.

It should be equally clear that the hard times on our farms demand attention. Crop surpluses abound. Our attempts at fashioning farm policy never seem to create stable markets nor an adequate return for those who work to feed our nation. These crop surpluses, along with wood wastes, should be put to use to help fuel our automobiles, creating new markets for farm products. We can grow part of our fuel, and replenish it each year from the land.

Many regions of our country also have an abundance of by-products from forestry operations which should be converted to alcohol. Wood chips, bark, sawdust and other forms of wood waste can be effectively used to help power our motor vehicles.

Advances in biomass technology also hold out the promise of converting urban refuse to alcohol. Each day American cities dump millions of tons of potential energy into the sea, into our rivers and into smoldering pits. Common sense dictates that we do all we can to convert these wastes to alcohol fuels.

Mr. President, enactment of the Gasohol Motor Fuel Act will be a giant step toward solving these pressing problems. This bill establishes an expeditious yet prudent timetable for bringing gasohol into the market. The secretary of energy is directed to formulate a program which will commence blending alcohol from renewable resouces into gasoline by 1981. The percentage of alcohol blended is steadily increased until a 10 percent alcohol–90 percent gasoline blend becomes available nationwide.

This bill puts the burden for production and distribution of renewable resources alcohol where it belongs, directly on our oil refineries. They have their distribution network in place for liquid fuels and the corporate strength to rapidly commercialize the gasohol concept. It is doubtful that any significant gasohol distribution will occur without placing such requirements on the oil companies themselves.

Passage of the act could result in a reduction of our need to import oil by one-fifth. New and needed markets for surplus farm products will be opened. Wood wastes and urban refuse could be put to use to help reduce our enormous oil import needs.

The technology to support this bill is available. Although improvements can be made in the production of alcohol from renewable resources, we must avoid the pitfall of "studying" the concept to death. Most of all, we must avoid the Department of Energy syndrome of publicly financed pilot plants, demonstration projects, and another horde of federal employees to perpetuate the experiment without ever getting the job done.

Those who argue that alcohol from renewable resources is too expensive forget that each gallon of fuel that we grow replaces a gallon of fuel that we import at prices which will only go higher. A gallon of gasoline made from oil or coal can never be replaced. A gallon of alcohol from renewable resources can be replaced as long as the soil lasts and the sun shines.

Experience both in the United States and abroad with the use of gasohol demonstrates that it works. The blended mix raises the octane rating, may yield improved mileage and significantly reduce pollution emissions. What is required is a definite decision to begin to grow a portion of our energy needs.

I urge my colleagues to join with me in the commencement of such an undertaking now.

I ask unanimous consent that this bill be printed in the *Record.*

There being no objection, the bill was ordered to be printed in the *Record,* as follows:

S. 2533

Be it enacted by the Senate and House of Representatives of the United States of America in Congress assembled,

Short Title

Section 1. This Act may be cited as the "Gasohol Motor Fuel Act of 1978."

Findings

Sec. 2. (a) The United States is currently importing large quantities of crude oil.

(b) A substantial portion of this crude oil is needed for the production of gasoline sold in interstate commerce.

(c) Renewable resources in the United States can provide a sufficient source of alcohol suitable for blending with gasoline to decrease the need for imported oil.

Definitions

Sec. 3. As used in this Act the term —

(1) "alcohol" means methanol, ethanol, or any other alcohol which is produced from renewable resources and which is suitable for use by itself or in combination with other fuels as a motor fuel.

(2) "alcohol-blended fuel" means any fuel consisting of a mixture of gasoline and alcohol motor fuel.

(3) "alcohol motor fuel" means alcohol produced for use as a motor fuel.

(4) "commerce" means any trade, traffic, transportation, exchange, or other commerce —

(A) between any State and any place outside of such State; or

(B) which affects any trade, traffic, transportation, exchange, or other commerce described in paragraph (A).

(5) "motor fuel" means any substance suitable as a fuel for self-propelled vehicles designed primarily for use on public streets, roads, and highways.

(6) "refiner" means, for purposes of this Act, any person engaged in the refining of crude oil to produce motor fuel, including any affiliate of such person, or any importer of gasoline for use as a motor fuel.

(7) "Secretary" means the Secretary of Energy.

(8) "United States" means each State of the several states and the District of Columbia.

(9) "ultimate purchaser" means, with respect to any item, the first person who purchases that item for purposes other than resale.

(10) "renewable resource" means any substance which is a source of energy, and which is available in an inexhaustible supply in the foreseeable future.

Program

Sec. 4. The Secretary shall establish pursuant to this Act a program to promote the use of alcohol-blended fuels in the United States. The purpose of the program shall be to replace gasoline used as a motor fuel with an alcohol-blended fuel containing the maximum percentage of alcohol motor fuel as is economically and technically feasible for use as a motor fuel.

Study

Sec. 5. (a) The Secretary, in consultation with the Secretary of Transportation, the Secretary of Agriculture, the Secretary of Commerce, and other appropriate agencies, shall conduct a study to determine —

(1) the most suitable raw materials, other than petroleum or natural gas, for the production of alcohol motor fuel; and

(2) the nature of the alcohol motor fuel distribution systems and the various production processes, using feedstock other than petroleum and natural gas; that will be necessary for the rapid development of an alcohol motor fuel industry. Such study shall identify ways to encourage the development of a reliable alcohol motor fuel industry and shall identify the technical, economic and institutional barriers to such development, and shall include an estimation of the production capacity of alcohol motor fuel needed to implement the provisions of this Act.

(b) The Secretary shall report to the Congress not later than 6 months after the date of enactment of this Act on the results of the study described in subsection (a), together with such legislative recommendations as may be appropriate to further the purposes of this Act.

Production Goals

Sec. 6. The Secretary shall, by rule, within 6 months after the completion of the study in Section 5, set production goal for the production of alcohol motor fuel in the United States in each of the calendar years 1981 through 1990. In setting such goals, the Secretary shall take into account the availability of reliable sources of alcohol produced from renewable resources. The production goal for alcohol motor fuel for calendar year 1981 shall be not less than 1 percent by volume of the projected consumption of gasoline used as a motor fuel in the United States for that year. The production goal for alcohol motor fuel for calendar year 1985 shall be not less than 5 percent by volume of the projected consumption of gasoline used as a motor fuel in the United States for that year. The production goal for alcohol motor fuel for calendar year 1990 shall be not less than 10 percent by volume of the projected consumption of gasoline used as a motor fuel in the United States for that year.

Alcohol-Blended Fuel Requirements

Sec. 7. (a) The total quantity of gasoline sold annually in commerce in the United States by any refiner for use as motor fuel shall contain, on the average, not less than the percentage alcohol motor fuel by volume set forth for the calendar years shown in the following table:

Calendar year	Percentage alcohol motor fuel by volume
1981	1%
1982	Determined by the Secretary under subsection (b) of this Section.
1983	Determined by the Secretary under subsection (b) of this Section.
1984	Determined by the Secretary under subsection (b) of this Section.
1985	5%
1986	Determined by the Secretary under subsection (b) of this Section.
1987	Determined by the Secretary under subsection (b) of this Section.

1988	Determined by the Secretary under subsection (b) of this Section.
1989	Determined by the Secretary under subsection (b) of this Section.
1990	10%

(b) Not later than July 1, 1980, the Secretary shall prescribe, by rule, the percentage alcohol motor fuel by volume required to be contained, on the average, in the total quantity of gasoline sold annually in commerce in the United States in calendar years 1982 through 1984 and 1986 through 1989 by any refiner for use as a motor fuel. Such percentage shall apply to each refiner, and shall be set to reach such calendar year at a level which the Secretary determines (A) is technically and economically feasible, and (B) will result in steady progress toward meeting the percentage alcohol motor fuel by volume required pursuant to this Section for calendar year 1990.

(c) Each refiner shall report annually to the Secretary the percentage alcohol motor fuel by volume contained on the average in the total quantity of gasoline for use as a motor fuel that refiner sold during the preceding calendar year.

Enforcement by the Secretary

Sec. 8. (a) Any person who violates any requirement of Section 7(a) is subject to a civil penalty of not more than $1 per gallon for each gallon of fuel sold that is not in compliance with Section 7(a). Such penalties shall be assessed by the Secretary.

(b)(1) Before issuing an order assessing a civil penalty against any person under this Section, the Secretary shall provide to such person notice of the proposed penalty. Such notice shall inform such person of his opportunity to elect within 30 days after the date of such notice to have the procedures of paragraph (3) (in lieu of those in paragraph (2)) apply with respect to such assessment.

(2)(A) Unless an election is made within 30 calendar days after receipt of notice under paragraph (1) to have paragraph (3) apply with respect to such penalty, the Secretary shall assess the penalty, by order, after a determination of violation has been made on the record after an opportunity for an agency hearing pursuant to section 554 of title 5, United States Code, before a hearing examiner appointed under section 3105 of such title 5. Such assessment order shall include the hearing examiner's findings and the basis for such assessment.

(B) Any person against whom a penalty is assessed under this paragraph may, within 60 calendar days after the date of the order of the Secretary assessing such penalty, institute an action in the United States court of appeals for the appropriate judicial circuit for judicial review of such order in accordance with chapter 7 of title 5, United States code. The court shall have jurisdiction to enter a judgment affirming, modifying or setting aside in whole or in part, the order of the Secretary, or the court may remand the proceeding to the Secretary for such further action as the court may direct.

(3)(A) In the case of any civil penalty with respect to which the procedures of this paragraph have been elected, the Secretary shall promptly assess such penalty.

(B) If the civil penalty has not yet been paid within 60 calendar days after the assessment order has been made under subparagraph (a), the Secretary shall institute an action in the appropriate district court of the United States for an order affirming the assessment of the civil penalty. The court shall have authority to review *de novo* the law and facts involved, and shall have jurisdiction to enter a judgment enforcing, modifying, and enforcing as so modified, or setting aside in whole or in part such assessment.

(C) Any election to have this paragraph apply may not be revoked except with the consent of the Secretary.

(4) If any person fails to pay an assessment of a civil penalty after it has become a final and unappealable order under paragraph (2) or after the appropriate district court has entered final judgment in favor of the Secretary under paragraph (3) the Secretary shall recover the amount of such penalty in any appropriate district court of the United States. In such action, the validity and appropriateness of such final assessment order or final judgment shall not be subject to review.

Alcohol Distillation Fuel Requirements

Sec. 9. (a) Any person constructing a facility to distill alcohol for motor fuel use shall use fuel sources which are renewable.

(b) The Secretary shall, 6 months after enactment of this Act, promulgate, by rule, procedures for certifying that any facility built for alcohol distillation pursuant to this Act comply with the following priorities of fuel use:

(1) First priority for fuel sources to operate such distillation facilities shall be given to renewable energy resources.

(2) Last priority for fuel sources shall be given to petroleum, petroleum derivatives and natural gas.

(c) The Secretary may by waiver authorize the use of subsection (b)(2) fuel sources upon finding that it would be economically or technically infeasible to comply with the requirements of subsections (a) and (b), above.

Procedures for Rulemaking

Sec. 10. Any rulemaking by the Secretary pursuant to this Act shall be, unless otherwise provided in this Act, in accordance with section 501 of the Department of Energy Organization Act of 1977.

Authorization of Appropriations

Sec. 11. There is authorized to be appropriated to the Secretary to carry out Section 5 and Section 6 not to exceed $1 million for fiscal year 1979.

Chapter 14

Refutation

* The Nature of Refutation
* General Refutation
* Specific Issues of Refutation
* Conclusion
* References
* Practicum

Many lay people have the mistaken impression that the responsibility for refuation of arguments and evidence rests primarily upon the negative advocates within any debate encounter. After all, they reason, since the negative's major responsibility is to deny the adoption of the resolution, it is obvious that the negative will mainly indict the affirmative's position, whereas the affirmative will do its best to maintain a viable defensive posture. If the negative refutes enough of the affirmative's case, the negative wins the debate; if the affirmative sufficiently defends itself against this negative refutation, then the affirmative wins the debate.

Such an attitude is completely wrong.

Both affirmative and negative advocates utilize refutation in competitive debate; both must be skillful in refuting opposing arguments so that their own position can withstand the arguments offered by the opposing team. Therefore, refutation is not something unique to negative speakers; *all* debaters must develop refutation skills so that their debate encounters will be as productive as possible. This chapter is designed to acquaint you with the basics of refutation.

The Nature of Refutation

The significance of refutation to effective argumentative communication has been recognized since the time of the fabled rhetoricians in ancient Greece. Protagoras of Abdera, considered the father of debate, organized contests between his pupils that stressed the refutation of opposing arguments. Perhaps the most important basic handbook on rhetorical theory, Aristotle's *Rhetoric*, devotes a significant amount of space to the refutation of arguments, with suggestions offered as to how certain types of arguments may be overturned successfully.[1]

Refutation serves two basic purposes, and often these purposes coexist. First, refutation acts as a direct method of argument, allowing the advocate to launch a head-to-head indictment of the argumentative position of her opponent. For example:

Argument: Poverty is a growing problem in the United States.

Refutation: The number of poor has declined since 1966.

The initial argument that poverty is a growing problem in the United States is met directly by the refutative argument that the number of poor has declined since 1966, exemplifying a piece of refutation designed primarily to deny the argumentative position of the other speaker.

The second type of refutative argument is designed to support your initial position by refuting the refutative argument of your opponent:

Argument: Poverty is a growing problem in the United States.

Refutation: The number of poor has declined since 1966.

Refutation: That is incorrect. Although the percentage of the poor within the population has decreased, the actual number of poor has increased by more than two million in the past fifteen years.

You should see that the second refutative argument was intended not only to deny the preceding statement but also to resupport the initial argument that poverty is a growing problem in the United States. It exemplifies a piece of refutation that *both* denies the argument of the opponent and simultaneously supports your own initial line of argument.

Theoretically, the give and take of arguments within a competitive round of debate should constitute a building process as arguments are presented, refuted, resupported, rerefuted, and so forth, all the way through the encounter. Refutation directly aids this building process by subjecting argumentative positions and evidence to direct and careful critical examination. Debate should exemplify refutation from the first negative constructive speech through to the end of the debate. Essentially, the 1NC speaker attempts to refute the basic justification for change stated by the 1AC speaker; the 2AC speaker attempts to resupport the justification for change by refuting the arguments of the 1NC speaker; and so on. Hopefully this chain of refutation will advance and extend the major arguments within the debate, allowing the critic-judge to make the best possible reasoned decision.

The refutation of another's argument or supporting piece of evidence, then, is both a destructive and constructive activity. Refutation does serve to destroy the arguments and evidence of your opponent; refutation may, simultaneously, serve to resubstantiate your initial arguments and evience by denying the counter-argument and counterevidence issued by your opponent. Importantly, the practice of refutation is something that both affirmative and negative advocates must employ. No single debater or debate team should attempt to occupy a purely defensive position; all debaters should try to destroy the case made by the other team. Refutation is the best method for accomplishing this goal.

Before considering the general and specific natures of argumentative refutation, one final point needs to be made concerning the overall nature of refutation: the critic-judge must be made aware of *exactly* what you are refuting and how you are refuting it. Far too many debaters assume that their attempted refutational arguments are so clear that it would be obvious to anyone (a favorite phrase of some debaters) what argument was being refuted and how it was being refuted. This, of course, is a most dangerous assumption; the truly effective debater will not take this chance. Instead, he will follow these three steps to ensure clear and effective presentations of refutational arguments:

1. Indicate specifically what argument or piece of evidence presented by your opponent you intend to refute. If possible, repeat or synthesize the argument or evidence so the critic-judge will know what you intend to consider.

2. Clearly explain what is wrong or incorrect about your opponent's argument or evidence, specifically countering his point with your own evidence and analysis as directly as possible.

3. Finally, and this is the point generally forgotten by many debaters, explain to the critic-judge how your evidence and analysis refute your opponent's argument and evidence, further explaining the significance of this refutation to the overall debate.

By following these three steps, your refutational arguments will be clear and effective, making them as direct as possible to the point under consideration. Contest debate is an exercise in oral communication and, as such, all materials presented must be aimed toward the critic-judge. Therefore, refutational arguments must be developed and delivered for and from the perspective of the critic-judge.

General Refutation

Generally, refutation centers upon either an argument presented by a debate opponent or the evidence cited in support of that argument. Since chapter 10 was devoted entirely to the examination of fallacious argument, this portion of this chapter concentrates upon the refutation of evidence, the materials used to substantiate arguments.

Evidence ought to be examined carefully, because it provides the substantive underpinning to arguments issued by you, your debate colleague, and your opponents. As has been noted previously, an argument not supported by evidence is nothing more than an assertion, and reasoned decision making requires that arguments be fully supported by evidence to serve as the basis for the making of those decisions. Mere assertions, then, are not worth very much; it is imperative that your major positional statements be substantiated by appropriate evidence.

Since evidence is so important to decision making in general, and to the operations of competitive debate in particular, you need to examine both your own evidence and the evidence offered by others to determine its argumentative worth. Specifically, for refutational purposes, each piece of evidence should be examined critically to determine its value in supporting arguments. If you are able to dispute the evidence that supports an argument, then you effectively have refuted the argument itself by eliminating that argument's foundation. Analogically, the process of eliminating an argument's evidence is akin to a well-made tackle in football, causing the ball carrier's body to fall as his feet are knocked out from under him. An argument, too, will fall when its supportive evidence is knocked away.

In examining the value of evidence, you essentially test the viability of that evidence, and there are four general tests that ought to be considered in attempting to refute your opponents' evidence. These same tests ought to be applied to your own evidence before you enter the debate round to be certain it will stand up to the refutational indictments of your opponents.

General Tests

In examining all evidence, there are four general tests to consider:

1. Is the evidence up-to-date? Finding research material is not that difficult. Certainly, any library, even of modest size and content, contains a virtual plethora of potential sources of evidence for most any argument on any debate topic. However, it is imperative that the evidence be current, reflecting the up-to-date situation. For example, evidence from a source published in 1957 dealing with the number of poor in the United States would be of no value in a late 1970s debate. Obviously, many things have happened since 1957 that would make that piece of evidence so out-of-date that it would not serve the advancement of argument twenty or more years after the fact. Therefore, you must be certain that your evidence is current, that it reflects the way things are *now*.

If you are able to show that your opponents' evidence is dated, or if you are able to update your opponents' evidence by presenting more current evidence, then you can deny the viability of your opponents' evidence. Because of that fact, it is essential that you continue to do debate research throughout the academic year, that you not depend entirely upon evidence gathered at the start of the debate season. Evidence recorded in September may not be temporally pertinent the following January.

2. Is the source of the evidence credible? Each piece of evidence comes from somewhere, has some type of source. Often, the source will be a specific person, such as the author of a book or of an article in a magazine or scholarly journal. At other times, a piece of evidence will come from a very general source that is not ascribed to a specific individual, such as an article in a newspaper or an

unsigned article in a major news magazine. Regardless of the particular source, you ought to consider the viability of that source before accepting the evidence as stated. Because of the importance of source credibility, an entire subsection is devoted to this topic ("Source Tests") later in this chapter.

3. Is the evidence clear? The primary reason that evidence is utilized in formal argumentative encounters is to provide support for arguments used to advance a position. In so doing, the evidence presented needs to be clear so that those listening to the evidence can (*a*) understand what the evidence says and (*b*) understand equally well how the evidence actually supports the intended argument. Unclear or confusing evidence, therefore, does not serve as adequate support for arguments, but many debaters try to get by through the use of such unclear evidentiary materials. Specifically, in dealing with inherently complex and possibly confusing debate topics, such as economically oriented topics, much evidence seems to be rambling gobbledygook. In such instances, you ought not to accept any evidence you do not understand; you should challenge or question the viability of any piece of evidence that is structurally unclear. Evidence is of no value unless it clearly relates to the argument it is intended to support, and you should remind the critic-judge of that fact.

4. Is there a sufficient amount of evidence? Of course, the issue of evidence sufficiency is a large value judgment; it is not an issue that can be settled easily by conjuring up a number, saying that each argument must be supported by *x* pieces of evidence. Instead, you need to support every argument with an amount of evidence of sufficient specificity and quantity to cause a reasonable listener to accept the validity of that argument. Therefore, each argument needs to have several pieces of evidence as support, although only two or three need to be presented initially, saving the other evidence as backup for later speeches. In refutation, you need to assess the quantity of evidence used by your opponents in supporting their arguments, challenging your opponents to resubstantiate their positional statements with more evidence from additional sources. An argument or entire case position supported by little evidence or evidence from few sources indicates that that argument or case may be of minimal significance.

Facts Tests

After applying the four previous general tests of evidence, you need to consider the two general tests of facts, the examination of specific instances utilized by your opponents to support their arguments. Since contest debate essentially is an exercise in inductive reasoning (specific examples and arguments lead to a general conclusion as stated within the debate resolution), it is critical that those specific instances utilized to justify argument be examined to determine their argumentative viability.

First, are the facts and examples cited true or hypothetical? Too many debaters treat hypothetical examples as if they actually had happened, but, of course, a hypothetical example is only the creation of the speaker. Do not allow yourself or the critic-judge to be tricked into believing that such hypothetical examples are real; challenge your opponents to provide actual, not "what if" or "suppose that," examples.

If the example cited is real, challenge your opponents to show other examples to prove that their evidence is not atypical, that the example illustrates a widespread situation. One example does not prove much; one example, by itself, is relatively insignificant — a point you should make very clear to the critic-judge.

Second, are all the examples cited? Perhaps your opponents have cited only those instances that support their position, neglecting to mention those other instances that support your position. The use of counterexamples negates the impact of those initial examples, indicating that the overall situation is quite complex and not as clear-cut as your opponents would have the critic-judge believe.

Source Tests

The vast majority of evidence presented within a typical intercollegiate or interscholastic debate round is opinionated evidence, the type of evidence from authorities on the areas covered by the debate resolution. Because of this, you need to assess carefully the sources or authorities cited by your opponents in the presentation of their evidence. You must also remember that the mere publishing of a book or of an article within a book or magazine does not demonstrate that the author is qualified to write on his subject. On the contrary, many published experts are, in fact, not experts at all; many people have written books and articles without knowing anything about their subjects. Therefore, you need to examine most critically all sources cited by your opponents, and you need to do the same to the sources you wish to cite. Five tests of source credibility should be applied.

1. Is the source an expert? You ought to be certain that John

Doe knows what he has written about, that he is not someone who has paid some book publisher a few thousand dollars to have his ideas published — something that can be done rather easily. You need to know who the source is to challenge your opponents to prove that the source is credible to speak on the topic under discussion. If your opponents cannot certify their source's credibility, then you may argue that that piece of evidence has no value because it comes from an untrustworthy source.

2. Is the source trained in research?[2] This is an important issue when the source of information presents materials that resulted from the completion of some type of behavioral or experimental study. Again, literally anyone may conduct experimental study, but you need to know that the individual was trained in doing research for the results of the study to have validity.

3. Is the source prejudiced vis-à-vis the material presented as evidence? This question goes right to the heart of the issue of source credibility in determining the rhetorical viability of the piece of evidence. If you can demonstrate that the source is prejudiced, that she has "an axe to grind," then you will be able to blunt the supposed objectivity of the source's information. For example, in debating the topic of comprehensive medical care (or socialized medicine, as many described the topic), evidence from the head of the American Medical Association would be considered prejudicial in nature because of the AMA's well-known opposition to national health care proposals. That does *not* mean that that type of evidence is blithely disregarded; it means that such evidence must be taken with the proverbial grain of salt, because it is apt to be skewed in favor of the source's prejudice.

4. Is the source guilty of exaggeration? This question, too, goes to the heart of source credibility, dealing with the specific trustworthiness of the source of information. If you can demonstrate that (*a*) the information contained in your opponent's evidence is grossly exaggerated or (*b*) that the source has been guilty of exaggeration in the past, then you will be able to diminish the reliability of the source and her information. The more you know about the source's background and previous mistakes, the better you will be able to question this issue.

5. Finally, is the source guilty of positional inconsistency? If you can demonstrate that the source has shifted her position on the topic under consideration, showing the source flip-flopping from one position to another, then you can deny source credibility. During the 1976 presidential campaign, for example, opponents of Jimmy Carter constantly accused him of "waffling" on the issues,

indicting him for changing his position on major public issues to court favorable public opinion and contending that you never knew where Carter really stood on any of these issues. The intent of that indictment was to destroy Carter's credibility, something that ultimately was not successful, but you may attempt to deny source credibility in analyzing the sources of information offered by your opponents.

Statistics Tests

The great English prime minister Benjamin Disraeli might have been thinking of future American contest debate rounds when he noted the existence of "lies, damn lies, and statistics." Most debate encounters are showcases of statistical data from both affirmative and negative advocates, and both the speakers and the critic-judge can easily become lost in this swirling sea of percentages, ratios, and multiple-digit numbers. Because a primary issue in the making of decisions is *significance*, most affirmative teams attempt to justify their rationale for change upon some statistically based argument:

> Under the affirmative proposal, the United States will save thirty billion dollars per year.
>
> Every night, tens of thousands of American children cry themselves to sleep hungry.
>
> For every rapist sentenced to jail in the present system, eight thousand more go unpunished.

And on, and on. To many debaters, coaches, and critic-judges, the issue of significance has become a game of statistical comparisons and contrasts: the affirmative unloads its barrage of statistical data, and the negative counterattacks with its barrage of statistics. Novice debaters often wish they carried pocket calculators to keep pace with this statistical swirl.

However, you must remember that statistics, of and by themselves, are meaningless inherently. Numbers mean nothing unless and until someone puts some sort of value upon them, interprets them for argumentative power. In examining the statistical analyses of your opponents, remember the observation of Disraeli, because it is very easy to mislead people through the use of a barrage of numbers. Therefore, all statistical data ought to be scrutinized most carefully, and the following three statistics tests should be considered:

1. How were the statistics gathered and compiled? You ought to ask how the statistical data was arrived at: were materials counted

exactly one by one, or was a guess made according to some type of sampling procedure? Most national statistics, such as the monthly report on the unemployment rate, are but educated guesstimates of the real situation. How were these estimates made? How reliable has this statistical data been in the past? Those kinds of questions deal directly with the validity of the statistics thrown at you, and you should challenge your opponents to be able to prove the validity and reliability of their statistical evidence.

2. Do other studies confirm or verify these statistics? Conducting meaningful and accurate experimental studies is a most difficult task, requiring a high degree of study and expertise. Therefore, besides questioning the methodology followed in conducting such studies, you ought to determine whether or not the resultant statistical data is atypical. Perhaps your opponents have cited the only study that confirms their position. What about the results of other statistical studies?

3. Finally, in dealing with percentage data — a favorite type of statistical data in contest debate rounds — always ask: percent of what? For example, you might have heard this statistical position on a national television advertisement: "Sixty percent of doctors surveyed recommended the use of [Brand X] for the alleviation of headache pain." Now that is pretty impressive, isn't it? Sixty percent!

But, 60 percent of what? How many doctors were surveyed? The commercial does not tell you that, but that is a primary issue in determining the viability of that percentage. If, for example, only ten doctors were surveyed, then 60 percent of that number would be only six doctors, and that certainly is not too impressive. Therefore, percentages may be quite misleading unless you know or find out how many people actually were interviewed in arriving at a percentage.[3]

Every one of the preceding tests of evidence — general tests, tests of facts, tests of sources, and tests of statistics — ought to be considered in attempting to refute the evidence of your opponents. Again, if you are able to deny the validity of your opponents' evidence, you will deny those arguments supposedly supported by that evidence. Refutation of evidence, then, is a crucial part of your overall refutation of your opponents' case.

Specific Issues of Refutation

Essentially, every speech following the first affirmative constructive is a speech of refutation. Note the responsibilities of the seven remaining speeches within a traditionally structured debate round:

1NC: to deny the affirmative proposal by *refuting* the rationale for change

2AC: to resupport the affirmative rationale for change by *refuting* the indictments lodged by the 1NC speaker

2NC: to deny the viability of the affirmative plan by *refuting* its workability, practicality, and advantageousness

1NR: to deny the affirmative rationale for change by reissuing 1NC attacks and *refuting* 2AC responses

1AR: to resupport the affirmative plan by *refuting* 2NC plan attacks and to resupport the affirmative rationale for change by *refuting* 1NR arguments

2NR: to deny the entire affirmative case by reissuing major negative arguments and by *refuting* affirmative responses to those arguments

2AR: to resupport entire affirmative case structure by *refuting* major negative attacks against both the affirmative rationale for change and the affirmative plan

Thus, the materials pertaining to the refutation of evidence and the analysis of fallacious argument (discussed in chapter 10) are of pertinence to all speakers within an academic debate and to all speeches following the presentation of the basic affirmative case within the 1AC speech.

Besides these matters of evidence and argument, refutation centers on those specific issues that determine the outcome of the overall debate: harm, significance, inherency, topicality, solvency, feasibility, and advantage or disadvantage. Refutation and counterrefutation upon those issues make up the majority of arguments that occur within a debate; the resolution of those specific issues will determine who wins and who loses the debate encounter.

In offering refutation on those issues, it is essential that nothing be taken for granted in dealing with the critic-judge. That is why the importance of each refutative argument must be explained before the argument is presented, leaving nothing to chance and not assuming that the critic-judge will be able to recognize the importance of your efforts. You need to take a few minutes to explain, for example, the importance of inherency in an affirmative's rationale for change, and then you prove that the affirmative has failed to meet this responsibility by refuting the built-in inherency position in the affirmative case structure. But you must first preview your refutation by explaining the significance of your forthcoming argument. Each refutation argument should be explained so you will be certain the critic-judge is aware of what you are doing and why what you are doing is important.

Conclusion

Refutation is a primary component of all debate encounters; it lies at the heart of intercollegiate and interscholastic contest debate. By critically examining both the arguments and evidence offered by your opponents, you will isolate those issues, both general and specific, that merit your refutational arguments. Since refutation is the major component of seven of the eight contest debate speeches, it is a sound idea for debaters to engage in refutation exercises, practicing the refutation of arguments heard quite frequently within debates on that year's debate resolution. Effective refutation wins most contest debates; because of that, refutation ought to be studied and practiced most diligently.

References

1. See Aristotle, *The Rhetoric*, trans. Lane Cooper (New York: Appleton-Century-Crofts, 1932), pp. 177–181.

2. Arguments centering on the methodology followed in conducting both field and experimental studies are very difficult to develop and to communicate clearly to the critic-judge with precision. Therefore, before launching into attacks against the research abilities of your opponents' sources, you must be certain that you know enough about research methodology to handle this line of argumentation adequately. This is not an area for argument based on content ignorance.

3. For an excellent exemplification of how statistics may be manipulated to be misleading or to lead us to completely erroneous conclusions, see Darrell Huff, *How to Lie with Statistics* (New York: W. W. Norton, 1954).

PRACTICUM

1. You may engage in very simple refutation exercises even while relaxing at home during the evening. Turn on your television set and carefully watch the commercials that take up so much of prime time television programming:

- Is evidence presented in support of the products or services proffered by the commercials?
- What type of evidence is used most heavily in those commercial messages?
- After applying the tests of evidence to those commercials, have you found them to be viable or nonviable examples of public argument?

2. The following essay is an example of an extended refutational argument. Read it very carefully. Does it perform an adequate job of refuting the arguments presented in the essay? What do **you** now think about the operations of the Central Intelligence Agency? (The essay is from the ***Journal of Thought***, November 1977, pp. 308–318. Used by permission.)

The Debate over the CIA: The Case for Maintenance

James Edward Sayer

Since its inception via the National Security Act of 1947, the Central Intelligence Agency (CIA) has been a primary issue of concern for many people in the post–Second World War era. Initially created to serve as the focal point of this country's intelligence-gathering activities, the CIA has, in its thirty-year history, additionally taken on covert paramilitary and subversive operations that have served to bring the agency under Congressional and popular scrutiny and criticism. These "cloak-and-dagger" missions have thrown a shroud of secrecy around the CIA, and these covert actions, as well as the CIA itself, have become increasingly unpalatable to many people.

From the mid-1950s on, there were some in Congress who publicly expressed concern about the operations of the CIA and their role in the shaping of American foreign policy. Other congressmen, like Montana's Senator Mansfield, called for increased congressional control over the agency and its clandestine operations, but such outcries resulted in little change from the status quo. The CIA was seen by members of the Washington power structure as a unique resource of the presidency, believing that the CIA should be allowed to operate freely in the defense of American national security, responsible only to the president of the United States.

The abortive Bay of Pigs invasion caused another massive outcry against the CIA, and President Kennedy felt compelled to create the Foreign Intelligence Review Board (FIRB), an advisory body composed of civilians,to observe the operations of our intelligence-gathering agencies — in effect, "to snoop on the snoops." In actual practice, however, the FIRB had no real power as it was but an advisory body. Tempers cooled, the Cuban disaster was quickly forgotten in the wake of the Cuban missile crisis "victory," and the CIA went on about its business.

However, the CIA's support of the "secret war" in Laos, the bankrolling of the "Phoenix" program in Vietnam, domestic surveillance by operatives within the

United States, the agency's shadowy involvement in the Watergate fiasco, and the increasing feeling that the CIA was involved in the assassination of President Kennedy as well as in the planned executions of foreign leaders of state have thrust the agency back into the national spotlight. Many articles and books have appeared that supposedly "expose" the CIA's operations and attitudinal biases, and both houses of Congress seem to be engaged in a sort of race to see who can create the greater number of investigative subcommittees to examine putative CI errors — both past and present.

Perhaps the most interesting aspect of this renewed interest in the CIA has been the large body of literature produced on the subject. An interested individual could gather a score of books written about the CIA in just the past several years. What is even more interesting is the fact that the current CIA debate via the nation's publishing houses is being largely carried on by former-CIA personnel or others connected with the intelligence services. For the anti-CIA forces, one may read Victor Marchetti and John Marks' "The CIA and the Cult of Intelligence" or L. Fletcher Prouty's "The Secret Team." Both works detail the fabulous blunders of the CIA's clandestine operations, and the claim is made that the agency has served counterproductively in furthering American interests.

For the pro-CIA forces there are a number of books and articles by Miles Copeland and Harry H. Ransom, two authors who contend that we must have the CIA and its clandestine services to fight the communist-terrorist menace with the appropriate medicine. As one would expect, various CIA success stories are told and documented, resulting in the conclusion that the United States is better off having the CIA than it would be without it.

Unfortunately, throughout all of these recent publications there has been a strong current of writer bias. Marchetti and Marks, as well as Prouty to some extent, are disillusioned about the CIA and they transmit their unhappiness into print. After having to go through a hell-like process of censorship, forced upon them by the CIA itself, it comes as no surprise that the Marchetti and Marks work is highly negative toward the CIA. On the other hand, Copeland and Ransom enjoyed favorable contact with the agency and the general intelligence-gathering community, and their works manifest a most definitely favorable bias. In short, how one will feel about the CIA and its operations is a function of literature contact; it all depends upon whose book you happen to read, regardless of the issues involved.

Therefore, in an effort to shift the current confrontation over the CIA into an area where it belongs, I shall examine the main issues and points of contention involved, not the attitudinal biases and prejudices that have been the benchmark of the controversy up to this time. Since this writer has no bias either way toward the CIA, this debate can be viewed objectively upon the merits of the arguments in question. The best way to examine the confrontation is to review the main points of both forces before offering any conclusionary analysis.

First, the anti-CIA position, or those who want to eliminate all clandestine operations, if not the CIA, altogether. The arguments that fall within this position easily can be delineated into three categories: the lack of CIA covert operation necessity; the resultant counterproductivity of such operations; and the philosophical hypocrisy of covert activities.

At a theoretical level, the first anti-CIA argument, that it is no longer a necessary tool of America's foreign policy arsenal of the 1970s, strikes directly at the source of the rationale provided for the agency's creation. The 1947 National Security Act created the CIA to serve as the main funneling device in our intelligence-gathering efforts aimed at controlling the spread of international communism. As the years went by, however, it was discovered that the CIA could quite easily function as an operations agency as well, one that could take a direct hand in combatting communism all over the globe. Thus, the agency took part in the overthrow of the communist-leaning Premier Mossadegh of Iran in 1954, in actions against the Viet Minh both before and after the French collapse at Dienbienphu, and in minor operations as in Guatemala and Peru. These examples of CIA-sponsored successes are often pointd to by pro-CIA spokemen as illustrations of the usefulness of covert activities.

However, critics such as Marchetti and Marks now claim that similar covert activity is no longer necessary because the CIA aims its operations at the Third World countries, not at the two main communist threats: the Soviet Union and Red China. Since, they argue, only these two great superpowers pose any real threat to the security of the United States, the CIA's operations are a colossal waste of time. The agency has outlived its usefulness in mounting covert operations; they should, therefore, be discontinued.

The second main anti-CIA argument posits the claim that covert operations result in unjustified harms to both the citizens and governments of the United States and other nations. Often, this argument is composed of three subarguments: CIA covert activity causes or needlessly escalates wars, causes wanton wholesale killing of innocent individuals, and results in political blackmail when such operations fail.

As far as the causation or escalation of war argument is concerned, critics have tended to use Vietnam as an illustration of this indictment. Specifically, Marchetti and Marks and David Wise in "The Politics of Lying" have attempted to draw a connection between CIA cover activity and the escalation of the war in Vietnam. According to their analysis, CIA operations in North Vietnam prompted the attack on the American destroyers in Tonkin Gulf in August 1964, which, in turn, led to the passage of the vague Gulf of Tonkin resolution whereby President Lyndon johnson committed the full-range of this country's war powers to the struggle. Thus, the United States, because of the CIA, took the first step down the slippery slope to Southeast Asian disaster.

Along with this anti-CIA and anti–Vietnam war argument comes the contention that covert operations lead to needless suffering and the murder of innocent people trapped by clandestine warfare. Two examples are generally cited to support this indictment: the CIA's sponsorship of the "Phoenix" program in South Vietnam and supposed widespread slaughter of innocents that occured after the collapse of the Allende regime in Chile via military coup. Both examples provide the most concrete evidence of the harm of CIA covert activities.

During the struggle in Vietnam one of the most effective Viet Cong campaigns was the terrorist program designed to prevent a strong alliance between the South Vietnamese villagers and the Saigon government. Through the use of physical violence, the Viet Cong were able to terrorize the countryside, preventing effective South Vietnamese/American "control" of the majority of the country's land area. To combat this obstacle, the CIA, with military support, began the "Phoenix" program in the late 1960s, a counterterrorist program designed to rid the countryside of communist agents and sympathizers. Some twenty-thousand villagers and officials were killed during the operation of this program. CIA critics have charged that this was nothing more than unjustified mass murder, a program as reprehensible as the initial communist terrorist program that brought "Phoenix" into existence.

Similarly, these critics have abhorred the reported mass executions and jailings of Marxist sympathizers after the Chilean coup that toppled Salvador Allende from power. The CIA is blamed for this postcoup suffering because of the agency's support of labor factions whose slowdown of the economy resulted in the socioeconomic chaos that led to the coup. The CIA's pumping of some eight million anti-Allende dollars into the Chilean political turmoil is seen as the prime causative factor in the overthrow of the Allende government and subsequent civil wronging promulgated by the junta. Thus, these two examples are cited as current illustrations of how CIA operations result in harm to innocent individuals.

The third supportive subargument is the contention that unsuccessful operations can lead to the blackmailing of the United States government. Since the main strength of CIA covert missions is their secretiveness, disclosure of such operations would damage the very rationale for their undertaking. Hence, it is argued, operations that are discovered can be used by the country involved to force concessions from the United States to keep such operations secret. This threat of political blackmail creates the unpleasant spectre of American dollars being bilked from our treasury to prevent covert disclosure.

The final major anti-CIA argument posits the value judgment that covert actions are a hypocritical contradiction of this country's basic democratic ideals and underpinnings. Marchetti and Marks claim that such covert operations have "no place in a democratic society" and are "contrary to the most basic American ideals." Again, the overthrow of Chilean President Salvador Allende is used to exemplify this supposed philosophical contradiction. On the one hand, the argument goes, the United States is committed to the support of all democratically elected governments throughout the world; we espouse the cause of national self-determination. However, this philosophical committment is directly denied by such operations as the CIA's Chilean venture, wherein a great amount of money was spent in the overthrow of the popularly elected Allende regime.

Taken as a whole, it can be seen that the three major anti-CIA arguments cover a wide range of issues, from operational failures of covert missions to the philosophical hypocrisy of such covert activities. In all cases, however, the same general conclusion is reached: CIA covert operations are counterproductive, doing more harm than good to United States foreign policy. CIA critics tend to draw on-balance comparisons that indicate the disadvantageousness of field operations. Therefore, they contend, the CIA should get out of the dirty business of covert actions altogether. Their need no longer exists; they are but an anachronism of the Cold War. There are some who believe that the Agency itself must be dismantled.

What of the pro-CIA forces? What do they have to say about the agency and its activities? Not surprisingly, most of the pro-CIA spokesmen, like the majority of their antagonists, are either current or former intelligence personnel. The best method for analyzing and evaluating the pro-CIA arguments is to juxtapose them with the anti-CIA arguments.

Covert operations are no longer necessary

To this first argument, the advocates of CIA covert activity respond that there still exists the need for clandestine capabilities. Specifically, they turn to five separate reasons that justify the continued use of covert powers: (*1*) the need to influence events in a volatile world situation; (*2*) to serve as an effective Cold War weapon; (*3*) to deal directly with the Soviet Union's KGB; (*4*) to combat contemporary terrorists groups; and (*5*) to provide the United States with a critical foreign policy tool that is one step short of full-scale war. Because of their significance, each supportive argument needs to be examined individually.

Covert action proponents claim that clandestine capabilities need to be maintained and occasionally utilized to deal with the current world situation. While 90 to 95 percent of the CIA's activities involve only pure "intelligence," i.e., information gathering, the remaining 5 percent capacity is needed to ensure our ability to respond to immediate crises. Since we cannot know what will happen in the future, the pro-CIA advocates contend that we must have a flexible system of response, including the use of covert operations. Even the generally critical *Time* magazine has conceded that we cannot limit ourselves to mere information gathering, concluding that "trying to influence events may at times be necessary."

Closely related to the above argument is the contention that CIA covert operations serve as an effective Cold War weapon. Not only do covert activities include military and paramilitary operations as in Laos and South Vietnam, they also include the transfer of money, equipment, and weaponry that can be used to influence the settlement of political turmoil. Even staunch CIA critics Marchetti and Marks have admitted that "...the CIA's clandestine Services have, over the years, enjoyed considerable success." The example of the Chilean coup, constantly mentioned by the anti-CIA forces, can be used to exemplify the effectiveness of covert activities in waging the Cold War.

Besides serving as a general foreign policy tool, CIA advocates additionally claim that covert actions are needed to deal with the Soviet union's covert operations service — the KGB. Young Hum Kim noted in *The Central Ingelligence Agency* that we must be prepared "to use the techniques of covert political warfare" to thwart communist expansion. Time reported that the KGB attempted governmental subversion or overthrow in several nations during recent years: the Congo (1963), Ghana (1966), Mexico (1971), and Yugoslavia (1974). The CIA has been quite effective in preventing the culmination of KGB operational goals, a point admitted by most CIA critics. Therefore, to offset the designs of the KGB, CIA proponents contend that covert capabilities must be maintained.

However, an even more dangerous situation is created

by the world's numerous terrorist organizations. Not tied to any one political philosophy or entity, these bands of individuals can strike almost anywhere at any time for any reason they desire. Strong CIA supporter Miles Copeland has envisioned the possibility of a terrorist group's attempting to cut us off from needed resources and raw materials — oil, uranium, the various metallic resources of Southeast Asia and South America, etc. Plus, there is the increasing fear that a terrorist group might secure the necessary hardware to build nuclear weapons or attempt to seize an existing American nuclear arsenal. To combat this threat it is asserted that covert operations must be utilized. Besides gathering data on the infrastructure, goals, and operations of terrorist groups, it may be necessary to infiltrate these organizations and to eliminate some of their leaders. While such operations are truly "dirty business," CIA advocates contend that this is highly superior to the situation created by a group like Black September's gaining access to nuclear materials.

Perhaps tying all the previous arguments together is the final contention that CIA covert missions provide a viable foreign policy tool that is one step short of war. Not only do covert operations allow us to combat Soviet designs without running the risk of setting off World War III (a point often made by Copeland), they also provide us with flexiblity in crisis situations. Therefore, "flexibility" serves as an important justification for the continuation of CIA policies and activities.

Covert operations are counterproductive

As noted before, the second anti-CIA argument often consists of three subarguments declaiming the harms of CIA covert missions — the causation of war, the wanton killing of innocents, and the political blackmail of the United States. As each is supported by recent evidence and examples, each subargument will be examined individually.

Opponents of the CIA contend that it was the agency's operations in North Vietnam that led to the Tonkin Gulf incident that caused the escalation of the war. If this contention is accurate, most of the lives and treasure expended from 1965 to 1973 could be billed to the CIA.

However, as CIA proponents point out, there is no clear causal connection drawn in this scheme of events. The United States already had a sizable military detachment in Vietnam prior to Tonkin Gulf — in fact, the war had been growing in intensity for some six months prior to the incident. In addition, David Wise, the leading advocate of the CIA–Vietnam war connection, provides other evidence that indicates President Johnson wanted to enlarge the war prior to the Tonkin Gulf attack. If this is accurate, then the CIA's covert actions were irrelevant in the escalation of the war. Any excuse would have sufficed to implement the existing predisposition to widen the conflict.

Have CIA covert operations caused the unjustified deaths of innocents as in Vietnam under the "Phoenix" program and in Chile after the Allende coup? Pro-CIA forces quickly point out that "Phoenix" was aimed at the elimination of Viet Cong members and sympathizers, not just any villagers who got in the way. As Miles Copeland has noted, "Its surgical precision cost fewer lives than the shotgun methods used by the South Vietnamese" prior to the inception of the "Phoenix" program. Although no one relishes the thought of killing more than twenty thousand people, Vietnam most definitely was a war zone in which the communists had killed many more civilians under their terrorist program begun in the early 1960s.

As far as the Chilean episode is concerned, pro-CIA advocates have tended to argue that the agency cannot be blamed for Salvador Allende's downfall. While it is admitted that the CIA pumped eight million dollars into anti-Allende labor groups, it is also argued that the causes of his downfall existed prior to the CIA's involvement: the rapid deterioration of the economy due to mismanagement and inadequate planning, the loss of investment money after Allende's expropriation of foreign copper interests in 1970, and the dictatorial manner in which Allende dealt with political dissidents and other non-Marxist South American nations. In short, the CIA-Chile connection is denied much the same way as the CIA-Vietnam connection: inadequate causality to prove harm or to justify recriminations against the agency.

Finally, these pro-CIA writers claim that the threat of blackmailing the United States when covert operations backfire is ludicrous. Although such missions, by their inherent nature, require secrecy to be effective, no great harm will be engendered by their eventual disclosure. Add to this the fact that the CIA has become the whipping boy for all malcontents throughout the world, and it can be seen that public accusation of CIA malevolence adds nothing new to the world political scene. Even as long ago as 1966, the *New York Times* reported that "the agency has been accused of almost anything anyone wanted to accuse it of." Blackmail is only viable against an individual or organization of unsullied reputation; the CIA certainly does not fit this description.

Covert operations contradict American ideals and values

This final point of conflict brings arguments of political philosophy into direct clash with arguments of supposed "real world" reality. CIA critics assert that the United States has no business snooping about and influencing the internal affairs of other countries. Americans cherish their privacy and demand that their lives receive minimal interference from outside sources. Why do we not conduct our foreign policy activities in accordance with this domestic view?

Pro-CIA advocates counter this argument with the observation that we would not need the CIA at all if the entire world minded its own business. Unfortunately, there are groups and governments that continually disrupt world peace and security, endangering the tranquillity that most people desire. Thus, to secure as much peace as possible, the influencing of events may be occasionally necessary. CIA covert operations provide an effective foreign policy tool in the achievement of this goal at a lesser price than full-scale warfare. The realities of life in the thermonuclear age make the CIA and its covert operations essential to continued existence.

Conclusion

Having briefly presented the main anti-CIA covert operations arguments and their rebuttal statements, a few observations about this ongoing debate are in order. First, the difficulty with the overall conflict lies in its value-oriented nature. That is, so much of what one feels about the

CIA and covert operations is dependent upon individual value judgments that it is impossible to analyze the arguments the same way that movements of chess pieces might be analyzed. Each individual's value system will play a large role in the evaluation of the current debate over the CIA.

Second, the debate has not received equitable space and coverage in the nation's mass media. It is much easier for the American consumer of ideas and information to secure anti-CIA material than that of the opposite viewpoint. Newspaper headlines, quick magazine pieces, and the like have tended to paint an unrealistic picture of CIA actions. Materials from the mass media create the impression that all the CIA does is engage in cloak-and-dagger James Bond–type stuff. However, these covert operations play a minor role in the agency's overall work effort, but the American public rarely sees the entire story. Much of the current misinformation and misanalysis to be found in the current CIA debate is due to skewed analysis and reporting by the mass media.

Finally, this writer would like to offer his own on-balance analysis of the debate and the value of CIA covert operations. While no one can accept gleefully the idea that clandestine operations are useful and necessary, the realities of the 1970s force us to make that conclusion. In a world filled with terrorist groups, continuing communist agitation, and threats to the peace and security of the Free World, we are much better off with the CIA than we would be without it. Although it is true that the CIA has bungled missions and has become overzealous in carrying out certain assignments, these failures and excesses do not justify the dismantling of the agency. Closer cooperation between the White House and Congress, and greater oversight by the Congress, can eliminate errors of thought and action by the CIA. In our zeal to purge ourselves of everything unseemly in the wake of Watergate, we must not allow ourselves to throw out the immense good provided by the CIA to rid ourselves on the few items of error. The on-balance analysis of arguments clearly shows that the merits of the debate lie with those supporting the continued existence and operation of the CIA.

Footnotes to Essay

Copeland, Miles. *The Game of Nations.* New York: Simon and Schuster, 1970.

Kim, Young Hum. *The Central Intelligence Agency.* Lexington, Mass.: D.C. Heath, 1968.

Kirkpatrick, Lyman B. *The Real CIA.* New York: Macmillan, 1968.

Marchetti, Victor, and Marks, John. *The CIA and the Cult of Intelligence.* New York: Alfred A. Knopf, 1974.

McGarvey, Patrick. *CIA: The Myth and the Madness.* New York: Saturday Review Press, 1972.

Ransom, Harry H. *Central Intelligence and National Security.* Cambridge, Mass.: Harvard University Press, 1958.

Ransom, Harry H. *Can American Democracy Survive Cold War?* Garden City, New York: Doubleday, 1963.

Wise, David, and Ross, Thomas B. *The Invisible Government.* New York: Bantam, 1964.

Wise, David. *The Politics of Lying.* New York: Random House, 1973.

Chapter 15

Forms of Debate

* **Traditional Tournament Debate Formats**
* **Additional Debate Formats**
* **Conclusion**
* **References**
* **Practicum**

There are or can be countless forms of debate, encompassing both formal and informal argumentative encounters and including both prepared and completely impromptu clashes over mutually agreed upon issues. You can debate with your parents, friends, teachers, or anyone else, and the formats utilized may be strictly adhered to or only loosely observed. Debates take place at religious gatherings, in scholarly conventions, and, of course, in the various state legislatures and within the United States Congress. Occasionally major political candidates take part in debates, such as Richard Nixon and John Kennedy in 1960 and Gerald Ford and Jimmy Carter in 1976. Even the courtroom advocacy found within criminal and civil trials may be considered a very specialized form of debate.

However, most formal debate today takes place within the academic setting, particularly the kinds of formal advocacy found within formal interscholastic and intercollegiate debate rounds. Therefore, the forms of debate discussed within this chapter are those directly pertinent to academic debate competition and to the use of debate as an instructional tool within a classroom setting. Such formats can easily be used, moreover, in nonacademic settings, since these various formats can be modified to meet the needs of specific audiences and occasions.

Traditional Tournament Debate Formats

Debate as a contest activity, complete with trophies and other similar prizes, is an important element of both high school and college and university extracurricular activities. Countless thousands of high school and college debaters take part in this year-long activity, and untold millions of dollars support this nationwide academic experience.[1] Because debate tournaments bring together competing debaters from a number of schools and often from various states, a uniform format for such contest activity is essential. At both the high school and college level, there are three formats used in contest debating: the traditional or Oxford format, the cross-examination format, and the Lincoln-Douglas format. This section examines each one of those most prevalent contest debate formats.

Oxford Debate

The Oxford or traditional debate format is the most prevalent structure found within both high school and intercollegiate debate tournaments, and it is the format with which novice debaters generally become most familiar as they begin their study of this form of argumentative communication. The preceding chapters have utilized the Oxford format in many examples, so the specific structure of an Oxford-style debate should look familiar to you by now:

Speech	Time Limit	
	High School	College
First affirmative constructive	8 minutes	10 minutes
First negative constructive	8 minutes	10 minutes
Second affirmative constructive	8 minutes	10 minutes
Second negative constructive	8 minutes	10 minutes
First negative rebuttal	4 minutes	5 minutes
First affirmative rebuttal	4 minutes	5 minutes
Second negative rebuttal	4 minutes	5 minutes
Second affirmative rebuttal	4 minutes	5 minutes
TOTAL	48 minutes	60 minutes

In an Oxford-style debate, each debater is responsible for presenting two speeches, a ten-minute constructive speech (eight minutes for the high school debater) and a five-minute rebuttal speech (four minutes for the high school debater.) The basic responsibilities for each speaker are those delineated in chapter 13, "Duties of Advocacy Speaking." The vast majority of academic debate contests in this country, at both the interscholastic and intercollegiate levels, utilize the Oxford format for tournament competition.

Cross-Examination Debate

The second most prevalent contest debate format is cross-examination, a style that has come into increasing use at both the high school and college levels during the past decade. Cross-examination debate allows the advocates to interact directly during the debate round, as each speaker asks and answers questions concerning the arguments and evidence presented within the contest.

Cross-examination debate has the following structure:[2]

	Time Limit	
Speech	**High School/ College**	**College**
First affirmative constructive	8 minutes	10 minutes
Negative cross-examination period	3 minutes	3 minutes
First negative constructive	8 minutes	10 minutes
Affirmative cross-examination period	3 minutes	3 minutes
Second affirmative constructive	8 minutes	10 minutes
Negative cross-examination period	3 minutes	3 minutes
Second negative constructive	8 minutes	10 minutes
Affirmative cross-examination period	3 minutes	3 minutes
First negative rebuttal	4 minutes	5 minutes
First affirmative rebuttal	4 minutes	5 minutes
Second negative rebuttal	4 minutes	5 minutes
Second affirmative rebuttal	4 minutes	5 minutes
Total	60 minutes	72 minutes

Within the cross-examination structure, each speaker has the responsibilities of asking questions during a cross-examination period and of answering questions during the cross-examination period immediately following his constructive speech. Therefore, each speaker must be prepared to defend his own arguments and evidence and critically question the arguments and evidence offered by the opposition. Because of the intricate and important nature of cross-examination debating, an entire chapter has been devoted to the skills of cross-examination: chapter 17, "Techniques of Cross-Examination."

Lincoln-Douglas Debate

This final major tournament debate format, Lincoln-Douglas, does not involve two-person debate teams as do the Oxford and cross-examination formats. Instead, as in the debates between senatorial candidates Abraham Lincoln and Stephen Douglas, only two debaters, one upholding the affirmative position and the other the negative position, take part in the contest. There are no debate partners or colleagues; the speaker must stand by herself in the argumentative encounter. Because of this factor, Lincoln-Douglas debate should be utilized only by the most experienced debaters.

Although there are a number of possible structures for a Lincoln-Douglas debate, a very popular structure incorporates the excitement of the give-and-take of cross-examination.

Speech	**Time Limit**
Affirmative constructive	10 minutes
Negative cross-examination period	3 minutes
Negative constructive	15 minutes
Affirmative cross-examination period	3 minutes
Affirmative rebuttal	5 minutes
Total	36 minutes

You should note that this format retains two of the most important elements of traditional two-person team debate contests. First, both speakers have an equal amount of speaking time with the affirmative advocate having two speeches totaling fifteen minutes, and the negative has one fifteen-minute speech. Second, the format has the affirmative both initiate and conclude the debate.

Lincoln-Douglas debate is an excellent format for classroom competition, because it provides plenty of time for postdebate analysis within the normal one-hour academic class period. Also, the Lincoln-Douglas format provides an interesting departure from the more traditional formats, adding a bit of excitement for the competing debaters. Because of that factor, coaches might wish to use the Lincoln-Douglas structure as a training device in intrasquad debates.[3]

Additional Debate Formats

Although the preceding three debate formats are the ones generally found at debate tournaments at both the interscholastic and intercollegiate contest levels, there are six other formats that may be utilized for training in argumentation or contest debate encounters.

Split-Team Debate

The split-team debate format, which is used very rarely, can be used to inject excitement and the element of the unknown into any interscholastic or intercollegiate debate tournament. Its structure is as its name implies: teams are put together by splitting up the regular tournament debate teams. For example, debater A from the University of Southern California might be teamed with debater B from Wright State University, debater C from Hutchinson Junior College might be teamed with debater D from Northern Arizona University, and so on. Debaters from different schools are teamed together for the duration of the tournament.

Of course, these new debate partners would have to decide quickly who would be the first affirmative speaker, the first negative speaker, whose affirmative case would be used, and other such issues so critical to the functional and successful operation of debate teams in contest situations. The major strength of this debate format is that it provides the debater with an unusual contest speaking situation, compelling her to react quickly in cooperating with a new partner. The concomitant weakness of this format is that teamwork generally is poor, and the quality of the overall debate is lower than normal — two factors caused by pairing two unfamiliar debaters with one another with little or no time provided for the development of a working teammate rapport. Because split-team debating puts a great burden on individual skill and the ability to adjust to new circumstances quickly, only very experienced debaters should be considered for this type of debate format.

Extemporaneous Debate

Another debate format that puts a great burden upon the debater to think and react quickly to unusual tournament circumstances is the extemporaneous debate format, wherein the topic for debate is not announced until a few hours before the start of the tournament.[4] Since it would be impossible to research an entirely new topic in an hour or two, a few hundred pieces of evidence often are given to each team at the time the topic is announced, allowing the debaters but a short time to organize this evidence and to develop an affirmative case from this evidence.

Those who favor extemporaneous debating claim that this format discovers who really can debate, finding out who can deal with basic argumentative issues after only the barest preparation. Unfortunately, this style of debate generally leads to superficial argumentation, weak or nonexistant argumentative extensions, and poor overall debate performances. If the goal is to discover who has best mastered debate style, then extemporaneous debate will meet this goal nicely. If, on the other hand, the goal of debate is to hear sound, solid, and well-reasoned arguments on important issues, then this debate format is to be avoided.

Heckling Debate

Somewhat similar to the cross-examination form is the heckling debate format, a structure that allows direct one-to-one verbal interaction among the competing debaters. Unlike cross-examination, however, heckling debate does not provide a specific period for the asking of questions; questions are posed during the presentation of a debater's constructive speech. Two rules control the timing and amount of heckling that may take place:

1. Questions may *not* be asked during the first three minutes and final minute of the constructive speech. In those instances where heckling is allowed during rebuttals, questions may *not* be asked during the first and last minute of a debater's rebuttal speech.
2. Only a limited number of questions may be asked, generally four during constructive speeches and two during rebuttal speeches.

Heckling provides the same opportunity to probe matters of argument and evidence as does cross-examination debate, with one significant difference: the debater answering questions does not know when the questions will be asked. This unknown factor puts more pressure upon the debater, creating a more realistic speaking situation, because, after all, in nonacademic settings questions may be asked of you anyplace at any time.

Moot Court Debate

This debate structure, often known as mock trial, is particularly useful in classroom settings as the academic year progresses. Moot court injects added interest into the study of a debate topic, and this format allows more than two or four people to take part in the controversy.

Basically, moot court is structured upon the criminal court system: the prosecution serves the role of affirmative advocacy, and the defense assumes the rule of the negative. Overall, twelve people are used in operating the moot court: two prosecutors, two defense attorneys, three prosecution witnesses, three defense witnesses, one bailiff, and one judge. The remaining members of the class serve as jurors.

Major lines of argument are presented by the main representatives of the prosecution and defense; evidence is presented by the expert witnesses for each side. These witnesses must be familiar with their material to withstand the rigors of cross-examination.

Here are the basic rules for running the moot court:

Rules for Moot Court

1st prosecutor:	gives five-minute introduction of points of contention
1st defense counselor:	gives five-minute introduction of points he hopes to prove

Prosecution (Affirmative) Witnesses:

1st prosecutor:	examines his first witness for five minutes
2nd defense counselor:	cross-examines for three minutes
1st prosecutor:	examines his second witness for five minutes
2nd defense counselor:	cross-examines for three minutes

1st prosecutor: examines his third witness for five minutes

2nd defense counselor: cross-examines for three minutes

Defense (Negative) Witnesses:

1st defense counselor: five minutes of questions

2nd prosecutor: three minutes of cross-examination

Rebuttals:

After all witnesses have been heard, the 2nd defense counselor gives a two-minute summary, followed by a two-minute summary by the 2nd prosecutor. Then, both the 1st defense counselor and the 1st prosecutor give three-minute summaries, in that order.

The *bailiff* will swear in every witness: "Do you swear (or affirm) that the testimony and evidence given in this court will be the truth to the best of your ability?" The bailiff will also call each witness.

If either the defense or prosecution feels that something is objectionable, an appeal should be made to the judge, stating upon what grounds the objection is lodged. The judge will rule in all cases.

Grounds for Objection:

1. irrelevant question
2. leading question
3. repetitious question
4. argumentative question

Moot court is an excellent device for involving an entire class in the debate activity, and it is also very effective in improving the participants' speaking abilities and sharpening their cross-examination skills. Students also learn a great deal about the operations of the American court system from this debate format.

Parliamentary Debate

Another excellent training device for the classroom is the parliamentary debate format, another structure that allows everyone in the class to participate. Although there are many varying forms of parliamentary debate, the following format serves classroom purposes well:

five members of the affirmative
five members of the negative
one chairman
audience

Each speaker is given five minutes for an initial or constructive presentation and three minutes for a rejoinder or rebuttal speech. Advocates speak alternately, with an affirmative speaker followed by a negative speaker and so on. During the course of the initial presentations, members of the opposing team, as well as members of the audience, may ask the speaker questions. No questioning is allowed during the rebuttal speeches. The chairman maintains decorum and prohibits inappropriate questioning by the opposition and the audience.

Parliamentary debate offers three advantages over traditional debate structures for the study of the principles of argumentation. First, parliamentary debate is more deliberative than adversarial in nature, making it much more relevant to the types of argumentative discussions engaged in by members of society. Most discussions are functionally deliberative, and the structure of parliamentary debate accentuates this real-life situation. Second, this form of debate applies the principles of negotiation and compromise, emphasizing group consideration and consensus. Finally, parliamentary debate is not so intricate or as jargonized as traditional debate formats. Ideas and thoughts predominate over form, thereby highlighting the important aspects of the study of argumentation.

The English have utilized the parliamentary debate form for many years; they prefer it to our highly competitive tournament debate structures. At least for teaching purposes, the parliamentary mode is a highly effective tool for the study of the basics of effective argumentative communication.[5]

Direct Clash debate

The last debate format to be considered here is direct clash debate, a structure rarely found in tournament competition but which is excellent for intrasquad practices. Direct clash focuses upon specific issues, with a decision rendered by the critic-judge at the conclusion of each clash. Thus, a direct clash debate consists of several specific clashes, with the overall debate continuing until one side wins three of the clashes.[6]

The following is the structure of a direct clash debate:

Preclash Stage	**Time Limit**
First affirmative defines terms of the topic, states those issues the affirmative wishes to debate	5 minutes
First negative accepts or rejects the affirmative definitions; accepts, rejects, or adds to those issues to be debated by the affirmative	5 minutes
First Clash	
Second affirmative presents and documents one issue critical to the affirmative position	4 minutes
Second negative refutes 2A speech	3 minutes
First affirmative resupports 2A speech	3 minutes
First negative recapitulates negative refutation to affirmative issue	3 minutes
The critic-judge announces the winner of the first clash	
Second Clash	
Second negative presents and documents one issue critical to the negative position	4 minutes
Second affirmative refutes 2N speech	3 minutes
First negative resupports 2N speech	3 minutes
First affirmative recapitulates affirmative refutation to negative issue	3 minutes
The critic-judge announces the winner of the second clash	

This pattern is maintained until one side has won three clashes; thus, a direct clash debate may contain as many as five separate clashes within its structure.

Because of the uncertain time factor, direct clash debate rarely is utilized in tournament competition. However, for pinpointing one's analysis on certain issues and for training debaters in how to deal with certain issues, there is no better teaching device than direct clash debate.

Conclusion

The popularity of academic debate has increased dramatically since the early 1950s. Countless thousands of students engage in debate contests at both the interscholastic and intercollegiate levels. Certainly, tournament debating is big business within the academic structures of American higher education. With so many debaters and debate tournaments, it is not surprising to find that uniform debate formats have emerged that allow for such national competition to be carried on so easily. Oxford, cross-examination, and Lincoln-Douglas formats are the three major structures by which contest debates are conducted.

However, your study of argumentative communication does not have to be limited by those three tournament debate formats. There are numerous possibilities for organizing and controlling debate encounters, and several other debate formats are delineated that might be more suitable for the study of the principles of debate in a classroom setting.

References

1. See James H. McBath, "Beyond the Seventies," *The Journal of the American Forensic Association* 8 (Spring 1972): 175–177.

2. See J. Stanley Gray, "The Oregon Plan of Debating," *Quarterly Journal of Speech* 12 (April 1926): 175–180.

3. The popularity of the Lincoln-Douglas debate format has been on the upswing since the use of that structure for the nationwide Bicentennial Youth Debates in 1976.

4. See Russell R. Marks and W. Barnett Pearce, "The Protagoras Memorial Debate Tournament," *The Journal of the American Forensic Association* 7 (Spring 1971): 284–287.

5. Parliamentary debate has received increased study for possible use in intercollegiate debate tournaments as exemplified by Action Caucuses held at the conventions of the Speech Communication Association in 1977 and 1978.

6. See Edwin H. Paget, "Rules for the Direct Clash Debate Plan," *Quarterly Journal of Speech* 23 (October 1937): 431–433.

Practicum

1. Here is an interesting and challenging project for you and your classmates to undertake. The televised debates between presidential candidates in 1960 (Kennedy versus Nixon) and 1976 (Ford versus Carter) were praised by political analysts as being very useful in raising the political consciousness of the American people. However, very few were happy with the variable formats used within these debates. Your task is to devise a format for future presidential debates:

- Would you favor using the Oxford format, with the presidential candidates teamed with their respective vice-presidential candidates?
- Would you favor using the Lincoln-Douglas format outlined within this chapter?
- Or would you prefer an entirely new and different format? If so, what would that format be?

2. The "Lincoln-Douglas" debate format has its roots in a historical event. In 1858, Stephen A. Douglas and Abraham Lincoln were campaigning for a seat in the United States Senate, and several head-to-head debates were held as part of that general campaign.

The following is an extract of the very first Lincoln-Douglas debate of 21 August 1858, held in Ottowa, Illinois. Examine the arguments presented by both speakers. With whom would you agree? Which speaker was the better argumentative advocate?

Mr. Douglas won the Senate seat, but his long sought prize, the presidency, eluded him. On the other hand, Mr. Lincoln emerged from these debates as a respected national figure; two years later, he was elected president of the United States.

Mr. Douglas's Opening Speech

Ladies and Gentlemen, — I appear before you to-day for the purpose of discussing the leading political topics which now agitate the public mind. By an arrangement between Mr. Lincoln and myself, we are present here to-day for the purpose of having a joint discussion, as the representatives of the two great political parties of the State and Union, upon the principles in issue between those parties; and this vast concourse of people shows the deep feeling which pervades the public mind in regard to the questions dividing us.

Prior to 1854, this country was divided into two great political parties, known as the Whig and Democratic parties. Both were national and patriotic, advocating principles that were universal in their application. An old-line Whig could proclaim his principles in Louisiana and Massachussets alike. Whig principles had no boundary sectional line: they were not limited by the Ohio River, nor by the Potomac, nor by the line of free and slave States, but applied and were proclaimed wherever the Constitution ruled or the American flag waved over the American soil. So it was and so it is with the great Democratic party, which, from the days of Jefferson until this period, has proven itself to be the historic party of this nation. While the Whig and Democratic parties differed in regard to a bank, the tariff, distribution, the specie circular, and the sub-treasury, they agreed on the great slavery question which now agitates the Union. I say that the Whig party and the Democratic party agreed on the slavery question, while they differed on those matters of expediency to which I have referred. The Whig party and the Democratic party jointly adopted the compromise measures of 1850 as the basis of a proper and just solution of the slavery question in all its forms. Clay was the great leader, with Webster on his right and Cass on his left, and sustained by the patriots in the Whig and Democratic ranks who had devised and enacted the compromise measures of 1850.

In 1851 the Whig party and the Democratic party united in Illinois in adopting resolutions indorsing and approving the principles of the compromise measures of 1850 as the proper adjustment of that question. In 1852, when the Whig party assembled in convention at Baltimore for the purpose of nominating a candidate for the presidency, the first thing it did was to declare the compromise measures of 1850, in substance and in principle, a suitable adjustment of that question. [Here the speaker was interrupted by loud and long-continued applause.] My friends, silence will be more acceptable to me in the discussion of these questions than applause. I desire to address myself to your judgment, your understanding, and your consciences, and not to your passions or your enthusiasm. When the Democratic convention assembled in Baltimore in the same year, for the purpose of nominating a Democratic candidate for the presidency, it also adopted the compromise measures of 1850 as the basis of Democratic action. Thus you see that up to 1853–1854 the Whig party and the Democratic party both stood on the same platform with regard to the slavery question. That platform was the right of the people of each State and each Territory to decide their local and domestic institutions for themselves, subject only to the Federal Constitution.

During the session of Congress of 1853–54 I introduced into the Senate of the United States a bill to organize the Territories of Kansas and Nebraska on that principle which had been adopted in the compromise measures of 1850, approved by the Whig party and the Democratic party in Illinois in 1851, and indorsed by the Whig party and the Democratic party in national convention in 1852. In order that there might be no misunderstanding in relation to the principle involved in the Kansas and Nebraska bill, I put forth the true intent and meaning of the act in these words: "It is the true intent and meaning of this act not to legislate slavery into any State or Territory, or to exclude it therefrom, but to leave the people thereof perfectly free to form and regulate their domestic institutions in their own way, subject only to the Federal Constitution." Thus you see that up to 1854, when the Kansas and Nebraska bill was brought into Congress for the purpose of carrying out the principles which both parties had up to that time indorsed and approved, there had been no division in this country in regard to that principle except the opposition of the Abolitionists. In the House of Representatives of the Illinois legislature, upon a resolution asserting that principle, every Whig and every Democrat in the House voted in the affirmative, and only four men voted against it, and those four were old-line Abolitionists.

In 1854 Mr. Abraham Lincoln and Mr. Lyman Trumbull entered into an arrangement, one with the other, and each with his respective friends, to dissolve the old Whig party on the one hand, and to dissolve the old Democratic party on the other, and to connect the members of both into an Abolition party, under the name and disguise of a Republican party. The terms of that agreement between Lincoln and Trumbull have been published by Lincoln's special friend, James H. Matheny, Esq.; and they were that Lincoln should have General Shields's place in the United States Senate, which was then about to become vacant, and that Trumbull should have my seat when my term expired. Lincoln went to work to Abolitionize the Old Whig party all over the State, pretending that he was then as good a Whig as ever; and Trumbull went to work in his part of the State preaching abolitionism in its milder and lighter form, and trying to Abolitionize the Democratic party, and bring old Democrats handcuffed and bound hand and foot into the Abolition camp. In pursuance of the arrangement the parties met at Springfield in October, 1854, and proclaimed their new platform. Lincoln was to bring into the Abolition camp the old-line Whigs, and transfer them over to Giddings, Chase, Fred Douglass, and Parson Lovejoy, who were ready to receive them and christen them in their new faith. They laid down on that occasion a platform for their new Republican party, which was thus to be constructed. I have the resolutions of the State convention thus held, which was the first mass State convention ever held in Illinois by the Black Republican party; and I now hold them in my hands and will read a part of them, and cause the others to be printed. Here are the most important and material resolutions of this Abolition platform:

1. *Resolved,* That we believe this truth to be self-evident, that, when parties become subversive of the ends for which they are established, or incapable of restoring the government to the true principles of the Constitution, it is the right and duty of the people to dissolve the political bands by which they may have been connected therewith, and to organize new parties upon such principles and with such views as the circumstances and the exigencies of the nation may demand.

2. *Resolved,* That the times imperatively demand the reorganization of parties, and, repudiating all previous party attachments, names, and predilections, we unite ourselves together in defense of the liberty and Constitution of the country, and will hereafter co-operate as the Republican party, pledged to the accomplishment of the following purposes: to bring the administration of the government back to the control of first principles; to restore Nebraska and Kansas to the position of free Territories; that, as the Constitution of the United States vests in the States, and not in Congress, the power to legislate for the extradition of fugitives from labor, to repeal and entirely abrogate the fugitive-slave law; to restrict slavery to those States in which it exists; to prohibit the admission of any more slave States into the Union; to abolish slavery in the District of Columbia; to exclude slavery from all the Territories over

which the general government has exclusive jurisdiction; and to resist the acquirement of any more Territories unless the practice of slavery therein forever shall have been prohibited.

3. *Resolved,* That in furtherance of these principles we will use such constitutional and lawful means as shall seem best adapted to their accomplishment, and that we will support no man for office, under the general or State government, who is not positively and fully committed to the support of these principles, and whose personal character and conduct is not a guarantee that he is reliable, and who shall not have abjured old party allegiance and ties.

Now, gentlemen, your Black Republicans have cheered every one of those propositions; and yet I venture to say that you cannot get Mr. Lincoln to come out and say that he is now in favor of each one of them. That these propositions, one and all, constitute the platform of the Black Republican party of this day, I have no doubt; and, when you were not aware of what purpose I was reading them, your Black Republicans cheered them as good Black Republican doctrines. My object in reading these resolutions was to put the question to Abraham Lincoln this day, whether he now stands and will stand by each article in that creed, and carry it out. I desire to know whether Mr. Lincoln to-day stands as he did in 1854, in favor of the unconditional repeal of the fugitive-slave law. I desire him to answer whether he stands pledged to-day, as he did in 1854, against the admission of any more slave States into the Union, even if the people want them. I want to know whether he stands pledged against the admission of a new State into the Union with such a constitution as the people of that State may see fit to make. I want to know whether he stands to-day pledged to the abolition of slavery in the District of Columbia. I desire him to answer whether he stands pledged to the prohibition of the slave-trade between the different States. I desire to know whether he stands pledged to prohibit slavery in all the Territories of the United States, north as well as south of the Missouri Compromise line. I desire him to answer whether he is opposed to the acquisition of any more teritory unless slavery is prohibited therein. I want his answer to these questions. Your affirmative cheers in favor of this Abolition platform are not satisfactory. I ask Abraham Lincoln to answer these questions, in order that, when I trot him down to lower Egypt, I may put the same questions to him. My principles are the same everywhere. I can proclaim them alike in the North, the South, the East the East and the West. My principles will apply wherever the Constitution prevails and the American flag waves. I desire to know whether Mr. Lincoln's principles will bear transplanting from Ottowa to Jonesboro? I put these questions to him to-day distinctly, and ask an answer . . ."

Mr. Lincoln's Reply

My Fellow-citizens, — When a man hears himself somewhat misrepresented, it provokes him — at least, I find it so with myself; but, when misrepresentation become very gross and palpable, it is more apt to amuse him. The first thing I see fit to notice is the fact that Judge Douglas alleges, after running through the history of the old Democratic and the old Whig parties, that Judge Trumbull and myself made an arrangement in 1854 by which I was to have the place of General Shields in the United State Senate, and Judge Trumbull was to have the place of Judge Douglas. Now all I have to say upon that subject is that I think no man — not even Judge Douglas — can prove it, because it is not true. I have no doubt he is "conscientious" in saying it. As to those resolutions that he took such a length of time to read, as being the platform of the Republican party in 1854, I say I never had anything to do with them; and I think Trumbull never had. Judge Douglas cannot show that either of us ever did have anything to do with them. I believe this is true about those resolutions. There was a call for a convention to form a Republican party at Springfield; and I think that my friend Mr. Lovejoy, who is here upon this stand, had a hand in it. I think this is true; and I think, if he will remember accurately, he will be able to recollect that he tried to get me into it, and I would not go in. I believe it is also true that I went away from Springfield, when the convention was in session, to attend court in Tazewell County. It is true that they did place my name, though without authority, upon the committee, and afterward wrote me to attend the meeting of the committee; but I refused to do so, and I never had anything to do with that organization. This is the plain truth about all that matter of the resolutions.

Now, about this story that Judge Douglas tells of Trumbull bargaining to sell out the old Democratic party, and Lincoln agreeing to sell out the Old Whig party, I have the means of knowing about that: Judge Douglas cannot have; and I know there is no substance to it whatever. Yet I have no doubt he is "conscientious" about it. I know that, after Mr. Lovejoy got into the legislature that winter, he complained of me that I had told all the Old Whigs of his district that the Old Whig party was good enough for them, and some of them voted against him because I told them so. Now I have no means of disproving such charges as this which the judge makes. A man cannot prove a negative; but he has a right to claim that, when a man makes an affirmative charge, he must offer some proof to show the truth of what he says. I certainly cannot induce testimony to show the negative about things; but I have a right to claim that, if a man says he knows a thing, then he must show how he knows it. I always have a right to claim this, and it is not satisfactory to me that he may be "conscientious" on the subject.

Now, gentlemen, I hate to waste my time on such things, but in regard to that general Abolition tilt that Judge Douglas makes when he says that I was engaged at that time in selling out and Abolitionizing the Old Whig party, I hope you will permit me to read a part of a printed speech that I made then at Peoria, which will show altogether a different view of the position I took in that contest of 1854. [Voice: "*Put on your specs.*"] Yes, sir, I am obliged to do so. I am no longer a young man.

This is the repeal of the Missouri Compromise. The foregoing history may not be precisely accurate in every particular; but I am sure it is sufficiently so for all the uses I shall attempt to make of it, and in it we have before us the chief materials enabling us to correctly judge whether the repeal of the Missouri Compromise is right or wrong.

I think, and shall try to show, that it is wrong, — wrong in its direct effect, — letting slavery into Kansas and Nebraska, — and wrong in its prospective principle, — allowing it to spread to every other part of the wide world where men can be found inclined to take it.

This declared indifference, but, as I must think, covert real zeal for the spread of slavery, I cannot but hate. I hate it because of the monstrous injustice of slavery itself. I hate it because it deprives our republican example of its just influence in the world; enables the enemies of free institutions, with plausibility, to taunt us as hypocrites;

causes the real friends of freedom to doubt our sincerity, and especially because it forces so many really good men amongst ourselves into an open war with the very fundamental principles of civil liberty, — criticising the Declaration of Independence, and insisting that there is no right principle of action but self-interest.

Before proceeding, let me say I think I have no prejudice against the Southern people. They are just what we would be in their situation. If slavery did not now exist among them, they would not introduce it. If it did now exist among us, we should not instantly give it up. This I believe of the masses North and South. Doubtless there are individuals on both sides who would not hold slaves under any circumstances; and others who would gladly introduce slavery anew, if it were out of existence. We know that some Southern men do free their slaves, go North, and become tip-top Abolitionists; while some Northern ones go South, and become most cruel slave-masters.

When Southern people tell us they are no more responsible for the origin of slavery than we, I acknowledge the fact. When it is said that the institution exists and that it is very difficult to get rid of it in any satisfactory way, I can understand and appreciate the saying. I surely will not blame them for not doing what I should not know how to do myself. If all earthly power were given me, I should not know what to do as to the existing institution. My first impulse would be to free all the slaves, and send them to Liberia, — to their own native land. But a moment's reflection would convince me that, whatever of high hope (as I think there is) there may be in this in the long run, its sudden execution is impossible. If they were all landed there in a day, they would all perish in the next ten days; and there are not surplus shipping and surplus money enough in the world to carry them there in many times ten days. What then? Free them all, and keep them among us as underlings? Is it quite certain that this betters their condition? I think I would not hold one in slavery, at any rate; yet the point is not clear enough to me to denounce people upon. What next? Free them, and make them politically and socially our equals? My own feelings will not admit of this; and, if mine would, we well know that those of the great mass of white people will not. Whether this feeling accords with justice and sound judgment is not the sole question, if, indeed, it is any part of it. A universal feeling, whether well or ill founded, cannot be safely disregarded. We cannot make them equals. It does seem to me that systems of gradual emancipation might be adopted; but, for their tardiness in this, I will not undertake to judge our brethren of the South.

When they remind us of their constitutional rights, I acknowledge them, not grudgingly, but fully and fairly; and I would give them any legislation for the reclaiming of their fugitives which should not, in its stringency, be more likely to carry a free man into slavery than our ordinary criminal laws are to hang an innocent one.

But all this, to my judgment, furnishes no more excuse for permitting slavery to go into our own free territory than it would be for reviving the African slave-trade by law. The law which forbids the bringing of slaves from Africa, and that which has so long forbidden the taking of them to Nebraska, can hardly be distinguished on any moral principle; and the repeal of the former could find quite as plausible excuses as that of the latter.

I have reason to know that Judge Douglas knows that I said this. I think he has the answer here to one of the questions he put to me. I do not mean to allow him to catechise me unless he pays back for it in kind. I will not answer questions on after another, unless he reciprocates; but as he has made this inquiry, and I have answered it before, he has got it without my getting anything in return. He has got my answer on the fugitive-slave law.

Now, gentlemen, I don't want to read at any great length; but this is the true complexion of all I have ever said in regard to the institution of slavery and the black race. This is the whole of it; and anything that argues me into his idea of perfect social and political equality with the negro is but a specious and fantastic arrangement of words, by which a man can prove a horse-chestnut to be a chestnut horse. I will say here, while upon this subject, that I have no purpose, either directly or indirectly, to interfere with the institution of slavery in the States where it exists. I believe I have no lawful right to do so, and I have no inclination to do so. I have no purpose to introduce political and social equality between the white and the black races. There is a physical difference between the two, which, in my judgment, will probably forever forbid their living together upon the footing of perfect equality; and, inasmuch as it becomes a necessity that there must be a difference, I, as well as Judge Douglas, am in favor of the race to which I belong having the superior position. I have never said anything to the contrary, but I hold that, notwithstanding all this, there is no reason in the world why the negro is not entitled to all the natural rights enumerated in the Declaration of Independence, —the right to life, liberty and the pursuit of happiness. I hold that he is as much entitled to these as the white man. I agree with Judge Davis he is not my equal in many respects, —certainly not in color, perhaps not in moral or intellectual endowment, but in the right to eat the bread, without the leave of anybody else, which his own hand earns, he is my equal and the equal of Judge Douglas, and the equal of every living man. . . ."

Unit Five

Argumentative Communication: Communication Concepts

Chapter 16

Effective Argumentative Communication

* Verbal Effectiveness
* Physical Effectiveness
* Formal Debate Advocacy
* Conclusion
* References
* Practicum

This final unit of *Argumentative Communication* focuses entirely upon communication-related factors as they pertain to argumentation and debate situations. It was noted throughout chapter 2, "Argumentation as Communication," that the processes of argumentation and debate were but types of the overall human communication process, that argumentation and debate were but subsets of human communication transactions. That relationship might be expressed in terms of an umbrella's functionings. Human communication serves as the umbrella under which argumentation, debate, and all other forms of human communication fall.[1] Argumentation and debate are types of communication, and the practitioner of functional argumentative communication must remember this important relationship. No matter how skillful you may be, no matter how informed and intelligent your audience may be, argumentation and debate are processes of communication. Therefore, the tenets of effective human communication should be mirrored in the more specific process known as argumentative communication.

In examining the art of effective communication, our analysis is delineated into three major sections: verbal effectiveness, physical effectiveness, and formal debate advocacy. All three components fall under the human communication umbrella, and all three are important in the development and maintenance of functional, effective argumentative communication.

Verbal Effectiveness

To maximize speaking effectiveness, the argumentative communicator should be most concerned with five factors that combine to form verbal argumentative effectiveness: directness, conciseness, clarity, fluency, and organization.[2] Each factor is considered separately below.

Directness

In all argumentative situations, the advocate should deal directly with his audience, meaning that all arguments, as well as all supportive materials for those arguments, should be applied directly to that audience. For example, were you to advance the position that nuclear power plants should be closed, you might support your position by contending that nuclear power plants posed a safety threat to the American people. That supposed threat could be expressed one of these two ways:

Someone will die someday; someone will suffer the

horrors of nuclear radiation unless power plants are shut down.

You will die; *you* will suffer the horrors of nuclear radiation unless power plants are shut down.

Which approach had the greater impact upon you? Which approach made you stop and think about the possible dangers of nuclear power plants? Obviously, it was the second approach, because that manner of argument related the issue *directly* to you. This is a prime quality of effective argumentative communication: arguments are related directly to the audience to heighten persuasive impact. Instead of saying that "somebody" has a problem, say that "you," the members of the audience, have a problem. That approach drives your point home directly.[3]

Persuasion does not exist in a vacuum. Ideas are not considered, policies are not deliberated, and changes are not made without a rationale for such action. Since argumentative communication often is concerned with major personal and social issues, it is imperative that their import be demonstrated to those people consuming the arguments based on those issues. A need to listen must be shown to the listening audience, and that need can best be demonstrated by the advocate's relating directly to the members of his audience. Verbal directness, therefore, is a must.

Conciseness

Most of us dislike having to suffer through the ramblings of long-winded speakers. Teachers, preachers, and parents often bore us horribly with lengthy pronouncements on a variety of matters. At times it seems as if they say the same things over and over through needless repetition and explanation. Those are the times when we find our heads nodding and our thoughts wandering and it becomes a great chore just to stay awake, let alone to pay attention. The practitioner of effective argumentative communication should learn a valuable lesson from those all-too-frequent occurrences.

Arguments and their explanations should be expressed as concisely as possible, utilizing the least number of words needed to make those arguments and explanations clear and meaningful to the audience. Lionel D. Wyld has provided an example of verbose versus concise language style:[4]

Verbose

We solicit any recommendations that you wish to make and you may be assured that any such recommendations will be given our careful consideration.

Concise

Please give us your suggestions. We shall consider them carefully.

Whereas the verbose example contains twenty-four words, the concise example uses only ten words to make the same exact point. Your pieces of argumentative discourse should be like that example of conciseness—making a point without bludgeoning your audience into submissive boredom. Word economy is an important element of effective argumentative communication.

Clarity

Closely related to conciseness is the communicative notion of clarity, primarily a factor related to the language selected by the speaker in verbalizing arguments. To deal effectively with most audiences, you should keep this theorem in mind in word selection: the clearer, the better; the simpler, the better. More audiences will be able better to understand what you are saying if you adhere to that dictum.

All of us know individuals who appear to have eaten a dictionary for yesterday's dinner, people who tend to express themselves continuously in the most confusing and obscure polysyllabic language possible. Although this approach may appear to be impressive and awe inspiring in some cases, most of the time such language usage is totally counterproductive. Language serves as the primary vehicle for the transmission of messages from one person to another; therefore, it is quite critical that language not get in the way or block the functional human communication process. Language should facilitate understanding, not impede it.

The practitioner of effective argumentative communication should study her audience to determine the requisites of language clarity. An audience composed of subject-matter experts would be expected to understand more complex and technical language than would a general lay audience, for example. Thus, the topic and the makeup of the audience should be considered by the speaker in determining language appropriateness. In general, however, simple and common-usage language should be selected for the expression of arguments, language that provides the greatest clarity for the greatest number within the audience.

Fluency

To increase overall verbal effectiveness and make the presentation of arguments more pleasing to your audience, you should strive to make your speaking as fluent as is possible. Fluency may be defined as the smooth flow of language used by the speaker. If you take the time to listen to most public speakers, you will find that those people, at least many of them, do not have fluent deliveries. Instead, many speakers suffer from a great number of nonfluencies or vocalized pauses, and they may sound like this:

> We-ahhh-need to-ahhh-be concerned with-ahhh-the dangers posed by the-ahhh-polluted air that we breathe. Ahhh-unless something is done to-ahhh-clear our-ahhh-skies, we may all-ahhh-choke to death under-ahhh-a blacked-out sun.

Doesn't that-ahhh-sound very familiar? The most oft-used word in the American language may be "ahhh."

Generally, speakers fall prey to nonfluencies like "ahhh," "uhhh," and "ummm" because they are concerned primarily with their following thought. That is, while they are thinking about what to say next, they fill in their verbal blank by saying "ahhh." So, nonfluencies are used to tie ideas together while the speaker takes a momentary time-out to think.

Unfortunately, such nonfluencies have a disastrous impact upon a speaker's delivery, causing a roughness that is unpleasant for the audience and creating a distraction away from the speaker's message. If the speaker has many ahhhs in her speech, members of the audience may soon concentrate on those nonfluencies and not on the content of the message. When that happens, the speaker functionally has lost a portion of her audience. To prevent that from happening, the practitioner of argumentative communication should strive for a smooth and even delivery flow, one that is virtually free of those troublesome nonfluencies. An exercise designed to improve verbal fluency is included within the "Practicum" section at the end of this chapter.

Organization

The final component of verbal effectiveness is the proper organization of thoughts expressed within argumentative encounters. As a general rule of thumb, arguments, both major and trivial, should be organized and presented in a sequence that makes the greatest sense to the audience. Arguments should relate well one to another composing a compelling matrix of argumentative advocacy. Essentially, what you want to create is a chain of argument that builds or leads to the desired conclusion.

In debate contexts, an example of the inductive method of reasoning, specific arguments are linked to other specific arguments that lead to a generalized conclusion. The speaker ought to organize these specific arguments so that they interface well with one another and lead logically to the final conclusion. Thus, arguments are not presented in an arbitrary sequence; arguments are not presented in a stream-of-consciousness order. Instead, great care must be taken to develop an effective chain of argument that leads the audience to the conclusion you desire.

Similarly, subarguments within arguments should be organized carefully. A complex argument often is composed of many internal elements, and these internal elements must be functionally sequenced to create a clear and logical argument. The advocate who allots time to the organized presentation of arguments will find that his position is better understood by the audience, that he is held in higher regard by the audience, and that the persuasive impact of the arguments presented will be enhanced significantly.

Physical Effectiveness

Conjoined with the foregoing factors of verbal effectiveness are the elements of physical effectiveness in functional argumentative communication. As with verbal expression, the physical elements of oral advocacy must be studied and practiced so that they, too, serve to enhance the individual's communicative posture. All too often, however, physical delivery mannerisms tend to harm the speaker's impact, generally providing stimuli that distracts the audience's attention away from the context of her message. In examining the nature of physical delivery effectiveness, four factors will be discussed: eye contact, physical movement, gestures, and the use of the podium.

Eye Contact

One of the areas of greatest difficulty for beginning speakers is the maintenance of direct eye contact with their audiences. Many speakers find such visual interaction to be unnerving and a source of apprehension, often resulting in the speaker's trying desperately to avoid direct eye contact. That is why so many speakers deliver their messages while looking out the window, gazing at the ceiling just above their heads, or staring downward at the tops of their shoes. All of us have seen speakers who have exhibited these mannerisms.

However, direct eye contact with the audience is something quite necessary for the speaker, something that must be developed and maintained—for two reasons. First, eye contact allows the speaker to gauge the reactions of the audience to his message, enabling the speaker to read the audience's nonverbal feedback to the message presented.[5] From an early age, everyone becomes relatively adroit at being able to discern nonverbal feedback, often expressed by yawns (the person is bored), shifting about (the person is bored or uneasy), and by such ocular expressions as surprise, anger or hostility, and boredom.

Thus, you need to maintain direct eye contact with your audience to see what kind of impact your message is having upon them. Do they understand the message? Do they accept the message? Do you need to clarify or reexplain your point? The answers to these kinds of questions can be answered only by your being aware of audience feedback. Therefore, you must maintain direct eye contact with the audience.

The second reason necessitating eye contact is that it shows your audience you care about them, are concerned about their reactions to your message. Without direct eye contact, the speaker appears not to be concerned with her audience, and this is the surest way to lose audience attention and interest. Eye contact says, in effect, "Hey, I care about you. Listen to what I have to say, because it's for your benefit." Quite simply, a speaker who appears not to care about the audience will find that the audience will not care about her and the message will fall upon functionally deaf ears.

The effective advocate should maintain direct eye contact with her audience, accruing the advantages of seeing audience reactions to the message and establishing a positive speaker-audience rapport.

Physical Movement

In most formal speaking situations, it is expected that the speaker will be on his feet, not seated in a chair or on the edge of a table or desk. The whole notion of platform speaking infers that the speaker will be in front of the audience, unfettered by physical support. In such circumstances, many speakers are confronted by the issue of physical movement: how much physical movement is permitted while speaking?

The answer to that question hinges upon the matter of audience distraction. Simply, some movement is functional in that it keeps the speaker's body relaxed and additionally aids in the maintenance of audience attention and interest. Literally standing stationary in one spot for five or ten minutes both feels awkward to the speaker and appears awkward to the audience. However, some speakers take movement to the extreme, and this is where distraction takes place. Some speakers

1. pace back and forth furiously as if they were in a mini track meet

2. run 'round and 'round the podium or speaker's stand as if they were chasing some object
3. move about hesitantly or jerkily as if suffering from an attack of palsy.

Every one of the preceding movements does not aid the speaker or her audience. Instead, they provide gross visual distractions away from the speaker's message, causing the audience to concentrate upon the pacing, running, and jerky movements and not upon the content of the message.

Therefore, proper physical movement is that which serves to keep the speaker relaxed and the audience interested in the message. Physical movements should not call attention to themselves, should not distract away from the message. Too little movement is definitely better than too much movement.

Gestures

All of us use our hands while speaking—in formal situations and in informal everyday conversations. Our hands help us to express ourselves, to emphasize that which we say verbally. In argumentative communication settings, we should use our hand gestures as we do in other speaking situations—as natural expressers of our feelings and emotions.

In the nineteenth century, the formal study of hand gestures was part of what was called elocutionary training.[6] Under that system, speakers were taught that each separate feeling or emotion should have its own corresponding and separate hand gesture. Taxonomies were developed that said one's hands should be held in a clenched fist to exhibit anger or extreme seriousness, that the hands should be open with palms up to plead or entreat a point, and so on. Happily, contemporary oral communication instruction does not include those artificial dictates of the elocutionists. We do not force people to commit to memory a lengthy list of appropriate gestures for all speaking occasions.

Instead, gestures ought to be the natural expression of emotions that coincide with the speaker's message. Preplanned or orchestrated gestures are very artificial and phony; gestures should be natural and spontaneous.

Use of the Podium. The final physical delivery factor to be considered is the use of the speaker's podium.[7] The podium exists to aid the speaker in handling his notes while maintaining a direct rapport via eye contact with the audience. Because many speakers find it very difficult to hold their notes while speaking, the podium provides a tool that allows the speaker to have his notes at close proximity while maintaining a solid and fluent verbal flow.

Unfortunately, far too many speakers use the podium counterproductively by:

1. holding onto the podium for dear life, thereby eliminating the natural use of hand gestures
2. hiding behind the podium from view of the audience
3. slamming the podium with force to emphasize a point, scaring and unnerving the audience
4. keeping their eyes glued to the notes on the podium, minimizing eye contact with the audience
5. lurching across the top of the podium during moments of great fervor like a snake striking from behind a rock

All such actions work against effective oral communication either by creating an unnecessary distraction or by diminishing the direct speaker-audience interrelationship.

The practitioner of argumentative communication should realize that the podium is intended to enhance communication, not impact negatively upon it. In fact, the less the podium is used, the better. The podium does present a distinct physical blockage between the speaker and his audience, cutting down the direct rapport that every speaker ought to try to create. Therefore, you should use the speaker's podium as sparingly as possible—and not at all if feasible. At a minimum, you should avoid those ineffective and counterproductive actions noted above.

Formal Debate Advocacy

There are six additional oral skills that need to be developed by the interscholastic and intercollegiate academic debater for maximum argumentative effectiveness.

1. *Presenting evidence*. Because evidence serves as the critical underpinning of your arguments, it is important that it be presented properly. Each piece of evidence should be presented by noting the author or expert citing the evidence, his qualifications, the source in which the evidence was printed, the date of publication, and the page number on which the evidence was located. Thus, the proper presentation of evidence would sound like this: "In support of that point, I turn to Arthur Ferndock, deputy undersecretary of state, who noted in *Wambat Magazine*, July fifteenth, nineteen seventy-nine, page nine, that. . . ." Such a complete citation guarantees that

evidence usage is ethical in nature and demonstrates that each piece of evidence has high credibility. The judge and audience know that the evidence comes from a reliable source of information and that the evidence is up-to-date. Each piece of evidence presented should note those five elements—author, author's qualifications, source, date of publlication, and page number.[8]

2. *Explaining evidence*. Besides merely reading each piece of evidence to the judge and audience, the debater ought to explain what each piece of evidence means. Far too many debaters assume that all evidence is self-explanatory, that there will be no confusion as to meaning or impact—a most untenable assumption. Instead, the debater should explain her evidence by (*a*) crystallizing or synthesizing the content of the piece of evidence, literally explaining what is meant by the evidence; (*b*) showing how the evidence applies to the argument under consideration, both in constructing and refuting arguments; and (*c*) demonstrating the impact of the evidence, showing how it supports your argument or refutes the argument of your opponent. Such a three-step process will make the presentation of your evidence more compelling and effective.

3. *Signposting*. The structure of your argumentative efforts should be highlighted via signposting—using phrases or complete sentences that tell the audience where you are organizationally and where you will be going. Each major issue addressed should be stated clearly so there is no confusion as to your intent:

> Let us examine inherency. The affirmative indictment does not present an inherent indictment against the present system. Please note that there is no structural barrier preventing the problem from being solved. As this next piece of evidence tells us. . . .

Hearing such a statement, the audience would be quite aware that you were going to deal with the issue of inherency. There would be no confusion as to your following argument's purpose. All major elements of your argumentative substructure should be similarly signposted to maximize communicative clarity.

4. *Summarization*. Each major argument, as well as the total argumentative position, should be summarized. These summaries crystallize what you have said, enabling you to have one last chance to make certain that the audience understands the nature of your position:

> Therefore, since I have shown that the purported problems are insignificant and that those difficulties can be alleviated by the normal operations of the status quo, please concur with me that there is no justifiable

rationale for change and that the affirmative proposal should not be adopted.

When you summarize your position, the listener is not left hanging in midair. Your total position is tied up neatly, making your position that much more impressive, well-organized, and persuasive.

5. *Flowsheeting*. Since contemporary academic debates are notable for their many lines of argument and great amount of evidence, it is impossible to keep track of what is going on without taking notes. Moreover, since the organization of argument and responses to argument is so essential, note taking must be a deliberate, planned activity.

The most efficient and effective method for taking notes on arguments and evidence is the use of a flowsheet, a structured note-taking evice. Using a legal pad or an art pad lengthwise, you may keep track of the debate's progress by organizing your notes into columns, one for each debate segment (see figure 16.1). Arguments issued by the first affirmative constructive (1AC), as well as the supporting evidence, are jotted down in order under the 1AC column. The same is done for the remaining seven speeches throughout the debate. Try to record as much information as possible.

The flowsheet allows the debater to see what arguments and evidence have been presented, thereby enabling him to plan later refutational and supportive arguments and evidence. The debate judge or critic may use the flowsheet to check the advancement of arguments and analysis, having a written record to use in determining the winner of each debate encounter.

6. *Audience Primacy*. Finally, the debater must remember that all arguments and evidence should be directed to the judge and audience. Far too many debaters address themselves to their opponents, essentially cutting the audience out of the communicative spectrum. Most academic debate situations have the affirmative and negative team tables set to the sides of the podium, and midway between the podium and the audience. It is very easy for the speaker at the podium to turn slightly and speak directly to the team of opposing debaters. After all, she is presenting arguments to be answered by these opponents. However, this is a tendency that must be avoided; the speaker's attention must be directed toward the judge and audience, for it is they who make the final decision, not the opposing debate team. As in all human communication transactions, the speaker must emphasize her audience.

Figure 16.1

1AC	1NC	2AC	2NC	1NR	1AR	2NR	2AR

Conclusion

Although argumentation and debate must be considered specialized forms of the human communication process, they are forms of communication and must be approached as such. Accordingly, those traits of effective public communication must be learned and exhibited by the practitioner of argumentative communication.

The advocate's verbal skills should encompass directness, conciseness, clarity, fluency, and a logical organization of argumentative materials. To enhance his physical aspects of delivery, the advocate should use effectively eye contact, movement, gestures, and the speaker's podium in interacting with the audience.

Finally, because argumentative communication includes the very specialized nature of academic debate, the advocate ought to be concerned with the proper presentation and explanation of evidence, with signposting and summarization of arguments, with taking notes on flowsheets, and with the necessity of directing her arguments and evidence to the audience.

References

1. The list for all human communication forms is virtually endless. It includes the very broad categories, such as speaking to persuade, as well as the more specialized categories, such as male-female communication.

2. For a fuller discussion of verbal effectiveness, see James Edward Sayer, *Functional Speech Communication* (Dubuque, Iowa: Kendall/Hunt, 1977), pp. 40–45.

3. This coincides with the nature and importance of identification mentioned earlier in this book.

4. Lionel D. Wyld, *Preparing Effective Reports* (New York: Odyssey Press, 1967), p. 26.

5. The significance of eye contact to the human communication process has received significant study during the past two decades. See, for example, Michael Argyle and Janet Dean, "Eye-Contact, Distance, and Affiliation," *Sociometry* 28 (1965), pp. 289–304.

6. See David H. Grover, "Elocution at Harvard: The Saga of Jonathan Barber," *Quarterly Journal of Speech* 51 (February 1965), pp. 62–67.

7. This discussion of the speaker's podium also includes speaker's stands and lecterns.

8. The National Forensic League (NFL) now demands that NFL-affiliated debaters provide such complete evidentiary citations in all debate rounds.

Practicum

1. Conduct this simple experiment to assess the verbal and physical delivery effectiveness of one speaker, perhaps one of your teachers. As you listen to his lecture, keep track of the following:

- How many vocalized pauses did he insert into his lecture material?
- Did the teacher indicate any pattern of organization to his material?
- Where did the teacher concentrate his eye contact?
- Did the teacher use the podium? If so, did he use it effectively or ineffectively?

Now, how would you assess that teacher's overall speaking effectiveness?

Every time ***you*** speak, your audience is making the same type of judgment regarding you. How would you rate your own speaking effectiveness?

2. To improve your verbal fluency, try using this technique, called go-go speaking:

- Have a friend devise a list of six unrelated nouns (cucumber, streetcar, baseball bat, bottle cap, ear lobe, pencil, for example).
- Have your friend recite the list to you, one word at a time.
- As you hear each word, start speaking about it — without taking time to think about what you are going to say.
- Go through the entire list in one sitting.

The purpose of this exercise is to maximize fluency by minimizing the number of vocalized pauses that so punctuate our speech. You might wish to speak to the beat of a metronome to maintain a fluent and rapid rate of delivery. After practicing this exercise several times, you will find that your overall communicative fluency has improved through the reduction of nonfluencies. Remember, don't think about what you're going to say, just say it!

Chapter 17

Techniques of Cross-Examination

* **Purposes of Cross-Examination**
* **Effective Cross-Examination Techniques**
* **Conclusion**
* **References**
* **Practicum**

One of the most interesting academic debate formats, derived from the operations of our legal system, is that of cross-examination debate.[1] Unlike the traditional or Oxford format that has each speaker communicate directly only with the audience, the cross-examination debate structure includes the interesting element of direct debater-to-debater verbal interaction. Thus, the cross-examination format more readily approximates real-life argumentative communication, for it is rare, indeed, that an advocate's arguments go unquestioned or unchallenged, directly, fairly, and immediately, by the advocate's opponent. This head-to-head contact also adds a spark of liveliness to an academic debate encounter that makes the debate more enjoyable to both participants and observers.[2]

This is the standard format for an interscholastic or intercollegiate cross-examination debate:

1st affirmative constructive	8 minutes or 10 minutes
Negative cross-examination	3 minutes
1st negative constructive	8 minutes or 10 minutes
Affirmative cross-examination	3 minutes
2nd affirmative constructive	8 minutes or 10 minutes
Negative cross-examination	3 minutes
2nd negative constructive	8 minutes or 10 minutes

Affirmative cross-examination	3 minutes	
1st negative rebuttal	4 minutes or	5 minutes
1st affirmative rebuttal	4 minutes or	5 minutes
2nd negative rebuttal	4 minutes or	5 minutes
2nd affirmative rebuttal	4 minutes or	5 minutes
Total:	60 minutes	72 minutes

High school debates tend to utilize the sixty-minute format; college debates generally utilize the seventy-two minute structure. Regardless of which format is used, one factor remains constant: each debater cross-examines one of her opponents, and each debater is cross-examined by one of her opponents.

To understand better the nature and proper functioning of cross-examination debate, it is necessary to examine (*a*) the purposes of cross-examination and (*b*) the techniques for effective cross-examination debating. The remainder of this chapter is devoted to those two main issues.[3]

Purposes of Cross-Examination

The cross-examination period exists to meet two purposes, and both purposes ought to be met to make every cross-examination effort as functional and as enjoyable as possible. Before examining those purposes, however, one nonpurpose of cross-examination needs to be addressed: it is *not* the purpose of the cross-examination encounter to have a debater browbeat and badger his opponent. All too often the examiner takes the offensive against the examinee in a manner similar to an attorney's examination of a hostile witness. The result of this offensive demeanor is predictable: the examinee clams up, virtually saying nothing, and the entire cross-examination period is a waste of time. It is imperative that debaters refrain from employing television-style attorney techniques (which, incidentally, exist only on television—they are not allowed in an actual courtroom), which tend to create communication breakdowns.

The main purpose of the cross-examination period is to allow the examiner to gain insights into arguments and evidence of the opposition that will be useful for later refutation. Instead of having to pose questions and ask that they be answered in the next opposition speech, cross-examination provides immediate feedback to those questions. An unclear piece of evidence can be explained, a questionable source may be probed, an intricate plan may be repeated—all these matters and more can be gleaned from effective cross-examination. It is no secret that many contemporary affirmative cases are noteworthy for their strategic vagueness; that is, the defense of the case depends upon the affirmative's greasing around the negative attack. Cross-examination allows the negative to force the affirmative into one specific position, to limit the affirmative's ability to slide around the negative attack. Conversely, cross-examination allows the affirmative to combat the negative spread by directly forcing the selection of the minor repairs to be offered as the negative inherency block. Therefore, the cross-examination period provides an excellent opportunity for concreteness and specificity in argumentation. Its direct nature gets to the heart of the issues in question by carefully examining the arguments, cases, and evidence of the opposition.

The secondary purpose of cross-examination is psychological: cross-examination can create a favorable impression of you while creating a less-than-favorable impression of your opponent. This is not merely a fringe benefit of effective cross-examination, it is a major purpose of the exercise; although it is certainly true that a favorable impression will not be *the* reason for winning a debate, it can be a difference in very close rounds. If a debater is successful in creating such a positive image, then the judge will tend to lean psychologically toward that debater. Since so many debates are won and lost on relatively few issues, any edge that one can gain will be beneficial. The creation of a favorable image is one positive edge that can be gained by effective cross-examination. The rhetorical concept of *ethos* is an important function of cross-examination technique.

We may conclude that the purpose of cross-examination is *not* to show how many jokes can be told in the guise of answering questions, *not* to waste everyone's time with irrelevant trivia, *not* to emulate television attorneys. Cross-examination can be and should be a positive aspect of the policy decision-making process that serves to facilitate consideration of important issues. With its twofold purpose in mind, cross-examination can be an added benefit to oral argumentation.

Effective Cross-Examination Techniques

Once the purposes of cross-examination debate have been internalized, the advocate must be concerned with the attitude to be shown during the cross-examination periods. Stated simply, the advocate should be outgoing, but not boisterous; confident, but not cocky; direct, but not harsh. In short, the advocate should be open, sincere, and honest in attitude, carrying herself in the manner of a poised, well-informed person.

Unfortunately, many debaters, especially during initial cross-examination practices, are frightened by the give-and-take of the cross-examination period. Instead of being secure in the debater-dominated dialogue with the judge, cross-examination forces the debater to take part in verbal exchanges with the opponent. That gaping hole in the affirmative substructure is now readily open to negative probing; that dated piece of evidence, strategically slurred during the constructive speech, can be examined during cross-examination. This lack of security (a security found in Oxford debate but not in real life) is frightening. The result: some debaters refuse to answer anything; some whimper throughout the cross-examination period; some overcompensate for their fright by being downright obnoxious—all because of the one-to-one dialogue with a debate opponent.

To offset this fear and resultant counterproductive attitude, the debater should keep the following three ideas in mind. First, every debater has had the same trepidations concerning cross-examination. Every debater has worried that he might say something that will totally destroy his team's argumentative position; every debater has feared looking like a fool. The point to be remembered is that a great deal of research, preparation time, and practice has taken place *before* one is ever part of a cross-examination debate. Hours of work have gone into the creation and defense of an affirmative case, and the same has been done for the negative files and blocks. It is absurd to think that one or two cross-examination questions can destroy a position or the debater who advances a position based on such predebate research and practice. Debaters should realize that a degree of uneasiness about cross-examination is natural, but thorough advance work can overcome the butterflies that all debaters experience.

Second, maintenance of a forthright, confident manner can be most effective by (*a*) helping the debater overcome her own internal anxieties, (*b*) aiding in the creation of a positive image so favored by judges, and (*c*) causing an opponent to drop a potentially damaging line of questioning. Questions should be answered in a clear, solid voice with the eyes and head up. Maintaining such a confident attitude cannot be overemphasized in its impact upon the debate round, and it is something that must be consciously worked upon.

For example, when asked a question for which you do not know the answer, a much more positive image is created by a clear, unaffected "I don't know" delivered directly to the judge. But what do most debaters do in this situation? All too often, when confronted by such a question, the debater will drop his eyes to the floor and quaveringly mumble, "I don't know." Such a response conveys the impression that the debater is ill-prepared and negligent for not being able to answer the question. A confident response has just the opposite effect.

Third, more effective cross-examination takes place if the debater has an open, positive attitude in both questioning and answering questions. That is, avoiding trick questions, filibustery answers, and other such time-wasters will immeasurably aid the cross-examination process. Functional cross-examination mandates that the debater be open, or at least appear to be open, in dealing with an opponent, refraining from attempts to conceal information. This does not mean, of course, that one fails to defend one's team's position adequately. It does mean, however, that such defense is made with minimal circular response patterns and a careful control over verbosity.

The greatest benefit may be gained if the debater is able to be viewed as an open, straightforward advocate, trying to present her position in an honest manner. Juxtapose this image with those created by debaters who ramble on endlessly in answering questions, speak in inaudible tones, attempt to badger their opponents, and so on. If you were judging a round, which debater would you prefer to watch? The answer is obvious, as is the need for the maintenance of an effective, positive attitude in cross-examination periods.

Perhaps the single greatest reason for the relatively low quality of so many academic cross-examination debates is the lack of preparation for cross-examination before the debate encounter begins. Debaters tend to wait until they are involved in a debate before preparing for the cross-examination, believing that they will be able to think of questions or answers on the spur of the moment. Unfortunately, very few individuals are able to put together effective cross-examination periods by utilizing such impromptu inspiration. Therefore, the following four general suggestions are offered to improve the quality of cross-examination questions and answers.

First, debaters should take turns answering questions in defense of their affirmative case. Questions should be tough and direct, avoiding no part of the case substructure. One's own case should be probed as closely and carefully as if the case belonged to someone else. Then, when engaged in actual competition, there is less chance that the debater will be surprised by a question for which he has no preset answer.

Second, debaters should practice asking questions and planning questions for others' affirmative cases. Some general questions may apply to all cases, but it is useful to have prepared questions for particular types of cases. Working from flowsheets of past debates is the most effective method for implementing this exercise.

Third, affirmatives should work very carefully at planning out their cross-examination of the first negative constructive speaker. Since they know what their case entails and how it may be defended best, proper predebate preparation allows the affirmative advocate to lead the negative speaker where they want her to go. Arrangement of pertinent questions in a series, proceeding from the general to the specific, can make the examination of the first negative an important weapon in the arsenal of affirmative case defense.

Fourth, the debaters should agree on some consistent system for recording responses received during cross-examination. Often, important admissions are lost because the examiner failed to note these responses. Trusting that you will be able to remember all important matters is sheer folly. We keep evidence cards to ensure the retention of vital debate data; the same should be done for information gathered through the cross-examination process.

Only by careful and extensive preparation can debaters make the most of cross-examination. Planning questions and answers will eliminate those embarrassing moments when you find you have nothing to say. Additionally, such preparation will eliminate "What do you think about . . ." and "Do you believe . . ." questions that do nothing more than invite your opponent to waste your time.

Having discussed effective cross-examination debate techniques from an attitudinal and general framework, we may now examine twenty specific tips or techniques—ten each for the cross-examiner and the cross-examinee.[4]

Cross-Examiner Techniques

1. The examiner always should stand while questioning the examinee, remembering to face both the examinee and the audience simultaneously. Being able to observe the nonverbal response of the examinee may provide clues as to the impact of the questions asked. Similarly, observing the nonverbal reactions of the audience allows the examiner to gauge its reactions to the viability and worth of those questions.

2. The examiner should not stand too close to the examinee, because such close proximity may give the appearance of physical intimidation and browbeating.

3. The examiner should speak clearly and loudly

enough for both the examinee *and* the audience to hear readily the questions asked. It is impossible for the listeners to detect hesitancy to answer a question on the part of the examinee if the question itself has not been heard.

4. The examiner must remember that her cross-examination period is not supposed to be like a rerun of the old *Perry Mason* television programs. The examinee should not be badgered; the examinee should not be verbally brutalized. The examiner should retain her good nature and sense of humor throughout the exercise.

5. The examiner should prepare some general questions beforehand that could be asked of all opponents. Specific questions should be constructed to deal particularly with the issues under consideration during this debate encounter that center upon the examinee's arguments and evidence.

6. The examiner should attempt to have a pattern to his questions that lead the line of questioning to some goal. At the very minimum, the questions can follow the organization of the examinee's constructive speech. Questions organized haphazardly tend to confuse everyone watching the debate encounter.

7. The examiner should be very careful in wording her questions. Simplicity and brevity should be the benchmarks for all questions. Double negatives create complete confusion in questioning the examinee: he won't understand the question; the audience won't understand the question; and you won't know how to interpret the examinee's answer.

8. The examiner should not allow the examinee to waste valuable cross-examination time by providing too lengthy answers. If the examinee appears to be trying to waste your time by filibustering, calling him by his first name will cause him to stop ("John!").

9. The examiner should not allow herself to be questioned by the examinee, a favorite trick of experienced cross-examination debaters. Should such a turnaround attempt be made, politely remind the examinee that this is *your* cross-examination period and that you will be more than happy to answer his questions when his cross-examination period occurs.

10. Finally, and perhaps most important, do not ask a question unless you have a pretty good idea what the answer will be. Goalless probing often results in the examinee's being able to score more points at your naive initiative. This is the number one tenet of all experienced trial attorneys.

Cross-Examinee Techniques

1. The examinee should stand during the cross-examination period, remembering to be positioned so that he may see both the examiner and the audience. Too often the examinee is effectively upstaged by the examiner. When this happens, the examiner has command of the physical setting, forcing the examinee to turn his back on the audience to deal directly with the examiner. The examinee should not allow this to happen.

Ideally, examinee and examiner stand equidistant from the audience. In this setup, both the examinee and the examiner can deal with one another and with the audience via direct and peripheral vision. No one is upstaged; no one is at a physical disadvantage.

2. The examinee should answer all questions in a strong, clear voice. Not only must the examiner be able to hear the responses, the audience must be able to hear them, too.

3. The examinee must remain relaxed and poised, combatting the tendency to be uptight and overanxious. Remember, one purpose of cross-examination is to enhance one's credibility to the audience. A polite and controlled style, sprinkled with an engaging sense of humor, will serve the examinee well.

4. The examinee should anticipate questions likely to be asked of him and be prepared with answers for those questions. In addition, the use of evidence in responding to questions will make such answers more compelling and persuasive, putting the examiner on the defensive.

5. The examinee should not answer a question that she does not understand. In such situations a request to reword or to explain the question should be made.

6. The examinee should not be afraid to say that he

does not know the answer to a question. Since it is literally impossible to know the answers to all potential questions the examiner might pose, there is nothing inherently damaging to admitting that one does not know the answer to a specific question.

7. The examinee should not allow herself to be pressured into having to give yes or no answers. Very few questions, in fact, can be answered so simply and broadly. If the examinee wishes to give a qualified yes or no answer ("Yes, but..."), the qualifying material should be stated first ("Because...therefore, my answer is yes") to prevent the examiner from cutting off the answer before the qualifier is given.

8. The examinee should exercise extreme care in responding to questions of a hypothetical nature created by the examiner ("Now what would happen if..."). The examinee should make it very clear in his answer that this is *only* a hypothetically based question, not a question based on fact or reality.

9. The examinee should not allow the examiner to make a speech in the guise of asking a question. The examiner's purpose is to ask questions, not to make speeches, a purpose conveniently forgotten by many examiners. Should the examiner launch into such a speech, the examinee should interrupt the statement by asking, "Is that a question?" thereby calling attention to the examiner's misconduct.

10. Finally, since the advocate will be cross-examined at the end of her constructive speech, primarily about the arguments and evidence within that speech, the evidence materials used should not be gathered up until the cross-examination period is completed. Many of those materials may prove to be useful in answering questions, so they should be left readily available for the examinee's benefit during cross-examination.

Conclusion

Cross-examination debate is a dynamic, lively, and interesting form of formalized argumentative communication. Its direct give-and-take nature corresponds more closely to real-world argumentative encounters than does Oxford-style debate. However, many cross-examination debates are not as functional as they should be, because many advocates do not realize that cross-examination's two major purposes (to probe for weaknesses in one's opponent's evidence and arguments; to enhance one's credibility with the audience) can be fulfilled only through thorough preparation and practice.

The techniques of effective cross-examination must be studied and practiced, and only through directed experiences can those techniques be learned adequately.

References

1. To study the development of cross-examination as it is applied to academic debate, see Everett L. Hunt, "Dialectic: A Neglected Method of Argument," *Quarterly Journal of Speech* 7 (June 1921): 221–232; J. Stanley Gray, "The Oregon Plan of Debating," *Quarterly Journal of Speech* 12 (April 1926): 175–180; and Darrell R. Parker, "The Use of Cross-Examination in Debate," *Quarterly Journal of Speech* 18 (February 1932): 97–102.

2. Although high schools have employed the cross-examination debate format extensively for a number of years, it was only in the mid-1970s that intercollegiate debates adopted the cross-examination format for the National Debate Tournament (NDT), the super bowl of intercollegiate debate competition.

3. See William J. Holloran and Charles W. Kneupper, "Cross-Examination as Policy Inquiry," *Debate Issues*, October 1976, pp. 8–10; and James Edward Sayer, "Effective Cross-Examination Debating," *Debate Issues*, December 1978, pp. 14-15.

4. See James Edward Sayer, "Functional Cross-Examination," *Debate Issues*, February 1976, pp. 5–8.

Practicum

1. Watch or listen to a presidential news conference broadcast, a type of cross-examination communication situation wherein the members of the press (the examiners) ask questions of the president (the examinee). At the conclusion of the press conference, answer these questions:

- Did it appear that the members of the press had prepared questions or developed questions on the spot to deal with an issue previously mentioned by the president?
- Did it appear that the president had pat answers for many of the questions asked?
- Did the president attempt to twist questions to meet better the answers he intended to give?
- Were the questions adequately specific to elicit significant responses from the president?
- Overall, how would you rate the president's performance in handling questions put to him? How would you rate the quality of the questions posed by the members of the press?

Finally, if you had the responsibility to monitor the president's communication behaviors, what changes would you suggest to improve the president's performance within a news conference setting?

2. The following is an extrapolated condensation of the cross-examination of a witness before the House Committee on Un-American Activities in the late 1940s. At that time, the committee was investigating the possible subversion of Hollywood groups, such as the Screen Writers Guild, by Communists. Unfortunately, the following excerpt shows how cross-examination can be nonfunctional when the examiner attempts to harass and browbeat the examinee. As you read this material, ask yourself if you would like to trade places with the examinee. Would you have reacted to the examiner differently?

Examiner: Are you a member of the Screen Writers Guild?

Examinee: I want to be cooperative about this but there are limits to my cooperation. I don't want to help you smash this particular guild, or to infiltrate the motion-picture business in any way, to control what the American people can see and hear in their motion-picture theaters.

Examiner: Now, don't do like the others, if I were you, or you will never read your statement. I would suggest —

Examinee: Mr. Chairman, let me —

Examiner: — you be responsive to the question.

Examinee: I am —

Examiner: The question is: Are you a member of the Screen Writers Guild?

Examinee: I understood I ***would*** be permitted to read the statement, Mr. Chairman. . . .

Examiner: Are you now, or have you ever been, a member of the Communist Party?

Examinee: Well, I would like to answer that question, too.

Examiner: The charge has been made that the Screen Writers Guild which you are a member of, whether you admit it or not, has in it members of the Communist Party. This committee is seeking to determine the extent of Communist infiltration in the Screen Writers Guild.

Examinee: Yes.

Examiner: Now, are you, or have you ever been, a member of the Communist Party?

Examinee: It seems to me you are trying to discredit the Screen Writers Guild through me, and the motion-picture industry through the Screen Writers Guild, and our whole practice of freedom of expression.

Examiner: If you and others are members of the Communist Party, you are the ones who are discrediting the Screen Writers Guild.

Examinee: I am trying to answer the question by stating, first, what I feel about the purpose of the question which, as I say, is to discredit the whole motion-picture industry.

Examiner: You won't say anything "first." You are refusing to answer this question.

Examinee: My understanding is, as an American resident —

Examiner: Never mind your understanding! There is a question: Are you, or have you ever been, a member of the Communist Party?

Examinee: I could answer exactly the way you want, Mr. Chairman —

Examiner: No —

Examinee: — but I think that is a —

Examiner: It is not a question of our wanting you to answer that. It is a very simple question. Any real American would be proud to answer the question, "Are you, or have you ever been, a member of the Communist Party?" — any ***real*** American.

Examinee: It depends on the circumstances. I could answer it, but if I did, I would hate myself in the morning.

Examiner: Leave the witness chair!

Examinee: It was a question that would —

Examiner: Leave the witness chair!

After reading this cross-examination transcript, what image do you have of the examiner? Of the examinee? What significant information was uncovered? Would you not agree that that method of questioning was counterproductive?

Chapter 18

Strategic Argumentative Communication

- **The Nature of Strategy**
- **General Elements of Strategy**
- **Refutational Elements of Strategy**
- **Conclusion**
- **References**
- **Practicum**

This final chapter in *Argumentation and Debate* is devoted entirely to the notion of strategy, the concept that arguments will be more effective if the advocate follows some prepared plan in presenting his own arguments and refuting the arguments of others. Earlier chapters have delineated such strategy-related matters as case construction ("How should I best organize my arguments to achieve maximum effect?") and the effective delivery of arguments ("What speaking skills do I need to develop to present arguments in an interesting and persuasive manner?"). This chapter concentrates upon the general methods to be used to secure a strategic advantage in argumentative communication encounters.

From the time of the ancient Greek rhetoricians to the present, teachers of public communication skills have noted that there are three major purposes of public communication attempts: to inform, to please or entertain, and to persuade.[1] Oral reports, expository speeches, and most classroom lectures are designed to inform; humorous stories, anecdotes, and comedic monologues are designed to please or entertain; argumentative communication, however, is designed to persuade. Although argumentation and debate activities certainly are informative and—if presented properly—may be entertaining, the primary purpose of all argumentative communication endeavors is to persuade, to convince someone that your arguments and conclusionary positions are superior to those advanced by others. To help ensure that your arguments get through to your audience, and to help you blunt the arguments of your opponents, it is essential that you think and act strategically. This chapter details such strategic considerations.

The Nature of Strategy

In general, strategy may be defined as the advocate's overall plan of attack, the method to be used in effectuating the advocate's goal.[2] In most argumentative communication settings, the advocate is faced with a number of potential problems:

1. How may I gain the attention of my audience?
2. How may I convince my audience to listen to me?
3. How should I present my arguments so that my audience will understand them?
4. How should I present my arguments so that my audience will believe them?
5. How should I motivate my audience to implement my ideas?

Of course, in any given situation, the advocate may face more or fewer problems than we have listed. Regardless of the circumstances, however, to maximize argumentative communication effectiveness it is imperative that the advocate have a strategy in mind both before and during the communicative act.

It might seem to you that the notion of strategy is very specialized and might not apply to you in your normal daily activities. That simply is not true. For example, you may have the goal of having a good job with a high degree of financial security. How do you achieve this goal? Perhaps your thoughts have run like this:

> To get a good job, I'll need to have the right kind of training, the right kind of education. Let's see, I'll go to college and then to graduate school to get an M.B.A. Along the way I'll get involved in an internship or cooperative education program to get some practical experience. Then, after five or maybe six years of college, I'll be able to get a good job with a good future, because I'll have the training and experience to succeed.

Those thoughts exemplify the nature of strategy. You had a literal game plan to ensure future career success. You thought strategically in planning ahead, and your future actions (going to undergraduate school and then to M.B.A. work in graduate school) would implement that preplanned strategy. All of us think and act strategically in varying degrees when we try to persuade someone to marry us, when we try to convince our boss to give us a raise, and when we plan and undertake myriad actions in our daily lives.

If you are honest with yourself, you might admit that those times that have been the most disastrous to you have occurred when you did not prepare, when you did not plan ahead. Activities engaged in haphazardly and without forethought often turn out poorly; actions taken without goals often end counterproductively. For maximum advantage, we learn fairly early in life that we need to plan and to be prepared; this most certainly is true for all our argumentative communication endeavors.

When an attorney goes into the courtroom, she has a plan in mind for the prosecution or defense of the individual facing the bench. Although we do not need to be concerned with depositions, lengthy argument briefs, and all the other accouterments of the legal profession, we do need to think and act strategically to make our daily argumentative efforts as effective and functional as possible.[3] Therefore, the remaining materials in this chapter are designed to acquaint you with general and refutative elements of strategy that will enhance your effectiveness as an advocate.

General Elements of Strategy

This section emphasizes some very general strategic matters that serve as an overview to all argumentative communication efforts. Four such general elements of strategy are detailed.

1. *Physical matters.* In formal argumentative communication situations, it is important that the advocate be aware of and take advantage of the physical elements of the situation that may work to his advantage. Factors such as lighting, acoustics, and space should be studied so the advocate may take advantage of this knowledge. Elements of delivery such as physical movement and vocal intensity are mediated by these physical factors, and the advocate should allot sufficient time to examine these factors to develop a plan to meet them. Speakers who do not speak loud enough to be heard in a large auditorium have failed to plan properly, have failed to study the physical locale before beginning to speak.

In contest debate situations, it is very effective to be the first debate team in the contest room, because you are able to arrange the room as you want it and to be prepared to speak before your opponents even show up. Then, your opponents, seeing you are ready to proceed, will feel rushed and will not be completely mentally ready for the contest; then your debate will begin with your holding a significant psychological advantage. If you are in the room first, you will not be so rushed, you will not be forced to catch up with your opponent.

One final physical matter needs to be mentioned. In formal debate encounters, sit facing your audience, not facing your opponent, or staring off into space. By facing your audience, be it one person or several hundred people, so that you will be able to see audience reactions and to gauge reactions to your opponent's arguments and conclusions. Seeing such reactions will enable you to decide which arguments your audience seems to accept and reject, helping you to plan your own constructive and refutative approaches. To take advantage of this nonverbal feedback, you need to face your audience throughout the entire debate encounter.

2. *Appearance*. No matter what the situation, no matter how heavy or emotional the issues debated, the advocate should attempt to appear cool and calm at all times. Overall, you wish to project the image of an informed, composed person, someone the audience can trust and believe. Therefore, you must remain calm and deliberate. Screaming, ranting, and other such histrionics certainly catch the audience's attention, but such actions do not inspire confidence or belief. On the contrary, they are distracting and downright revolting to most people.

When your opponent screams and jumps up and down, don't follow her lead. Create a very clear dichotomy of style by remaining cool and calm. That difference will be most compelling and persuasive to your audience. After all, what type of speaker do you tend to believe, one who rants and carries on or one who is calm, rational, and judicious? The answer to that question is obvious.

A second appearance-related factor is dress, how one is physically attired. Quite simply, all of us make judgments about others based on their physical appearance.[4] Therefore, you should dress so that your audience will find you credible and believable. A neat, well-groomed appearance is inherently more effective and persuasive than a sloppy, disheveled appearance. Since the nature of persuasive communication includes the packaging of the speaker, his *ethos* or image, you should dress appropriately to *contribute* to your appearance's impact, not to detract from it.

3. *Offensive posture*. To be in control of the argumentative communication situation is to be in the best possible position to secure argumentative acceptance and to win a round of competitive debate. The person or persons who control the flow of arguments also control the overall argumentative encounter and a significant portion of the encounter's eventual outcome. Therefore, to initiate

the line of arguments and to control future lines of arguments must be seen as a strategic advantage. Just as a military unit is in a better position to be in an offensive posture rather than a defensive one, so, too, is the advocate in a far better position if he serves as the precipitator of the argumentative flow.

In contest debate situations, it is said sometimes that the affirmative tries to build a fort around its policy position to fend off the attacks of the negative against that position. However, that type of scenario is untenable for the affirmative, because it allows the negative to control the debate, and sheer numerical odds indicate that at least some of the negative attacks will break through the affirmative defense perimeter. Instead of hiding within a fort, the affirmative should take the offensive directly against the negative positions and not merely try to blunt the negative attacks.

In all argumentative communication encounters, an offensive posture works to the advocate's strategic advantage, providing her with a modicum of control over the flow, direction, and result of each encounter.

4. *Effective listening*. Unfortunately, very few people are effective listeners, and this can prove to be quite detrimental in argumentative communication. Arguments are misinterpreted or missed entirely and possible counterarguments are lost because of poor listening habits.

To listen well, one must be prepared to listen and to listen critically. The exact wording of arguments and evidence must be considered, not just the impressions created by these materials. All too often, we are overly concerned with what *we* are going to say, and, as a result, we do not listen to what others are saying. We may hear, but we do not listen. Effective argumentative communication requires that we respond to the specific arguments and evidence of our opponents, and we can do this only if we listen carefully to our opponents' arguments and evidence. The advocate certainly must plan his arguments, organize his materials, and develop delivery skills for the presentation of arguments. The advocate also must develop the ability to listen; the advocate must look upon critical listening as a strategic tool.[5]

Refutational Elements of Strategy

This section details specific strategies designed for the refutation of others' arguments and evidence. As with the general strategic elements, the advocate must commit himself to these refutational strategies before argumentative communication takes place and to the implementation of these strategies during the argumentative encounter. Three such specific refutational strategies are considered.

1. *Assailing certain points*. One of the biggest mistakes made by novice debaters is attempting to defeat every point made by the opposing debaters. It is simply impractical to try to win every point, because (*a*) not every point is worth winning—some points may have absolutely no significance to the outcome of the encounter—and (*b*) not every point can be defeated. How, for example, could you refute the argument that poverty exists in the United States? To attempt to refute that statement would only cause the advocate to waste her time and to look like a fool.

Instead, the advocate should examine the total argumentative position of her opponent and decide which arguments to attempt to refute. Strategically, of course, arguments should be selected for refutation from this priority list:

priority one:	arguments that are critical to the outcome of the debate (inherency, significance, and so on)
priority two:	other arguments for which you have direct refutational evidence (specific in nature)
priority three:	other arguments for which you have indirect refutational evidence (general in nature)
priority four:	other arguments you may attempt to refute via reasoning and analysis

The advocate should attempt to maximize the number of priority one and two refutational arguments presented, relying only minimally on priority three and four arguments. The relative significance of each of your opponent's arguments should be assessed and then refuted appropriately. Remember, you do not need to refute *every* argument offered by your opponent; concentrate upon the most significant arguments.

2. *Using analysis*. Contrary to a mistaken impression often held by beginning debaters, not every refutational argument has to be substantiated by supporting evidence. After all, (*a*) some arguments are so absurd that they do not merit reading contradictory evidence against them, and (*b*) it is impossible to have evidence for every point that might be offered by your opponents.

In the case of absurd arguments, were you to be confronted with the argument that there is no poverty in the United States, you certainly could produce evidence to refute that point most directly, but why waste your time going through such an exercise? In such a situation, the response that it is obvious to everyone that poverty exists—all you have to do is look at many of our inner cities—would be sufficient refutation. There would be no need to recite several pieces of evidence attesting to a truism. No evidence is necessary to refute a nonsense argument.

In the latter case, it is not possible to have evidence to counter every argument you might hear. At the intercollegiate debate level, there are so many affirmative case variations that a truck would be needed to carry the evidence necessary to handle all those case possibilities. Since that is a bit impractical, remember this: the more obscure or bizarre a case is, the less significant it is; and little significance does not require evidence for adequate refutation. Your own analysis and reasoning will do nicely.

3. *Specific refutational techniques*. Besides being concerned with such matters as evidence sufficiency, source credibility, and fallacious argument, the advocate should consider three other refutational strategies:

- *Argumentative turnarounds*, often called turning the tables. Many arguments, especially conclusionary arguments, may be literally turned around to refute that which is claimed by your opponents. Specific examples also may be turned around to prove the exact opposite of what is claimed.
- *Evidentiary turnarounds*. Many debaters cite evidence without carefully inspecting the exact wording or the implications of that evidence. Such evidence may be turned around to refute the argument your opponents thought the evidence supported.
- *Humor*. There is no rule that mandates all debates to be totally somber affairs. On the contrary, the injection of humor not only adds interest and liveliness to the debate, but humor also is a potent refutational device, especially in dealing with absurd or bizarre arguments issued by your opponent. Several excellent examples of the use of humor in refutation may be found in the second item of the "Practicum" section of this chapter.

Conclusion

To perform effectively in all argumentative communication situations, it is essential that the advocate be prepared and plan ahead, that the advocate proceed strategically in the presentation and refutation of arguments. In general, the advocate should make strategic decisions regarding the physical layout in which the argumentative encounter takes place, the appropriate offensive posture to be maintained, the image he wishes to convey to the audience, and the critical listening habits to be employed throughout the encounter. More specifically, the advocate needs to make strategic decisions concerning the number of arguments to be refuted, the analysis of arguments, and the specific refutational techniques to be employed, including the use of argumentative turnarounds, evidentiary turnarounds, and humor.

References

1. From such ancient treatises as Augustine's *De Doctrina Christiana* to the many public communication texts of today, the three perceived purposes of public communication remain constant.

2. Roy V. Wood, *Strategic Debate* (Skokie, Ill.: National Textbook, 1972), pp. 4–6.

3. Of course, the more formal the argumentative communication encounter, such as contemporary intercollegiate debate, the more formal and detailed are the argumentative support systems.

4. Lawrence B. Rosenfeld, *Human Interaction in the Small Group Setting* (Columbus, Ohio: Charles E. Merrill, 1973), p. 188.

5. See Larry L. Barker, *Listening Behavior* (Englewood Cliffs, N.J.: Prentice-Hall, 1971).

Practicum

1. To help you develop your ability in deciding which arguments of your opponents to attempt to refute and which to leave alone, try this pick-your-point exercise:

- Have your colleague or some other person present a standard, ten-minute first affirmative constructive speech
- Now you are to refute that speech as if you were the first negative constructive speaker, except —
- You are given only four minutes to speak.

Since you have such a greatly reduced speaking time, you will be forced to pick your point, to select some points for refutation and exclude others.

This exercise will enable you to develop an important skill in selecting only the most important arguments for refutation, and this will result in your being a much more strategic and effective debater.

2. The following material is the transcript of the constructive speeches of a public two-man debate, a modified Lincoln-Douglas debate format, over the issue of capital punishment. Judge Alfred Talley supports capital punishment and famous courtroom attorney Clarence Darrow opposes that policy. (The Darrow-Talley debate took place on 26 October 1924 in New York City. The transcript of the debate was published originally as ***Debate on Capital Punishment*** by Haldeman-Julius Publications of Girard, Kansas, in 1924.) Note especially how Darrow uses humor to refute many of Talley's arguments. Do you find the use of humor makes the debate more interesting? Does Darrow use humor effectively? Does Darrow's humor adequately refute Talley's position?

Debate on Capital Punishment

Judge Alfred J. Talley
Affirmative

Clarence Darrow
Negative

Affirmative Presentation Address

JUDGE ALFRED J. TALLEY: Mr. Chairman, Mr. Lawes, Ladies and Gentlemen: More brilliant nonsense has been written about crime and criminals than upon any other subject under the sun. And if this afternoon furnishes an occasion when the people of this city, represented by so large and distinguished an audience, will begin to think, and then think right, upon the subject that is of such pressing importance, we will indeed be indebted to my friend, Mr. Darrow, for coming out from the West to New York and attracting an audience of this size.

Now, there isn't much difficulty in defining the terms of this debate. "Is Capital Punishment a Wise Public Policy?" There can't be any misunderstanding as to precisely the purport of this discussion.

A wise policy is that which is reasonably calculated to accomplish the end which is sought. And in a country, such as ours, that policy should have the approval of the majority of the people of a Republic. And capital punishment is the right exercised by the State to put to death one who has violated that law of the State which says, "Thou shalt not kill," and for a murder deliberated and premeditated upon, that penalty shall be imposed.

We need not consider the right of the nation to put to death one guilty of treason. Happily, since the days of Benedict Arnold, that crime, thank Heaven, has been of rare occurrence in this country of ours. And so all we need to concern ourselves with this afternoon is the question of the wisdom and the expediency and the utility of the State exercising the right to put to death one guilty of the crime of murder.

Now, homicide is the killing of a human being by the act or procurement or commission of the one who accomplishes the slaying. But not every homicide is murder. Bear in mind that in this State and in practically all of the States that adopt capital punishment—either without qualification, as in this state of ours, or, as was suggested by Mr. Marshall, where the question of penalty is left sometimes to the jury—the only kind of homocide that is punishable by death is what we designate as murder in the first degree. And that is the killing of a human being—which is neither excusable or justifiable, and which follows deliberation and premeditation upon the part of the killer.

So that no act done in the heat of passion, no act under provocation or occasion that might make it excusable or justifiable is punished in any of our States by the extreme penalty. But only that kind of killing which follows the mental operation requiring some apreciable length of time, which results in the death of a human being—that kind of slaying alone is punishable by death in any of our States.

Now, the sanest division of my side of this question today would seem to be to discuss, first, the right of the State to impose capital punishment and, then, the expediency and necessity of enforcing that kind of punishment.

In the heart of every man is written the law, "Thou shalt not kill." Upon the statute books of every civilized community is written the law, "Thou shalt not kill." And no one offends that precept through ignorance. It is fundamental that every man knows it is wrong and illegal to take the life of another man.

And we say to potential murderers in this country of ours, "If you have an intention to slay, your mental operation is that of a premeditated and deliberate effort to kill, if after that condition of mind is found to have been present in you, you take the life of another human being, then you shall be tried for that offense, and all the forms of law shall be observed. Twelve men, selected because of their lack of interest in the result save such as they may have as citizens of the community, shall be drawn from the highways and byways to constitute a Jury. A Judge shall preside to see that all the rights given by law to such a defendant as you will be observed. And when—and not until that time—these fellow citizens of yours shall declare that you were the one who accomplished this slaying and that it was not accomplished without deliberation and premeditation upon your part and you had neither right nor justification nor excuse to kill, when your twelve fellow citizens have thus declared and characterized your act, the law says that is murder, and the law says for that murder you should forfeit your life, because you have taken it upon yourself to take the life of another."

Is there anything barbaric or unnatural about a sovereign State making that declaration to its citizens? We must have not merely a declaration of a law, but we must have a sanction to that law if any State can hope to endure. Not merely the writing of prohibitory acts upon the statute books of any State is enough, unless back of that statute there stands a penalty for the violation of that law. And, in the absence of such a penalty, the law is a senseless and meaningless thing.

Those who would abolish capital punishment would give this notice to the potential murderer: "You who have snatched away the life of one who had a right to live, you shall be tried by a jury of your peers. The State will see to it that you are defended by able counsel if you are without means to employ one for yourself. And if it should happen that a Jury should determine that you are guilty of premeditative murder, you are then by reason of that verdict convicted of that crime, you shall not forfeit your life in return for the one which you destroyed, but you shall be incarcerated in a prison possibly — only possibly — for the rest of your life. And when you are sent to that prison you shall be put into a cell, into which the sunlight of which you have deprived your victim must ever come. You shall be given some light labor for a few hours a day — fewer than ever falls to the lot of the average man who must earn his bread by the sweat of his brow amongst law-abiding, nonkilling people of the community. And you are given this labor not for what it might produce, but primarily that your time might be profitably to yourself employed. And you shall be given entertainment. If you happen to kill in the State of New York, you will be provided with a moving picture show every night of the week, and at various times during the season prominent Broadway stars will bring up their companies and their paraphernalia for your entertainment. Your less fortunate brother, who has respected the law, must pay for that entertainment in the theaters of Broadway. But you, a ward of the State, will be provided with these without the necessity of paying for them at all. And you shall be given three meals a day — meals that will be supervised by a dietician employed by the State. And if you don't like those meals, if you don't like the prison fare, you may order that which you eat from a private cafeteria, such as we have under the splendid and able direction of a warden of a prison, as our friend, Warden Lawes, who graces this occasion this afternoon, whose last report shows that more than one-half of the prisoners today confined in Sing-Sing prison eat outside the prison fare, and that for the first six months of 1923 expended over $50,000 for that kind of food.

That is the notice that is given to the potential murderer in the State of New York. Has the State the right to impose capital punishment for first degree murder? Why, if Mr. Darrow, not content with annihilating me today with the force of his eloquence and logic, would at the conclusion of this debate — or, possibly, before it (he is moving closer to me) — attempt to take my life, I would resist that effort. And if it appeared to me, wisely or unwisely, that I was in imminent danger, I would slay him upon this platform. And neither God nor man would question my right to defend my life. Now if I, as an individual, have that right to kill in self-defense, why has not the State, which is nothing more than an aggregation of individuals, the same right to defend itself against unjust aggression and unjust attack?

Does anyone dispute the right of a nation to kill in the protection of its citizens? Why should the right of any State be questioned when it seeks to protect its citizens and their lives and property against unjust aggression.

Because, in the progress of civilization, the individual has delegated many of his privileges and powers to that which we call the State, we do not in these days leave private vengeance to the individual. We say we are citizens of no mean State or of a great Republic and that State or that Republic will protect our rights. We leave the sanction of the violated laws to the State, rather than take vengeance in our own hands as individuals.

Those who would seek to take away from the State the power to impose capital punishment seek to despoil the symbol of justice. They would leave in her hands the scales that typify that in this country at least all are equal before the law and that these scales must never tip from one side to the other, loaded on either side with power or influence of the litigant that comes to the temple of justice. They would leave over her eyes the bandage that tipifies that she must be no respecter of persons, but they would take from her hand the sword, without which the other symbols would be meaningless things. For if justice has not the right to enforce her edicts and her mandates, then her laws may be lost upon a senseless people.

The object of punishment of crime must be deterrent, and it must be vindicative — not vindictive in the sense of revengeful, but it must be imposed so that the law and its majesty and sanctity may be vindicated.

It will be argued, I am sure, as it has been argued countless times by those in favor of abolishing capital punishment, that it is not a deterrent to those who would commit crime; that it deters no one with murder in his heart from committing murder. I can read books without number in favor of that argument. I can delve into the works of Bocalley and Lombroso and Lawes and other men who have made intensive study of this question. But, ladies and gentlemen, please do not misunderstand me when I say that out of my own experience, as lawyer for defendant, as prosecutor for the State and as Judge of the greatest criminal court in all the world, I say that the only thing the criminal fears is the penalty of death that will follow his crime. And I need not read that in any book or any essay or any treatise. That is my experience of more than twenty-five years.

Who can say, and substantiate his assertion, that in this country of ours, shamed with ten thousand murders in every twelve months — who can say, with that criminal tendency upon the part of the American people, that stigmatizes us as to the most lawless nation on the face of the earth — who can say that, with murder in the heart of so many of our people, the number would not be twice as great or three times as great if death, which is still the king of terrors (more to criminals than the righteous man), were not maintained as the penalty for an unlawful killing?

Do you ladies and gentlemen have any appreciation of the homicide or the murder figures of this country of ours, of the amazing increase beyond all calculation that is shown year after year? Do you realize that in New York, our great Empire City, there is practically a murder every day? And we are a population of some six millions here. And in Mr. Darrow's splendid city of Chicago, with a population of about three million, there are more murders committed annually than there are in New York. And not only are these numbers appalling, but the increase in the annual rate is the thing that should make us pause.

In twenty-eight cities from which statistics were

available, in 1900 there were 609 homicides. That leaped in 1910 in these same twenty-eight of the principal cities of our country to 1,365. And for the period running from 1917 to 1921 those figures of twenty years ago — 609 homicides a year — reached the appalling figure of 8,946.

MR. DARROW (Interposing): Beg pardon. What is that last figure?

JUDGE TALLEY (Continuing): Eight thousand, nine hundred and forty-six. And I am reading from the statistics of Frederick M. Hoffman, Consulting Statistician of the Prudential Insurance Company of America, a statistician who is cited with approval by Warden Lawes.

WARDEN LAWES (Interposing): Who also does not believe in capital punishment.

JUDGE TALLEY: Who also does not believe in capital punishment. He is with Mr. Lawes and Mr. Darrow on that subject. And while his statistics are right, his conclusions are all wrong.

Now just let me give you an illustration of the homicides in our principal American cities. These figures are based upon 100,000 of the population — that is, so many murders for each 100,000 of the population. Out of courtesy to our visitor, I will refer to his city first.

In the period from 1912 to 1916 the figures in Chicago for 100,000 population were represented by nine and five-tenths per cent. They leaped in 1922-23 to twelve and seven-tenths per cent plus. In New York — wicked New York — the figures in 1912 to 1916 are represented by five and six-tenths per cent plus. In Memphis, Tennessee — (now bear in mind the figures, twelve per cent for Chicago and five per cent for New York) — the figures reached sixty-six and two-tenths per cent. They leaped in 1922–23 to twelve and seven-year they reached thirty-four and seven-tenths per cent. And in the city of Washington, the Capital of our great Republic — with twelve per cent in Chicago, five per cent in New York, the percentage in Washington reached thirteen and three-tenths per cent.

Now I cannot take the time to go over in detail these figures. I simply submit them to you as sketchily as time permits, with this suggestion to follow them: Is this the time to consider abolishing capital punishment when our country is disgraced by the number of murders that are committed upon our shores?

I say it is the time for sensible men and women to come to a realization that there is one way to deal with the criminal and the malefactor, and that is with certainty and severity. There is no other way in which the integrity of the people of this country or the sanctity of the law may be observed. I am in favor of abolishing capital punishment when the murderers of the country abolish its necessity.

Negative Presentation Address

MR. DARROW: I had this stand moved up so I could get next to the audience.

I hope I will not be obliged to spend too much time on my friend's address. I don't think I shall need to.

First, I deny his statement that every man's heart tells him it is wrong to kill. I think every man's heart desires killing. Personally, I never killed anybody that I know of. But I have had a great deal of satisfaction now and then reading obituary notices, and I used to delight, with the rest of my hundred per cent patriotic friends, when I saw ten or fifteen thousand Germans being killed in a day.

Everybody loves killing. Some of them think it is too mussy for them. Every human being that believes in capital punishment loves killing, and the only reason they believe in capital punishment is because they get a kick out of it. Nobody kills anyone for love, unless they get over it temporarily or otherwise. But they kill the one they hate. And before you can get a trial to hang somebody or electrocute him, you must first hate him and then get a satisfaction over his death.

There is no emotion in any human being that is not in every single human being. The degree is different, that is all. And the degree is not always different in different people. It depends likewise on circumstances, on time and on place.

I shall not follow my friend into the labyrinth of statistics. Statistics are a pleasant indoor sport — not so good as cross-word puzzles — and they prove nothing to any sensible person who is familiar with statistics.

I might just observe, in passing, that in all of these states where the mortality by homicide is great, they have capital punishment and always have had it. A logical man, when he found out that the death rate increased upon capital punishment, would suggest some other way of dealing with it.

I undertake to say — and you can look them up yourselves, for I haven't time to bother with it (and there is nothing that lies like statistics) — I will guarantee to take any set of statistics and take a little time to it and prove they mean directly the opposite for what is claimed. But I will undertake to say that you can show by statistics that the State in which there was no capital punishment have a very much smaller percentage of homicides.

I know it is true. That doesn't prove anything, because, as a rule, they are States with a less diverse population, without as many large cities, without as much mixtures of all sorts of elements which go to add to the general gayety — and homicide is a product of that. There is no sort of question but what those States in the United States where there is no capital punishment have a lower percentage than the others. But that doesn't prove the question. It is a question that cannot be proven one way or the other by statistics. It rests upon things, upon feelings and emotions and arguments much deeper than statistics.

The death rate in Memphis and in some other Southern cities is high from homicide. Why? Well, it is an afternoon's pleasure to kill a negro — that is about all. Everybody knows it.

The death rate recently in the United States and all over the world has increased. Why? The same thing has happened that has happened in every country in the world since time began. A great war always increases death rates.

We teach people to kill, and the State is the one that teaches them. If a State wishes that its citizens respect human life, then the State should stop killing. It can be done in no other way, and it will perhaps not be fully done that way. There are infinite reasons for killing. There are infinite circumstances under which there are more or less deaths. It never did depend and never can depend upon the severity of the punishment.

He talks about the United States being a lawless country. Well, the people somehow prefer it. There is such a thing as a people being too servile to law. You may take China with her caste system and much of Europe, which has much more caste than we. It may be full of homicides, but there is less bread and there is less fun; there is less opportunity for the poor. In any new country, homicide is more frequent than in an old country, because there is a high degree of equality. It is always true wherever you go.

And in the older countries, as a general rule, there are fewer homocides because nobody ever thinks of getting out of his class; nobody ever dreams of such a thing.

But let's see what there is in this argument. He says, "Everybody who kills, dreads hanging." Well, he has had experience as a lawyer on both sides. I have had experience on one side. I know that everybody who is taken into court on a murder charge desires to live, and they do not want to be hanged or electrocuted. Even a thing as alluring as being cooked with electricity doesn't appeal to them.

But that hasn't anything to do with it. What was the state of mind when the homicide was committed? The state of mind is one thing when a homicide is committed and another thing weeks or months afterward, when every reason for committing it is gone. There never can be any comparison between it.

We might ask why people kill. I don't want to dispute with him about the right of the State to kill people. Of course, they have got a right to kill them. That is about all we do. The great industry of the world for four long years was killing. They have got a right to kill, of course. That is, they have got the power. And you have got a right to do what you get away with. The words power and right, so far as this is concerned, mean exactly the same thing. So nobody who has any knowledge of philosophy would pretend to say that the State had not the right to kill.

But why not do a good job of it? If you want to get rid of killings by hanging people or electrocuting them because these are so terrible, why not make a punishment that is terrible? This isn't so much. It lasts but a short time. There is no physical torture in it. Why not boil them in oil, as they used to do? Why not burn them at the stake? Why not sew them into a bag with serpents and throw them out to sea? Why not take them out on the sand and let them be eaten by ants? Why not break every bone in their body on the rack, as has been done for such serious offenses as heresy and witchcraft?

Those were the good old days in which the Judge should have held court. Glorious days, when you could kill them by the million because they worshipped God in a different way from that which the State provided, or when you could kill old women for witchcraft! There might be some sense in it if you could kill the young ones, but not old ones. Those were the glorious days of capital punishment. And there wasn't a Judge or a preacher who didn't think that the life of the State depended upon their right to hang old women for witchcraft and to persecute others for worshipping God in the wrong way.

Why, our capital punishment isn't worth talking about, so far as its being a preventive is concerned. It isn't worth discussing. Why not call back from the dead and barbarous past the hundred and sixty or seventy odd crimes that were punishable by death in England? Why not once more reenact the Blue Laws of our own country and kill people right? Why not resort to all the tortures that the world has always resorted to to keep men in the straight and narrow path? Why reduce it to a paltry question of murder?

Everybody in this world has some pet aversion to something, and on account of that pet aversion they would like to hang somebody. If the prohibitionists made the law, they would be in favor of hanging you for taking a drink, or certainly for bootlegging, because to them that is the most heinous crime there is.

Some men slay or murder. Why? As a matter of fact, murder as murder is very rare; and the people who commit it, as a rule, are of a much higher type than others. You may go to any penitentiary and, as a rule, those who have been convicted of murder become the trusties; whereas, if you are punishing somebody as a sneak thief or a counterfeiter or a confidence man, they never get over it — never.

Now, I don't know how injustice is administered in New York. I just know about Chicago. But I am glad to learn from the gentleman that if a man is so poor in New York that he can't hire a lawyer, that he has a first-class lawyer appointed to defend him — a first-class lawyer appointed to defend him. Don't take a chance and go out and kill anybody on the statement made by my friend.

I suppose anybody can go out and kill somebody and ask to have my friend, Sam Untermyer, appointed. There never was such a thing. Here and there, a good lawyer may have defended people for nothing. But no court ever interferes with a good lawyer's business by calling him in and compelling him to give his time. They have been lawyers too recently themselves to ever work a trick like that on a lawyer. As a rule it is the poor and the weak and the friendless who furnish the victims of the law.

Let me take another statement of my friend. He said, "Oh, we don't hang anybody if they kill when they are angry; it is only when they act premeditatedly." Yes, I have been in courts and heard Judges instruct people on this premeditated act. It is only when they act under their judgment and with due consideration. He would also say that if a man is moved by anger, but if he doesn't strike the deadly blow until such time as a reason and judgment has a chance to possess him, even if it is a second — how many times have I heard Judges say, "Even if it is a second"? What does any Judge know about premeditation? What does anybody know about it? How many people are there in this world that can premeditate on anything? I will strike out the "pre" and say how many people are there that can meditate?

How long does it take the angry man for his passions to cool when he is in the presence of the thing that angers him? There never was a premeditated murder in any sense of psychology or of science. There are planned murders — planned, yes — but back of every murder and back of every human act are sufficient causes that move the human machine beyond their control.

The other view is an outworn, outlawed, unscientific theory of the metaphysics. Does anybody ever act in this world without a motive? Did they ever act without a sufficient motive? And who am I to say that John Smith premeditated? I might pemeditate a good deal quicker than John Smith did. My judgment might have a chance to act quicker than John Smith's judgment had a chance to act.

We have heard talk of justice. Is there anybody who knows what justice is? No one on earth can measure out justice. Can you look at any man and say what he deserves — whether he deserves hanging by the neck until dead or life in prison or thirty days in prison or a medal? The human mind is blind to all who seek to look in at it and to most of us that look out from it. Justice is something that man knows little about. He may know something about charity and understanding and mercy, and he should cling to these as far as he can.

Now, let me see if I am right about my statement that no man believes in hanging, except for a kick or revenge. How about my friend, Judge Talley here. He criticises the State of New York because a prisoner may be shown moving pictures. What do you think about it — those of you who think? What do you feel about it — those of you who have passed the hyena age? I know what they think. What do you think about shutting up a man in a penitentiary for twenty years, in a cell four feet wide and seven feet long — twenty years, mind! — and complaining because he had a chance now and then to go out and see a moving picture — go out of his cell?

A body of people who feels that way could never get rid of capital punishment. If you really felt it, you would feel like the Indian who used the tomahawk on his enemy and who burned him and embalmed his face with the ashes.

But what is punishment about anyway? I put a man in prison for the purpose of getting rid of him and for such example as there might be. Is it up to you to torture him while he is there? Supposing you provided that every man who went to prison should be compelled to wear a nail half an inch long in his shoe. I suppose some of you would do it. I don't know whether the Judge would or not, from what he said.

Is there any reason for torturing someone who happens to be in prison? Is there any reason why an actor or even an actress might not go there and sing? There is no objection to a preacher going there. Why not give him a little pleasure?

And they really get food there — what do you know about that? Now, when I heard him tell about what wonderful food they get — dietary food — did you ever know anybody that liked dietary food? I suppose the Constitution of the State of New York contains the ordinary provision against cruel and inhumane punishment, and yet you send them up there and feed them on dietary food.

And you can take your meals out! Now, some of you might not have noticed that I walked over and asked the Warden about it. The reason I did that is because I am stopping over here at the Belmont, and I didn't know but I'd rather go up and board with him.

Now, this is what I find out: that for those who have gained consideration by good conduct over a considerable period — how long, Mr. Lawes?

WARDEN LAWES: One year.

MR. DARROW: One year — they may spend three dollars a week for board. I pay more than that over here. They ought to pass some law in New York to prevent the inmates getting dyspepsia. And for those who attain the second class, they may spend a dollar and a dollar and a half a week. And for those below the second class, nothing can come from outside — nothing. A pure matter of prison discipline.

Why, I wonder if the Judge ever took pains to go up there. I will tell you. I have had some experience with people that know them pretty well. I never saw a man who wanted to go to prison, even to see the movies. I never saw a man in my life who didn't want to get out.

I wonder what you would have. Of course, I live in Chicago, where people are fairly human — I don't know, maybe I don't understand New York people. What would you have? Suppose you could tell yourselves how a person was to be treated while in prison — and it doesn't require a great amount of imagination. Most people can think of sme relative or good friends who are there. If you can't, most of you can think of a good many that ought to be there. How would you have them treated — something worse than being shut up in a cell, four by seven, and given light work — like being a Judge or practicing law — something worse than dietary food?

I will tell you. There is just one thing in all this question. It is a question of how you feel, that is all. It is all inside you. If you love the thought of somebody being killed, why, you are for it. If you hate the thought of somebody being killed, you are against it.

Let me just take a little brief review of what has happened in this world. They used to hang people on the cross-ways and on a high hill, so that everybody would be awed into goodness by the sight. They have tortured them in every way that the brain of man could conceive. They have provided every torture known or that could be imagined for one who believed differently from his fellowman — and still the belief persisted. They have maimed and scarred and starved and killed human beings since man began ponning his fellowman. Why? Because we hate him. And what has added to it is that they have done it under the false ideal of self-righteousness.

I have heard parents punish their children and tell their children it hurt the parent more than it did the child. I don't believe it. I have tried it both ways, and I don't believe it. I know better.

Gradually, the world has been lopping off these punishments. Why? Because we have grown a little more sensitive, a little more imaginative, a little kindlier, that is all.

Why not reenact the code of Blackstone's day? Why, the Judges were all for it — every one of them — and the only way we got rid of those laws was because Juries were too humane to obey the courts.

That is the only way we got rid of punishing old

women, of hanging old women in New England — because, in spite of all the courts, the Juries would no longer convict them for a crime that never existed. And in that way they have cut down the crimes in England for punishment by death from one hundred and seventy to two. What is going to happen if we get rid of them? Is the world coming to an end? The earth has been here ages and ages before man came. It will be here ages and ages after he disappears, and the amount of people you hang won't make the slightest difference with it.

Now, why am I opposed to capital punishment? It is too horrible a thing for a State to undertake. We are told by my friend, "Oh the killer does it; why shouldn't the State?" I would hate to live in a state that I didn't think was better than a murderer.

But I told you the real reason. The people of the State kill a man because he killed someone else — that is all — without the slightest logic, without the slightest application to life, simply from anger, nothing else!

I am against it because I believe it is inhumane, because I believe that as the hearts of men have softened they have gradually gotten rid of brutal punishment, because I believe that it will only be a few years until it will be banished forever from every civilized country — even New York — because I believe that it has no effect whatever to stop murder.

Now let's make that simple and see. Where do the murders come from? I would say the second largest class of what we call murders grow out of domestic relations. They follow those deep and profound feelings that are at the basis of life — and the feelings which give the greatest joy are susceptible of the greatest pain when they go a-riot.

Can you imagine a woman following a man around with a pistol to kill him that would stop if you said, "Oh, you will be hanged!" Nothing doing — not if the world was coming to an end! Can you imagine a man doing it? Not at all. They think of it afterwards, but not before. They come from acts like burglary and robbery. A man goes out to rob or to burglarize. Somebody catches him or stops him or recognizes him, and he kills to save himself. Do you suppose there was ever a burglar or robber since the world began who would not kill to save himself? Is there anybody who wouldn't? It doesn't make any difference who. Wouldn't he take a chance shooting? Anyone would do it.

Why, my friend himself said he would kill in self-defense. That is what they do. If you are going to stop them, you ought to hang them for robbery — which would be a good plan — and then, of course, if one started out to rob, he would kill the victim before he robbed him.

There isn't, I submit, a single admissible argument in favor of capital punishment. Nature loves life. We believe that life should be protected and preserved. The thing that keeps one from killing is the emotion they have against it; and the greater the sanctity that the State pays to life, the greater the feeling of sanctity the individual has for life.

There is nothing in the history of the world that ever cheapened human life like our great war; next to that, the indiscriminate killing of men by the States.

My friend says a man must be proven guilty first. Does anybody know whether anybody is guilty? There is a great deal implied in that. For me to do something or for you to do something is one thing; for some other man to do something is quite another. To know what one deserves, requires infinite study, which no one can give to it. No one can determine the condition of the brain that did the act. It is out of the question.

All people are products of two things, and two things only — their heredity and their environment. And they act in exact accord with the heredity which they took from all the past, and for which they are in no way responsible, and the environment, which reaches out to the farthest limit of all life that can influence them. We all act from the same way. And it ought to teach us to be charitable and kindly and understanding.

INDEX